THE ART OF
FILM PROJECTION

A Beginner's Guide

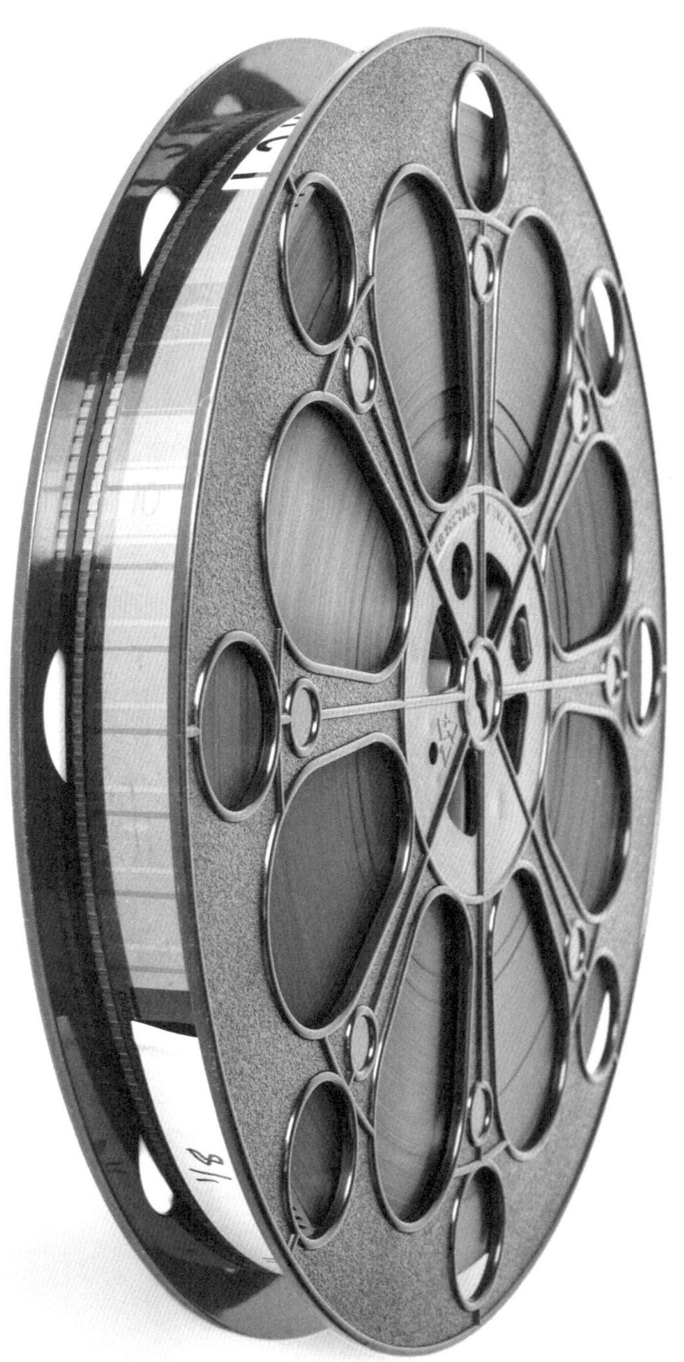

THE ART OF FILM PROJECTION

A Beginner's Guide

EDITED BY

Paolo Cherchi Usai
Spencer Christiano
Catherine A. Surowiec
and Timothy J. Wagner

FOREWORD BY

Tacita Dean
and Christopher Nolan

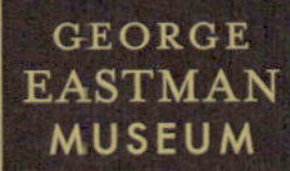

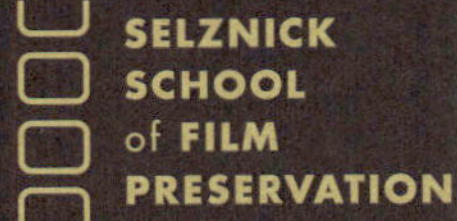

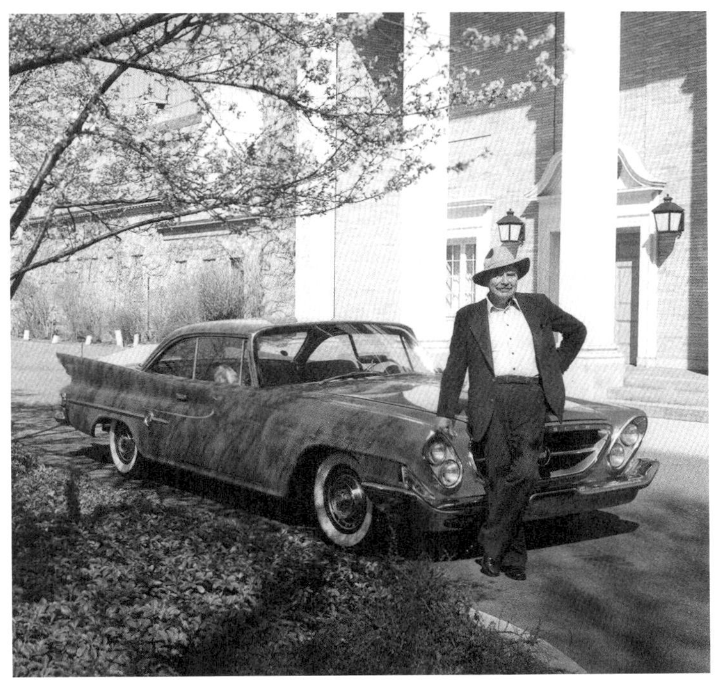

"My own hell would be to have a projector and all the films, but no one around to see them with me."

—JAMES CARD (1915–2000)

GEORGE EASTMAN MUSEUM

Published by the George Eastman Museum
900 East Avenue, Rochester, New York 14607

Publication of this book has been made possible by the George Eastman Museum Publishing Trust Endowment, which was established by Thomas Gosnell and Richard Menschel with funds donated by Thomas and Georgia Gosnell and the Horace W. Goldsmith Foundation.

Edited by Paolo Cherchi Usai, Spencer Christiano,
Catherine A. Surowiec, and Timothy J. Wagner

Foreword by Tacita Dean and Christopher Nolan

Project management by Amy Schelemanow

Proofreading by Joshua Boydstun

Photography and scanning by Elizabeth Chiang,
Sophia Lorent, Timothy J. Wagner, and Spencer Christiano

Design by Headcase Design

Indexing by Shelley Indexing Services

Typeset in Excelsior and Verlag

Printed on Magno Natural

Printed in Italy by Verona Libri

The George Eastman Museum is a member of **fiaf**
International Federation of Film Archives

ISBN: 978-0-935398-31-1

Library of Congress Control Number: 2019934903

TABLE OF CONTENTS

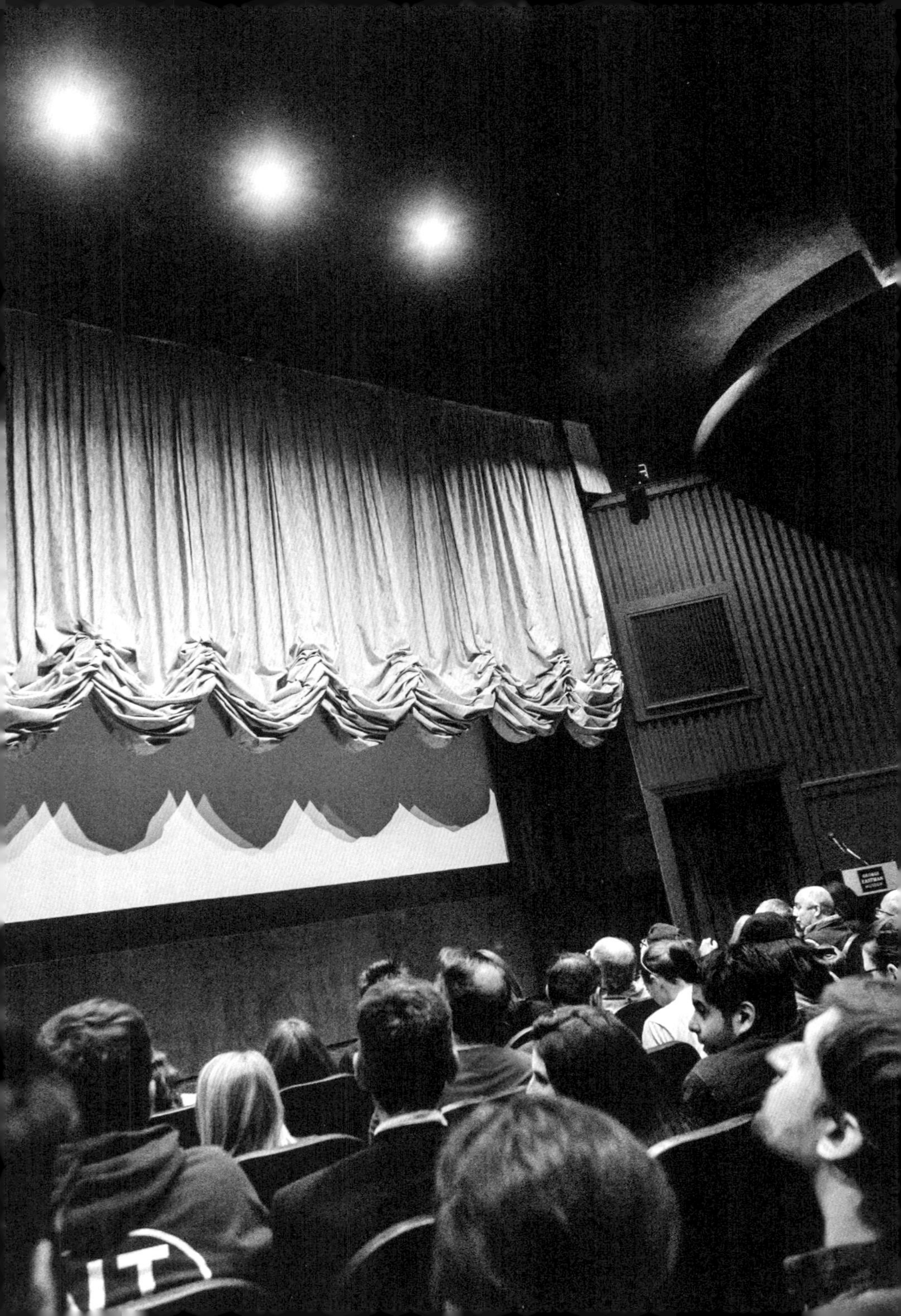

FOREWORD

O N **DECEMBER 8,** 1975, director Stanley Kubrick sent out a letter to all the projectionists of his film *Barry Lyndon*:

An infinite amount of care was given to the look of "Barry Lyndon"; the photography, the sets, the costumes; and in the careful color grading and overall lab quality of the prints, and the soundtrack – all of this work is now in your hands, and your attention to sharp focus, good sound, and the careful handling of the film will make this effort worthwhile.

In the current era of automated de-professionalised digital projection, Kubrick's letter comes across as an eccentric attempt to exert control on the uncontrollable, yet anyone who works with film can fully testify to Kubrick's insistence on communicating directly with his projectionist so as to ensure the very best possible projection of their work. Film projectionists are an integral part of the creative process: an impeccable projection is the ultimate fulfilment of a filmmaker's intention. The exhibition of the film is, after all, *the* point of contact with the audience; it is the culmination of months, if not years, of labour and endeavour and the final act of trust between like-minded professionals who are engaged in the collaborative business of making a film and who still insist on the very highest level of expertise that their profession requires.

The good projectionist has fallen foul of the same attitudes in cinema that make Kubrick's exactitude appear risible in today's world. The profession has become endangered or has been deskilled into non-existence, which is why this beginner's manual is so overdue. Projecting film prints correctly is a great responsibility and a great skill. When a print is mishandled, it can be easily destroyed. A filmmaker is dependent upon the projectionist's full understanding of how the images and sounds of a film should be perceived. We only notice a film's projection when it goes wrong. Good projectionists are trained to handle history; they must protect the prints in their care, and their greatest skill is to remain unnoticed.

Written with deep knowledge of all aspects of film exhibition acquired by experienced film projectionists, technicians, and museum curators, this book has been edited by the staff of George Eastman Museum with the active participation of students from the L. Jeffrey Selznick School of Film Preservation, who have learned the basics of film exhibition and would like to make their findings available to all. This manual is expressly addressed to non-specialists. Of course there have been many specialized publications on this topic; none of them, however, has attempted to explain the art of film projection in a language that is accessible to those who have never entered a projection booth or touched a strip of motion picture film.

Despite its appearance as a technical manual, this book is a cultural manifesto on the importance of film as creative work and a window through which to understand the materiality of film and its de-materiality as projected image. Cinema has never been reducible to just the reels of a film but is a contract between the maker and their audience made possible through the act of projection. Cinema will always be an art form that exists in three dimensions; it requires a projector and projectionist, as much as it needs the physical volume of the theatre and an audience to watch it. Knowledge of changeover cues, aspect ratios, and loop sizes is not the arcane information of a lost era but the expertise necessary to project a film correctly today. To disrespect the role of the projectionist is to disrespect cinema itself. *The Art of Film Projection* at last gives Stanley Kubrick's letter the context and seriousness it had briefly lost, while reaffirming the role of one of cinema's most unsung but essential professionals: the film projectionist.

TACITA DEAN

CHRISTOPHER NOLAN

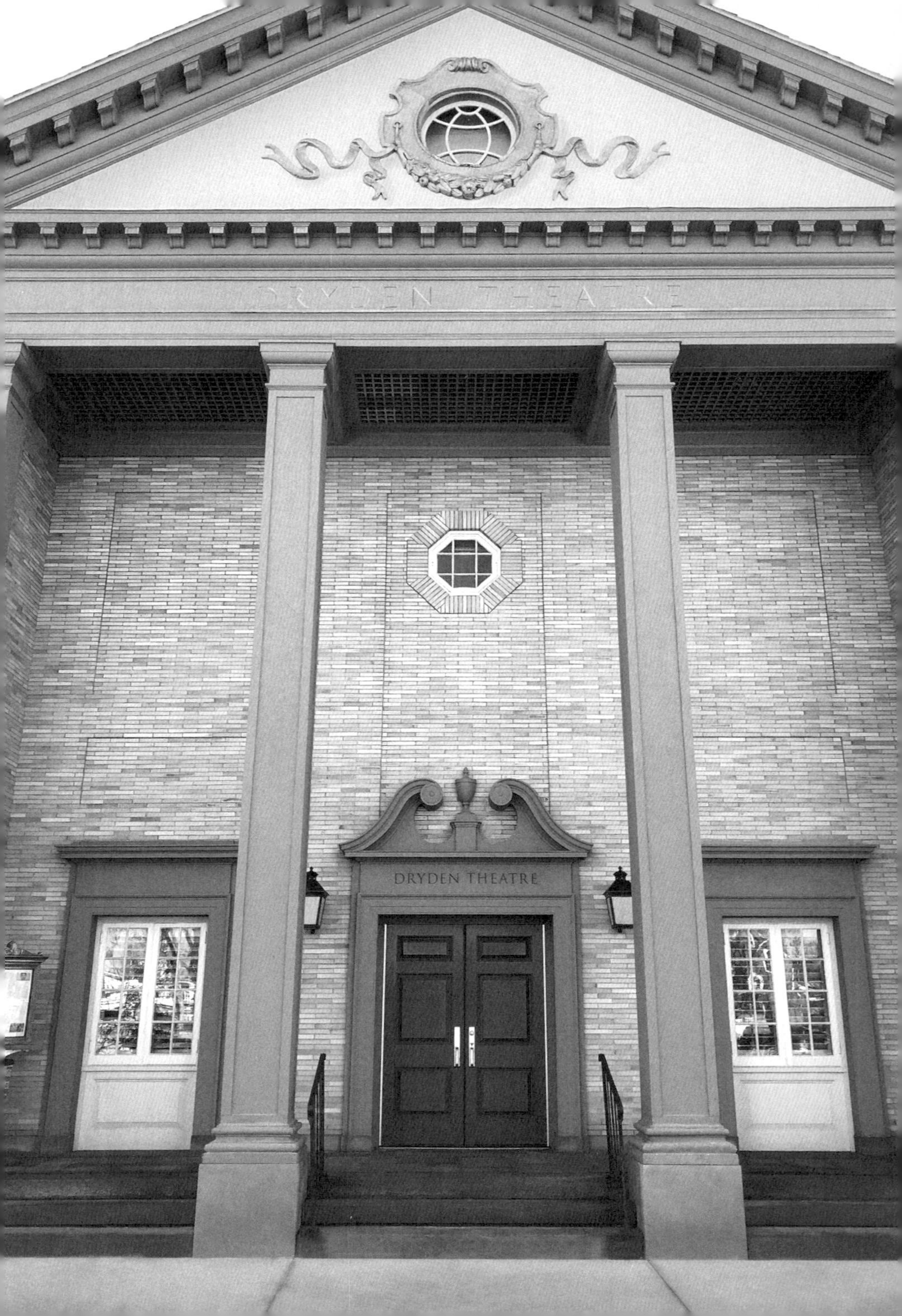

PREFACE

THIS BOOK IS the expression of a teamwork in a two-fold sense. First, it is the result of a collaboration between staff members of the Moving Image Department at the George Eastman Museum. Over several years, the museum's projectionists, curators, and film technicians have designed, discussed, and reviewed the text with the intent of making it as accessible and accurate as possible, mindful of our goal to highlight the importance of film projection in the preservation process and the art of cinema in general. The first draft of the text, written by Timothy J. Wagner, was reviewed by Spencer Christiano, with contributions from Benjamin Tucker (Chapter 9) and Paolo Cherchi Usai, who conceived and spearheaded this project. Spencer Christiano also drafted the afterword, supervised the final stages in the revision of the manuscript, and finalized the selection of the illustrations. Darryl G. Jones, Deborah Stoiber, Patrick Tiernan, and Samuel B. Lane provided invaluable suggestions in their respective fields of expertise and on the overall structure of the book.

The second aspect of the collective nature of this work is the crucial role played by the students of the L. Jeffrey Selznick School of Film Preservation, a certificate and graduate program held in partnership with the University of Rochester. Selznick School students and alumni — under the guidance of Assistant Curator Jeffrey L. Stoiber, administrator of the program — helped with their advice, questions, recommendations, and amendments to the text, with the shared objective of making the book a reliable training tool and a useful reference source. Among the many Selznick students who directly or indirectly contributed to the text were Javier Cámara Camaño, Kelli Shay Hix, David Rodriguez, Joshua Romphf, Heather Sabin, Katie A. Trainor, and Kyle Westphal. Their enthusiasm and commitment to this work is a testimony to the level of excellence achieved by the Selznick School Master of Arts and Certificate programs over the years.

Our heartfelt thanks go to Elizabeth Chiang and Sophia Lorent (at the George Eastman Museum) and Rachel Behnke for the photographs and frame enlargements reproduced in this book; William Duelly and Hannes Ziegenhorn for providing additional illustrations; Cynthia Rowell for her review of the first draft; Catherine A. Surowiec for her meticulous editorial work on the final version; and our colleague Amy Schelemanow, who followed the design and production process from beginning to end with matchless patience, creativity, and insight. We would like to express our gratitude to Dr. Bruce Barnes, Ron and Donna Fielding Director of the George Eastman Museum, for having made this book possible through his initiative and constant support.

This publication was made possible by the George Eastman Museum Publishing Trust Endowment. We are profoundly grateful for the foresight and generosity of Thomas Gosnell and Richard Menschel, who founded this endowment in 1990 to support the museum's publishing activities.

INTRODUCTION

FILM PROJECTION IS the ultimate achievement of film preservation. It is the synthesis of a process in which archivists, curators, and technicians gather their expertise and talents in order to conserve, restore, and exhibit motion picture film as a cultural artifact in a private or public collection. The cinematic event is in itself the realization of film curatorship, in that it brings to the screen the results of all previous work undertaken in order to showcase cinema as a living reality, an experience to be shared with present and future audiences. This book is, first and foremost, a guide on how to make this experience happen under the best possible conditions, so that the objects of preservation can be displayed as they should, and remain intact so that others can see them in the future as they are now. The following pages will necessarily adopt a technical language, but it should be clear from the outset that technology is intended here as a tool for the attainment of an aesthetic experience, rather than a goal in itself.

It must also be emphasized that this is an introductory manual, whose only aim is to present the essential aspects of film projection in clear, concise, and accessible terms, for the benefit of those who wish to acquire the skills necessary for the exhibition of museum, archival, commercial, and collectors' prints in general, as well as of new artworks made on film. It is emphatically *not* a compendium on the history and technology of film projection (references to names, dates, and film titles have therefore been kept to a bare minimum). There is a wealth of specialized literature on the subject, and this book has no ambition to compete with it. Those who are already familiar with the topic will only find here a brief – and deliberately simplified – summary of what they already know. As the projection equipment available to film screening venues is so varied, the instructions provided here are meant to serve as very basic guidelines that apply to most, but not all, projection machines. Those who wish to learn the operations of their equipment in greater detail should look for the specific texts on the apparatus at their disposal. We hope, however, that those technicians who have been acquainted for many years with the art of film projection will find these pages useful in explaining to others the most fundamental aspects of their job.

In writing this collective book, the team of museum professionals engaged in the project applied the same principles that inform their activities within our institution, and their collaboration with fellow projectionists and technicians of other film archives and museums. Before entering into the practical manifestations of these concepts in the pages that follow, it is worth giving a brief description of what they are.

We would like to begin by quoting what our esteemed Austrian colleagues Alexander Horwath (former Director of the Österreichisches Filmmuseum in Vienna) and Regina Schlagnitweit (who coordinated the Filmmuseum's exhibition programs) said in response to our question about their own approach to the projection of archival prints. When a print was about to be shown in their museum, they treated it as if it was the last existing copy in any format, and as if that was the last time they would be able to present it to their public. To further paraphrase Regina and Alex, they asked their projectionists to behave as if the print bestowed to their care was the only surviving trace of the film to be exhibited.

This is precisely what our book is about. Once upon a time, it may have been possible to think otherwise, both because it was easier to replace damaged prints, and because the so-called "wear and tear" to the film was regarded as part of its material evolution in the course of history.

Truthful as it is (prints were seldom treated kindly in the projection booths of commercial theaters), this portrayal of the past could never justify a similar attitude in a cultural organization, and is now alien from the *modus operandi* of a place where the cinematic heritage is preserved for posterity. When film prints were formally acquired as part of archive and museum collections, they should have been treated with the same respect and attention due to other artworks such as paintings, sculptures, and illuminated manuscripts. If they weren't, it was both because cinema was labeled as an "art of reproduction" (therefore justifying the "wear and tear" misconception), and because archivists and curators rarely thought of the projection booth as a place to apply the same exacting standards observed in every other area of their institutions.

For this reason, film projectionists have by and large been unfairly excluded or marginalized from the preservation projects undertaken by the rest of the staff, as if their role was simply to make visible what others had previously done. To compound this state of things, film projection was rarely a focus of attention in the academic world. The much welcome surge of interest in film technology as a scholarly subject, as testified by publications and conferences worldwide, is not a "comeback" – it is the belated recognition that cinema is neither made of "content" nor of mere "objects," but is a complex performance involving a creative work (the film), its carrier (the print), an apparatus (the projector), a physical environment (the theater and its screen), and the people in charge of exhibiting the work (the projectionists).

Films held in museums and archives are now much harder to duplicate in their original medium and format. Laboratory costs have dramatically increased; access to preservation negatives outside the collecting institution's premises has become very difficult, if not impossible. Even when the negatives are available, obtaining copies of good quality from a laboratory other than the one where the duplication work was originally done is extremely challenging if there is no information on the grading to be used for the creation of new elements. With the advent of digital technology, the very survival of motion picture stock cannot be taken for granted, but neither this nor the other facts mentioned above should be the reasons why it is important to ensure the physical integrity of projection prints. Their status as collection objects should have been a matter of priority from the very beginning of their presence in a collecting institution; the new evidence at our disposal about the economy, technology, and politics of film preservation has given an additional sense of urgency to what ought to have been part of a responsible approach to film conservation at its outset.

The second principle behind this book is an elaboration of the previous point, in positive terms. Because film preservation on *film* is now such a rare occurrence, and is so expensive to undertake, it makes no sense to waste so much energy and financial resources on the photochemical duplication of any given title if its brand-new projection print is damaged after a few screenings (or even in a single show, as projectionists know all too well). In early October 2016, the Cinémathèque française presented at the Pordenone Silent Film Festival (Le Giornate del Cinema Muto) a beautifully tinted print of the newly restored *Kean* (Alexandre Volkoff, 1924). A 35mm copy was struck at the Haghefilm laboratories in Amsterdam from the preservation negative; the black & white print was then sent to Prague, where it was manually tinted with a process very similar to the one used in the early decades of cinema. By all intents and purposes, that print is unique. (The film is also available in a high-resolution digital version, but the Cinémathèque française is to be applauded for having taken the hard route as well.) To make another copy would take a significant amount of time, money, and human effort. We would like to see that very same print shown again twenty years from now, and look as stunning as it is did in Pordenone.

This is by all means possible, with the necessary competence, patience, and goodwill. The point is illustrated by an anecdote reported by another eminent colleague in our field, David Francis, formerly Chief of the Motion Picture, Broadcasting and Recorded Sound Division at the Library of Congress in Washington, DC, and previously Curator of the British Film Institute's National Film Archive in London (now called the BFI National Archive). In 1965, a new 70mm Todd-AO print of *The Sound of Music* (Robert Wise, 1965) was screened in London at the Dominion Theatre on Tottenham Court Road (near the BFI's headquarters, where Francis was then employed). The film was a resounding success, and its tenure was extended indefinitely. At that point, the projectionists were offered – in Francis's recollection – a bonus of 10,000 British Pounds if they could make that one print last for the entire run of the film. By the end of its tenure at the Odeon, *The Sound of Music* remained unharmed after about 2,400 screenings. The projectionists received their bonus, and the BFI decided to ask for the print for the National Film Archive's collection, simply to show that a print would last a long time if projectionists were given the right incentive to keep it intact.

As nice as it would be to be able to remunerate film projectionists as much as they deserve, money is not the only thing that makes a print enjoy a long, productive life in a collecting institution. The care and dedication of its staff make the real difference. In another telling anecdote, Robert A. Ogie, Chief Projectionist at what was then called George Eastman House, screened the museum's 35mm print of *Bronenosets Potemkin* (*Battleship Potemkin*, Sergei M. Eisenstein, 1925) to a group of students in the late 1990s. The young viewers were stunned by the exceptional quality of the print and queried Ogie about its history and provenance. He first responded with a proud smile, and then added that the print had been acquired by the museum's founding film curator, James Card, sometime in the 1950s. Since then Ogie had been showing the very same print at least once a year; four decades later, it looked like new. "I was the one who projected that print every time," Ogie said, "and because the film could be found everywhere, nobody ever asked for our print to be loaned in over forty years." There was more than a touch of irony in Ogie's words, but his message came through loud and clear. With the proper maintenance and care, a film print can indeed be screened many times with no appreciable change to its original condition.

Films are preserved in order to be seen; this applies to both present and future audiences, who have equal rights to enjoy their beauty, now and one hundred years from now, which is what film preservation has always declared as its overarching goal. This book intends to show that this is not only possible but is also not too difficult to learn, once the key aspects of film projection are fully understood. One of its most underrated aspects has to do with what happens before and after the actual projection event. Print inspection is as important as the screening itself, because it is the phase in which the projectionist is given an opportunity to assess the condition of the artifact, prepare it for the screening, and verify its material status after the show, when the print is about to return to the climate-controlled vaults. Detailed condition reports before and after the exhibition of a work or object are customarily made by fine arts curators, who share them with the venue where the object is about to be, or has been, displayed. It is also normal for the receiving venues to examine, discuss, and agree upon the condition reports before the show takes place, as a gesture of understanding and respect for the work that has been previously done to protect the artifact.

This simple procedure can and should be implemented as a matter of course in the exhibition of archival films as well. Inspecting a print involves much more than rewinding it and checking that no tears or abrasions are present on the artifact; on average, a thorough print inspection takes at least half a day of work for a specialized technician. This important task has been unjustifiably neglected by collecting institutions, in the mistaken belief that such work is not a matter of priority. There is only one persuasive argument against this deep-rooted prejudice: print inspection is an aspect of curatorial work of no lesser value than all the others in a film museum. Even the humble act of rewinding a print is an act of curatorship, because it involves a set of decisions that affect the material condition of the film and its future life as a messenger of culture. Film projectionists are curators also because they are in charge of protecting and, when necessary, restoring the film apparatus that makes film exhibition possible. The thorough maintenance of projection equipment on an ongoing basis is in itself an integral part of the film preservation process; securing the availability of replacement parts for the equipment, and being able to build new ones if necessary, is like cleaning and tuning a musical instrument before and after a concert, replacing the strings of a violin or a guitar, or being able to manufacture new parts if necessary.

There is something self-defeating in the attitude that describes film projectionists as an endangered species. The only way to safeguard a form of cultural expression and prevent its premature extinction is to protect and cultivate its own environment. In a film museum or archive, this environment is a complex ecosystem that consists of film prints and negatives, climatized vaults, equipment, and the personnel working in the institution. This includes the projection booth and its staff. The conservation, restoration, and use of projection equipment should become a mandatory topic for all courses in film preservation; its practitioners should be called curators, and their unique role in championing the cause of cinema should not only be recognized once and for all, but also celebrated in museums, archives, festivals, film societies, and every venue where the history of cinema is presented to an audience. Insofar as collecting institutions have photochemical motion picture films in their collections, and to the extent that they wish to present them in their original medium and format, there is no other way to achieve this goal. It must be emphasized that the same curatorial criteria should be applied to the preservation and exhibition of digital-born works, where curatorship speaks a language that is technically different, but whose objectives are fundamentally the same as those pertaining to photochemical film.

Despite its unassuming look, this book is the result of a long planning process. Several drafts of the text were discussed, tested, and shared over many years with the students of the L. Jeffrey Selznick School of Film Preservation. For more than two decades, students and staff of the George Eastman Museum – film projectionists, technicians, and curators – learned from each other with their expertise and their questions, their long acquaintance with film artifacts, and the eager curiosity of those who touched these prints for the first time. They have seen nitrate film projected at the museum, both on a regular basis throughout the years, and at the Nitrate Picture Show, an event inaugurated in 2015, in which films made before the 1950s can still be appreciated in all their visual glory. Like fellow travelers, students and staff have written a joint diary of their experiences, leaving no stone unturned in order to make the art and science of film projection find its long-overdue place of prominence in the realm of film curatorship. As this is a team endeavor, all of its participants – faculty and students – take responsibility for any errors and omissions, in the awareness that writing a handbook for beginners is in many ways more difficult than addressing film specialists, as it must present complex issues in the simplest possible terms.

You, the reader, can help us by using this book. Touch film projectors. Learn how they work. Project film. Do not be afraid of making mistakes, and tell us what our mistakes were, so that we can improve upon this book in its future incarnations. Please do so by writing to selznickschool@eastman.org. Your direct feedback will be taken as the best reward for our efforts.

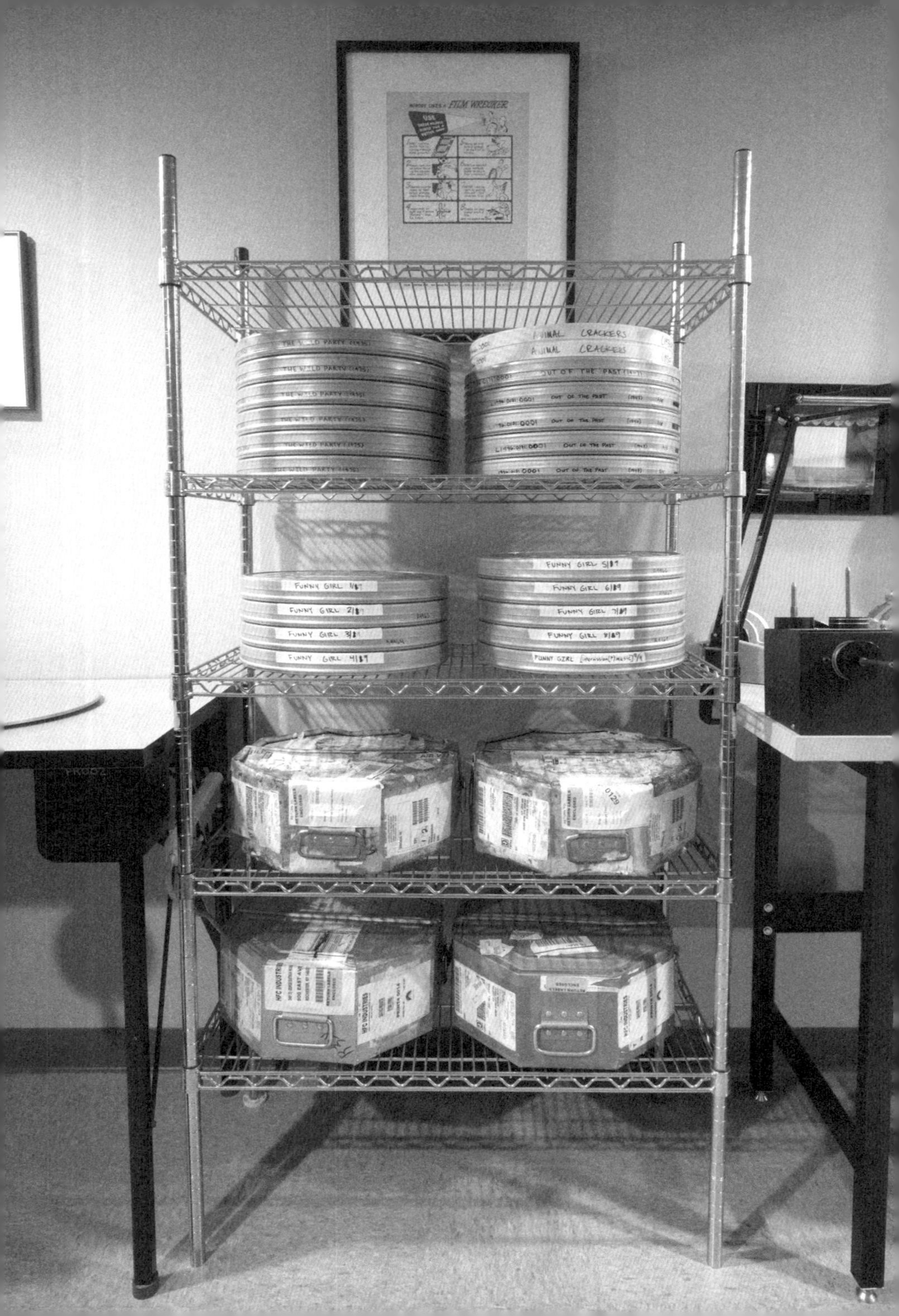
NOBODY LIKES A FILM WRECKER
USE
THE WILD PARTY (1929)
THE WILD PARTY (1935)
THE WILD PARTY (1945)
THE WILD PARTY (1955)
THE WILD PARTY (1975)
THE WILD PARTY (1945)
ANIMAL CRACKERS
ANIMAL CRACKERS
OUT OF THE PAST (1947)
OUT OF THE PAST (1947)
OUT OF THE PAST (1947)
OUT OF THE PAST (1947)
OUT OF THE PAST (1947)
FUNNY GIRL 1/89
FUNNY GIRL 2/89
FUNNY GIRL 3/89
FUNNY GIRL 4/89
FUNNY GIRL 5/89
FUNNY GIRL 6/89
FUNNY GIRL 7/89
FUNNY GIRL 8/89
FUNNY GIRL [intermission(?)music] 9/9
HPC INDUSTRIES

1

THE PRINT

I**N THE WORLD** of archival film projection, reason and passion are the elements that bind together the building blocks of cinema exhibition. A committed film projectionist raises the functional level of equipment operations to an art and craft, capable of seamlessly delivering the breadth and depth of cinema to an engaged audience in a manner consistent with the intentions of the filmmakers, while respecting the material integrity of the film as an artifact.

Archival projection encompasses several disciplines, including mechanics, optics, and electronics. An in-depth knowledge of film history, acquired skills, and sensory awareness (the senses of sight, sound, smell, and touch) are necessary components as well. The ability to coordinate these resources to present a successful screening is the hallmark of a professional film projectionist, who operates a complex piece of electro-mechanical equipment in a small room, while an adjacent audience becomes emotionally, intellectually, and psychologically engaged in a cinematic event. Somewhere between the

Fig. 1.1 – **Commercial 35mm film cans and shipping containers.**

projector and the audience, there is magic happening: nothing in the film archive field is more satisfying than being the person to create this enchantment.

Projectionists have three tools at their disposal to perform their magic: film, equipment, and a space for exhibition. We shall begin with describing the film object itself.

MOTION PICTURE FILM

Motion picture film stock is composed of a clear base material supporting a layer of **emulsion**, a light-sensitive layer which contains the image. Since around 1888, motion picture film stock has been manufactured worldwide by many companies on a variety of base materials, beginning with nitrate, followed by diacetate, triacetate, and, later, polyester. **Nitrate film**, which is flammable, is addressed in Chapter 10. The **35mm width** of commercial motion picture film stock was generally accepted as the **standard format** by the early 1900s.

Acetate film, also referred to as "**safety film**," was introduced around 1912 as a non-flammable, safer alternative for home, school, and industrial use. The early version of this base, cellulose diacetate, was available in several **gauges** (such as 28mm, 22mm, 16mm, 9.5mm, and 8mm), depending on the manufacturer and intended use. In the early 1920s, the Eastman Kodak Company promoted 16mm acetate safety film as a standard for home and school use; however, it wasn't until 1951 that Kodak discontinued the manufacture of nitrate film and began selling exclusively a new kind of acetate carrier (cellulose triacetate) for use as 35mm professional motion picture film. Kodak acetate film stock was manufactured in several chemical compositions over time. Other manufacturers of motion picture film are mentioned in the section "Film Stocks" in Chapter 4.

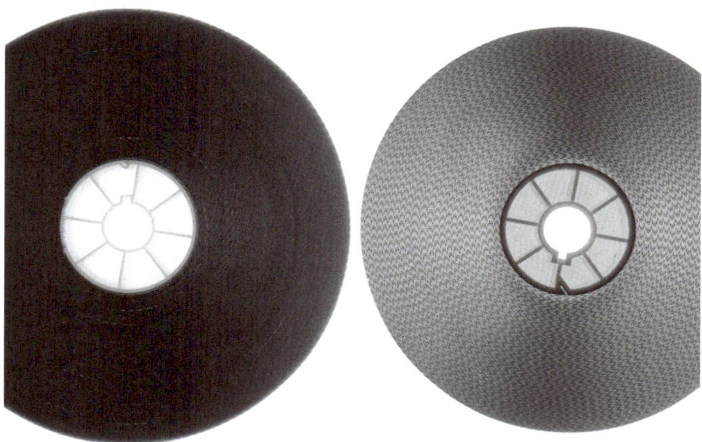

1.2 – **When held up to light, acetate film stock (left) appears opaque, while polyester film stock (right) is translucent.**

Polyester motion picture film stock was introduced in 1955, although it was not until the early 1990s that it began to replace triacetate film for use in mainstream theatrical exhibition. Thinner than acetate film, polyester holds superior strength and dimensional stability over acetate, and suffers from little to no shrinkage after several years.

The easiest method of determining whether a film stock is acetate or polyester is to hold a reel of film up to a light source and look through the film pack. *[Figure 1.2]* Acetate stock is typically opaque, while polyester stock is normally translucent (please note, however, that some 16mm acetate stocks can also appear translucent).

The two sides of the film are referred to as **the base and the emulsion**, with the photographic image residing in the emulsion. With acetate film stock, the base side generally appears shiny, while the emulsion side appears matte. When working with

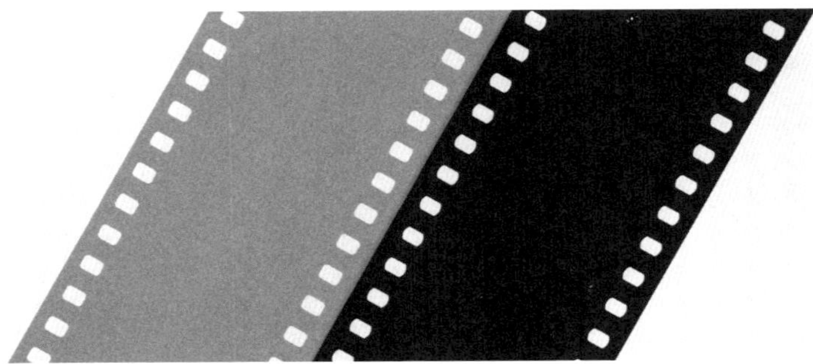

1.3 – **35mm film stock with Kodak Standard (KS) perforations (left) and Bell & Howell (BH) perforations (right).**

polyester stock, it can be difficult to distinguish the base from the emulsion. **To determine the emulsion side of a polyester film**, lay the film flat on a clean surface, with a light source reflecting off the surface of the film into the direction of your eyes. A black cloth underneath the film is helpful in minimizing distraction from the picture. The emulsion side will display a faint relief pattern along the surface, caused by the presence of an image within the emulsion. This pattern may be difficult to see at first: always remember to look at the surface of the film, rather than the image itself. Images with high contrast and straight lines (such as film credits with white letters on a black background) provide the most noticeable relief patterns. The base side, which is merely a flat piece of plastic, will not have any surface pattern to show (other than scratches and other possible damage).

Film inspectors should not use other methods of identifying the emulsion side which are likely to cause physical harm to the object, such as breathing on either surface of the film. With this method, a fog of moisture momentarily appears on the base side, then quickly evaporates. On the emulsion side, however, the moisture will be permanently absorbed without fogging the surface, damaging the film. Additionally, putting film between one's lips to determine the emulsion side (as the moisture sticks only to the emulsion, and not to the base) permanently damages film, leaving lip marks which cannot be removed by cleaning. It is also an unseemly thing to do. Please don't put film in your mouth!

Motion picture film can be printed so that the image reads correctly when you are looking through the emulsion (**A-wind**), or looking through the base (**B-wind**). Most 35mm projection prints are A-wind. Most 16mm projection prints are B-wind. Determining whether a print is A-wind or B-wind is best done when looking at text, preferably opening titles or credits.

Film stock is manufactured with either black & white or color emulsion, to produce either a positive or negative image. In most cases, **negative stock is used in motion picture cameras**. **Contact printing and optical printing** within the duplication process result in the creation of **positive copies for film projection**.

PERFORATIONS

Most 35mm motion picture stock has four perforations per frame, along both sides of the film. There are many kinds of perforations, depending on when and where the print was made, but only two are most frequently found on standard projection prints. Positive stock manufactured for projection has **positive perforations**, also known as **KS perforations (Kodak Standard)**, which have the shape of rectangles with rounded corners. Motion picture film manufactured for negatives and intermediate duplication has **negative perforations**, or **BH perforations (Bell & Howell)**, which are rectangular as well, but ever-so-slightly shorter in height and with slightly curved sides, looking like parentheses. *[Figure 1.3]*

Negative perforation stock, designed to accommodate rotary heads on contact printers, also has a shorter **pitch**, meaning that the perforations are closer together (vaguely approximating the look of a shrunken film). Most 35mm projection prints made between the early 1910s and the introduction of KS perforations in 1924 have Bell & Howell perforations. Before the late 1900s, perforations were made in a variety of shapes and sizes; this is because film producers were often purchasing raw sensitized stock, to be perforated with many different kinds of commercially available machines.

16mm motion picture film has one perforation per frame. It is available with perforations along one side of the film (single-perforation stock) or both sides (double-perforation stock). *[Figure 1.4]* 16mm prints with an audio track are single-perforation, while 16mm silent films may be printed on either single-perforation or double-perforation stock. When projecting 16mm film with vintage projectors, it is important to know whether the projector has a single-claw or double-claw advance mechanism, and whether it has teeth on just one side or both sides of the sprockets. Single-perforation film cannot be projected on a double-claw or double-tooth sprocket projector without damaging the film. As with 35mm film, 16mm motion picture film is also available in short- and long-pitch stocks; the pitch can vary depending on the stock.

PROJECTION SPEED

35mm and 16mm projection prints may be silent, or contain optical or magnetic audio tracks. The average projection speed in the silent era ranged between 16 and 18 frames per second, with significant variations relative to the country and the year of production (from 14 frames per second and below for many early films, to 20 frames per second and above in the late silent era). The optimal projection speed of a film is largely dependent upon how fast the camera was cranked during shooting.

1.4 – **16mm film stock with double perforation (left) and single perforation (right).**

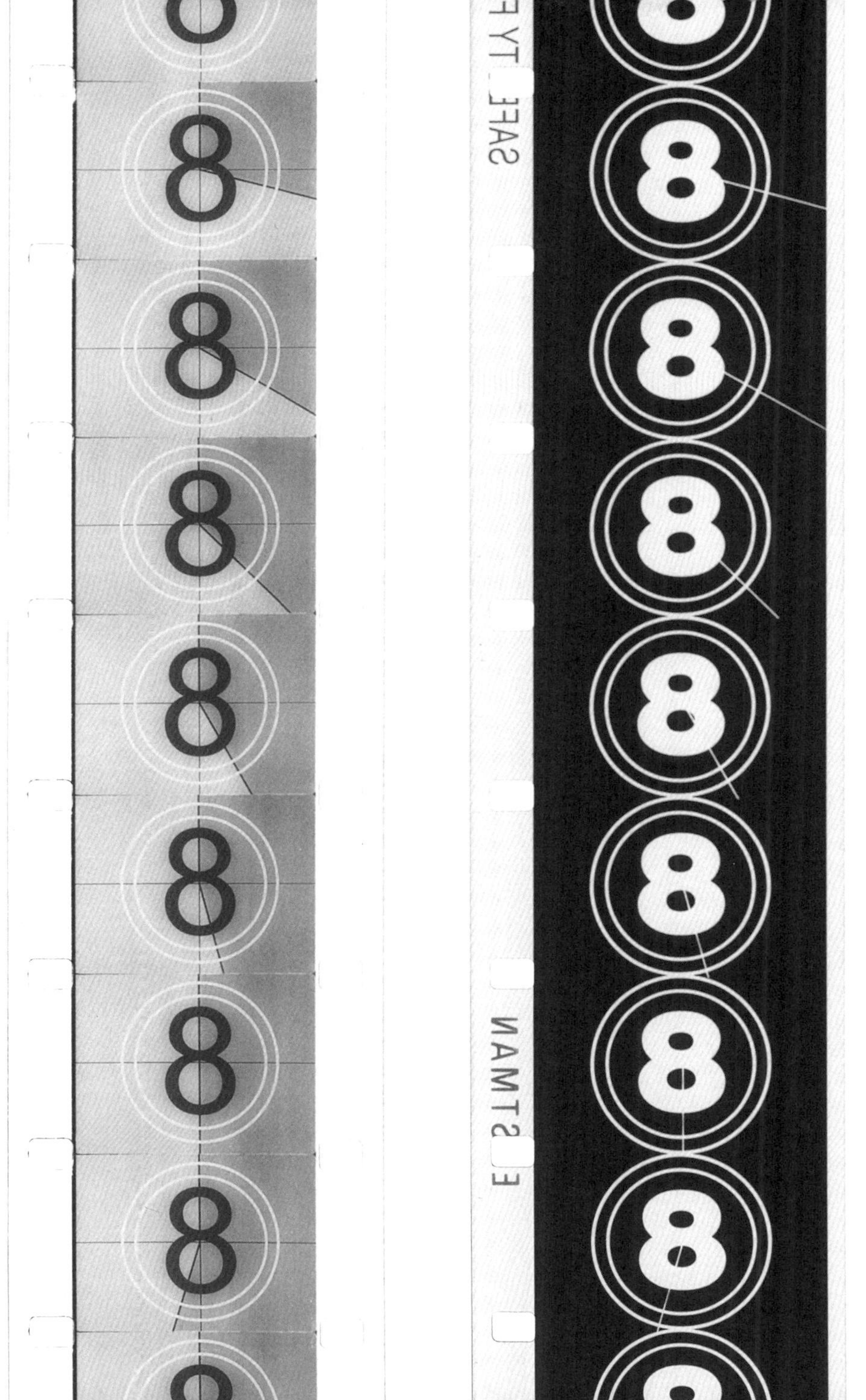
SAFE TYPE
EASTMAN

It is important to keep in mind, however, that **there is no single rule on the appropriate speed for silent films**, and that the most frequently used speed in a given territory was not necessarily common in other parts of the world. For instance, Japanese silent films of the early 1930s often look best when projected at 18 frames per second.

Contrary to common belief, there was no steady progression from slower to faster projection speeds from the early to the late years of silent cinema. **A projectionist should test projection speed prior to each screening**, ensuring that the movements of the characters onscreen are appropriate to the situation: an extra one or two frames per second sometimes helps to give the film an appropriate rhythm. Slapstick comedies made in the United States, in particular, may be best projected a touch faster than dramas. In any case, projectionists should exercise their best judgment (in consultation with curatorial staff and with musicians specialized in silent film accompaniment) in projecting silent films at speeds that facilitate a smooth, natural movement of the characters on the screen. In a few cases, projection speeds may vary within the same film.

Archival projection equipment should include a **rheostat** or a similar mechanism for varying projection speed with the greatest degree of accuracy. To avoid the "flicker" effect that is often derived from slower projection speeds, projectors that are used to show silent films should be equipped with a **three-blade shutter** (or a mechanism which approximates this effect, such as Kinoton's Variodrive shutter system). When a three-blade shutter is in use, it is advisable to enhance the output of the light source to compensate for the extra blade.

SOUNDTRACK

Sound films with optical or magnetic tracks should be projected at **24 frames per second**.

Magnetic audio tracks are less common than optical tracks, and require a projector to be equipped with a magnetic playback head.

Optical tracks may contain an analog or a digital signal. 16mm prints with optical tracks carry a mono, analog signal. 35mm prints can simultaneously accommodate up to four optical tracks: analog (mono or stereo), SRD (Dolby Digital), DTS (Digital Theater Systems, later known as Datasat Digital Entertainment), and SDDS (Sony Dynamic Digital Stereo). Further information on this topic is provided in the section "Soundtracks" in Chapter 4.

While the image portion of motion picture film is projected in an intermittent fashion to create the illusion of movement, the soundtrack (whether optical or magnetic) needs to be read in a smooth, continuous motion. To accommodate the mechanics necessary to meet these separate requirements, each image's accompanying audio information is printed a specified number of frames apart from the image. For 35mm optical tracks, the sound is printed 21.5 frames ahead of the corresponding picture. For 16mm optical tracks, the sound is printed 26 frames ahead of the corresponding picture. For 35mm magnetic tracks, the sound is printed 28 frames *behind* the corresponding picture (the only such case). For 16mm magnetic tracks, the sound is printed 28 frames ahead of the corresponding picture. These separations work in tandem with the designs of motion picture projectors, which must use separate mechanisms in different locations to project images and read audio tracks simultaneously.

ASPECT RATIO

The image area of motion picture film may be printed in a variety of aspect ratios, which determine the shape of the projected image. Multiple sets of lenses and aperture plates for film projectors are required to present the images properly, along with adjustable masking for the screen. Further information on this matter is covered in the section "Aspect Ratios" in Chapter 4.

REEL LENGTH

35mm motion picture films are typically shipped in containers holding several 2,000-foot reels. At a projection speed of 24 frames per second (or 90 feet per minute), a 2,000-foot reel accommodates approximately 22 minutes of running time. Table-top film counters, calibrated in feet or in meters depending on their country of manufacture (Europe: metres), are used to measure the lengths of film reels. 35mm motion picture film has 16 frames per foot, while 16mm motion picture film has 40 frames per foot.

DO'S AND DON'TS

ALWAYS

- Honor each projection print as if it were the last surviving element of the film. The copy can and should leave the projection booth in the same or better condition than it was before the screening.

- Test the projection speed of silent film prints prior to each screening.

NEVER

- Identify the emulsion and base sides of the print by placing the film in your mouth.

- Project single-perforation 16mm prints on double-claw or double-tooth sprocket projectors.

NOTES

NOTES

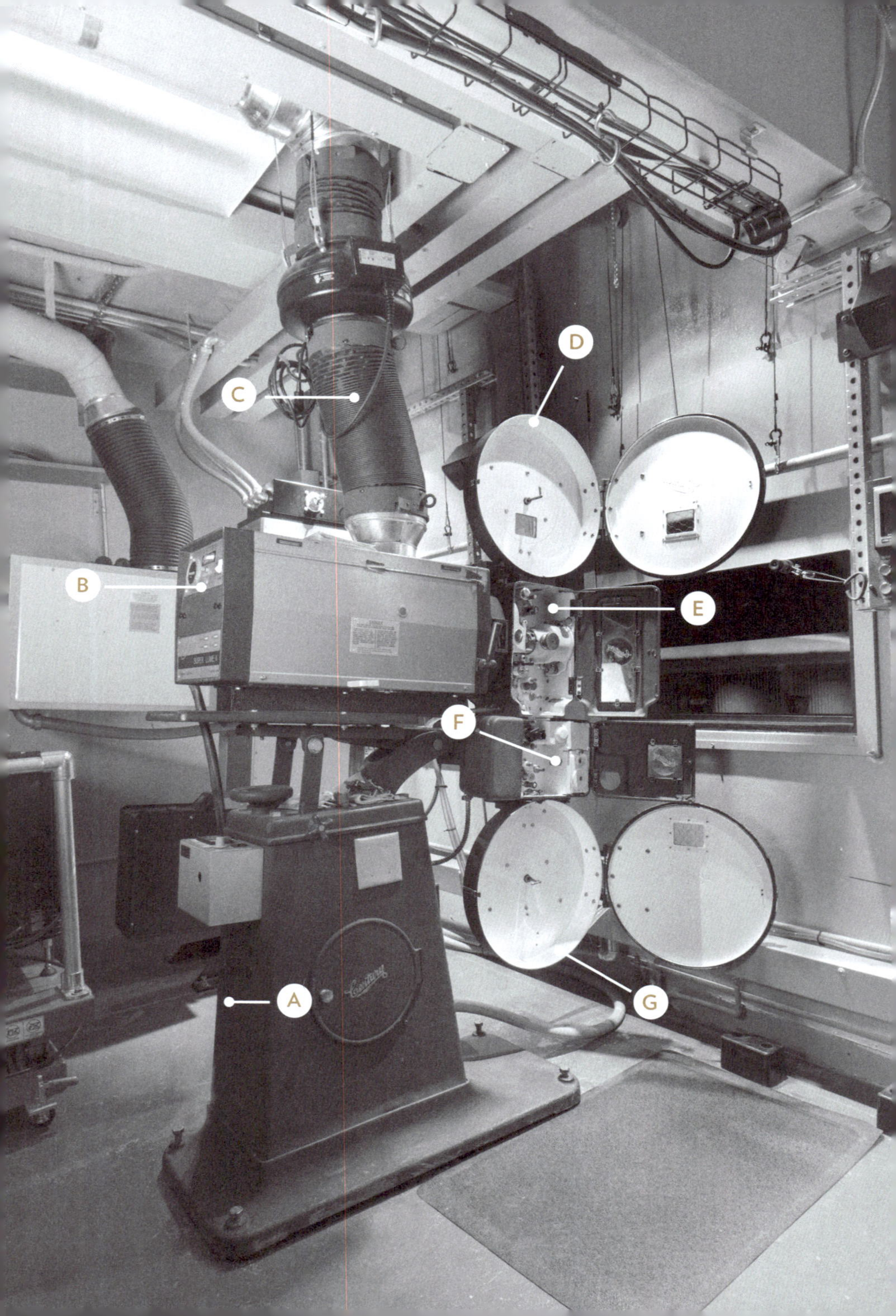

C
D
B
E
F
A
G
Century

2

THE PROJECTOR

MOTION PICTURE FILM projectors are made of components designed to project successive still images onto a surface, quickly enough to create the illusion of motion. Despite this simple description, the motion picture projector is a highly specialized, precision-built mechanism designed to perform precise functions.

Many brands and types of film projectors are used for the exhibition of cinematic works in various formats: Cinemeccanica, Kinoton, Ernemann, Norelco, Century, Bauer, and Simplex (as well as Eiko, Bell & Howell, and Eastman Kodak for 16mm projectors) are only a few of the most familiar. Describing them all is well beyond the scope of this introductory volume. Most of these machines, however, share the same basic configuration. The examples and illustrations presented in this book are related to three film projectors commonly used for archival prints: Century (Model C) and Simplex (Model PR-1014), from the United States; and Kinoton (Model FP 38 E), from Germany. Before operating any film projection equipment, please consult

Fig. 2.1 – **The main components of a Century Model C 35mm film projector (United States, ca. 1940):**

A. PEDESTAL B. LAMPHOUSE C. EXHAUST STACK D. FEED MAGAZINE
E. PICTURE HEAD F. SOUND HEAD G. TAKE-UP MAGAZINE

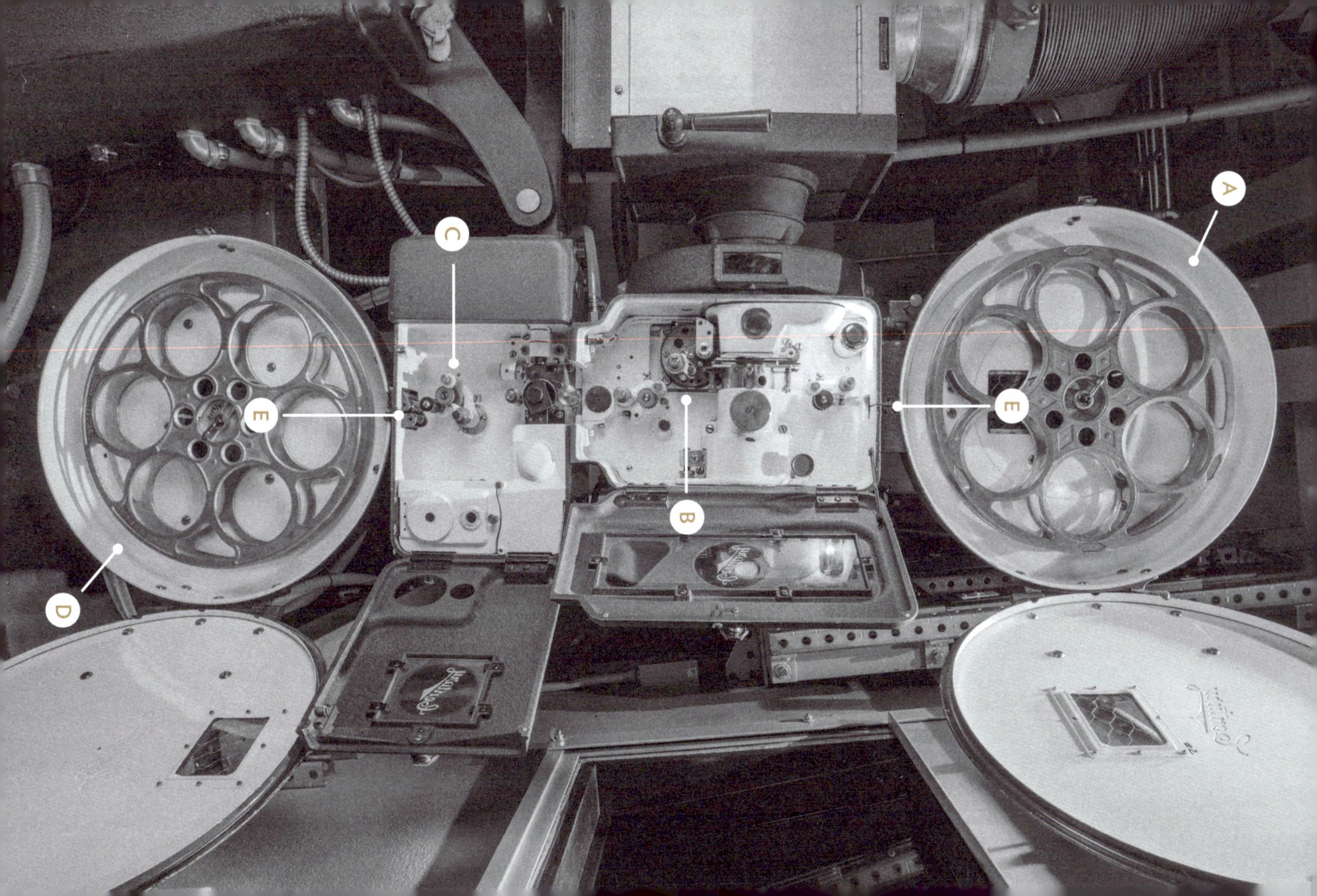

A
B
C
D
E
E

that projector's instruction manual, and verify that the manu-facturer's recommended practices are consistent with those described in this book.

THE PROJECTOR MECHANISM

Whether 16mm or 35mm, the front end of the projector contains all the moving parts and mechanisms required to make motion pictures come to life on the screen. In basic 35mm projectors, you will find (from the top down): a **feed magazine** or spindle; a **picture head**; a **sound head**; and a **take-up magazine** or spindle. *[Figure 2.2]*

Older 35mm projectors, designed to accommodate nitrate film, also feature a fully enclosed **film path** (including film magazines, and picture and sound heads), and **fire rollers** between the magazines and their adjacent components. Projectors designed to run safety film usually, but not always, feature an open film path, with spindles for feed and take-up reels, rather than enclosed magazines.

Magazine enclosures for 35mm projectors may be sized to accommodate 2,000-foot, 3,000-foot, or 6,000-foot reels. Sets of metal fire rollers are located between the feed magazine and the picture head, and between the sound head and the take-up magazine. These rollers are intended to prevent fire from reaching magazines containing flammable nitrate film, in the event of a film break. Further information regarding the projection of **nitrate film** is provided in Chapter 10.

2.2 – **Lateral view of a Century 35mm film projector with open compartments.**

A. **FEED MAGAZINE** B. **PICTURE HEAD** C. **SOUND HEAD**
D. **TAKE-UP MAGAZINE** E. **FIRE ROLLERS**

For projectors with open spindles, the distance of the spindles from the picture or sound head determines the reel size that can be accommodated. Feed spindles are tensioned to provide resistance, so that film reels don't freewheel and begin feeding film faster than the projector mechanism advances it. Take-up spindles incorporate some type of slip-clutch mechanism, so that the speed of the take-up reel adjusts (slows) as the reel advances and the diameter of the amount of film on the reel increases. To minimize damage to film prints, it is recommended to maintain a set of **metal house reels** in good condition for mounting and projecting films (never use the plastic reels often provided with the shipment of prints from commercial distributors). Using the proper metal reels for both feed and take-up prevents or at least minimizes the damage to film and projection equipment that can be caused by reels with warped or cracked flanges, sharp edges, and damaged spokes.

Given how the image and the sound are reproduced on motion picture stock, film projectors feature separate picture and sound heads. In general, after the film leaves the feed reel, it enters the picture head, where the image is projected with intermittent motion. The film then travels into the sound head, where the audio track(s) are read with continuous motion. Finally, the film travels to the take-up reel for winding.

THE PICTURE HEAD

[Figure 2.3]

The film is pulled into the picture head by the first of two or three constant-drive **sprockets**. **Pad rollers or pad shoes** (plastic or metal) hold the film against these sprockets, which turn at a continuous rate. The film then passes through the **gate and trap assembly**, where image projection occurs when each

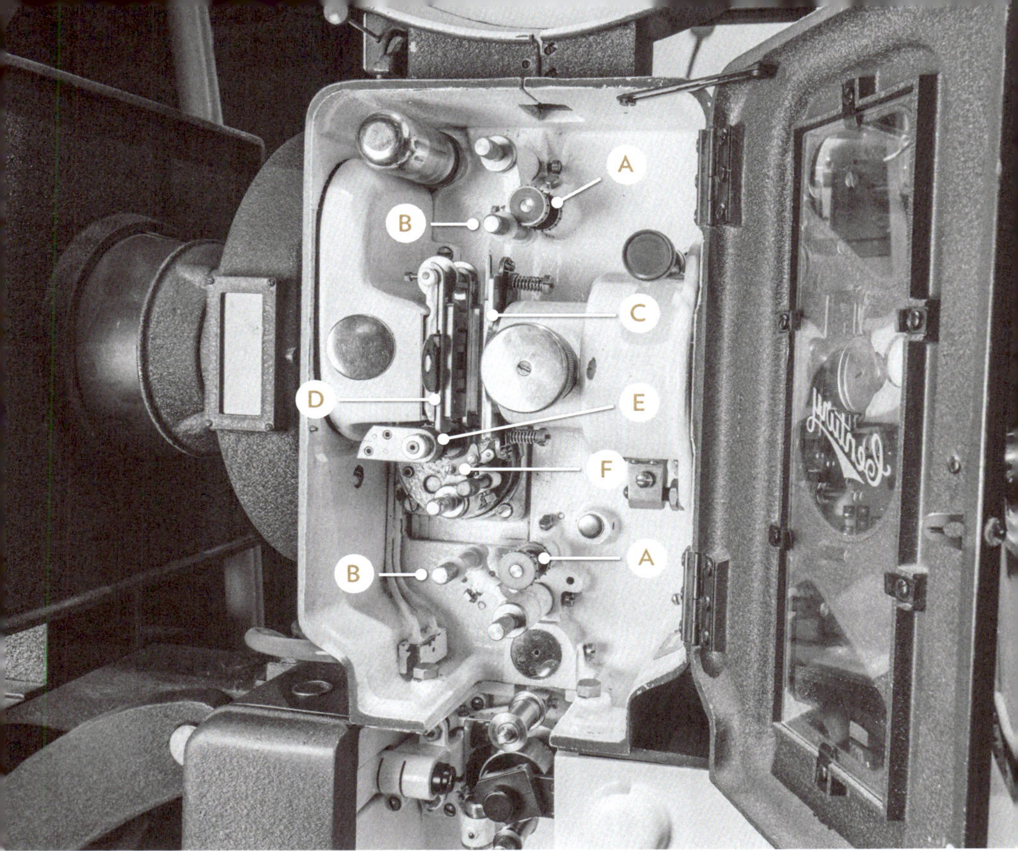

2.3 – Lateral view of the picture head in a Century 35mm film projector with open compartments.

A. DRIVE SPROCKETS   B. PAD ROLLERS   C. GATE   D. TRAP
E. INTERMITTENT SPROCKET   F. PAD SHOE

frame is momentarily brought to rest. This assembly (often referred to simply as the "gate") is a mechanism made up of several components, which include the film **trap**, the **gate**, and the **aperture plate**.

The static film **trap** (between the film and the lamphouse) guides the film and contains a slot for interchangeable aperture plates. The **gate** (between the film and the lens) is movable, to allow access to the film trap for threading. The flat or

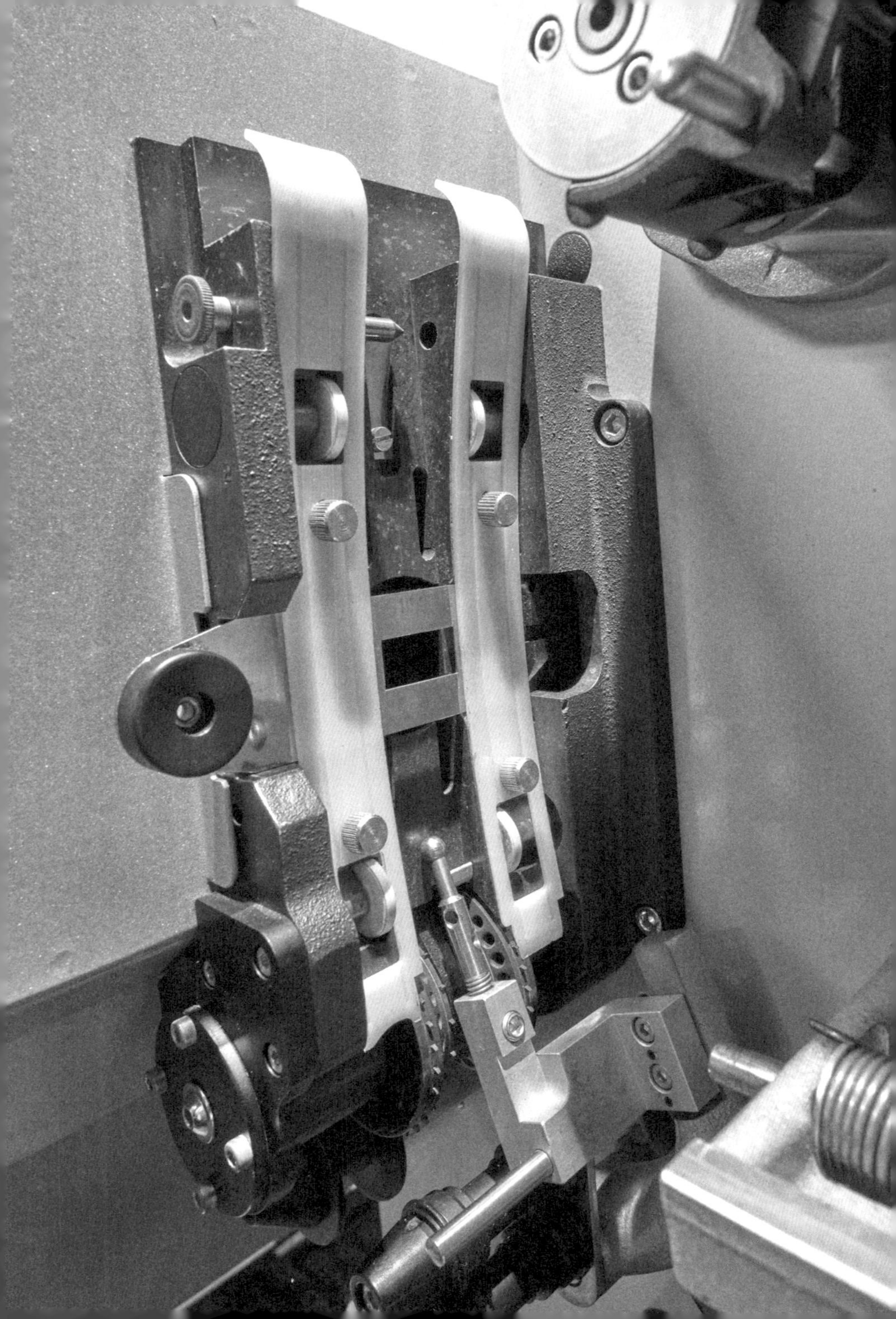

curved gate (usually made of metal) has an adjustable spring tension in order to hold the film flat against the trap once the gate is closed. It is important for the film to lay flat in the aperture in order to achieve a perfectly even focus. Curved gates are designed to relieve the effect of film **"flutter,"** or unsteadiness, and improve the focus stability of warped films. Some projectors of more recent manufacture feature Delrin (a synthetic polymer thermoplastic) film pressure **"skates"** in place of metal gates. *[Figure 2.4]*

The film gate may be flat or curved, and it may also have been manufactured to incorporate water cooling, a safety feature for projectors designed to protect the projector mechanism, avoid burning fingers on a hot gate and trap assembly, and prevent overheating the film stock. Water-cooled gates incorporate internal plumbing, connected to the building's water supply or to a closed, recirculating system in order to enable cool water to flow through the metal trap, which conducts heat from the intense light emanating from the lamphouse.

35mm projectors employ **aperture plates** to define the aspect ratio of the projected image. These metal plates may be found in multiple aspect ratios, as well as undercut or blank, to allow custom filing for each installation. Accommodating more than one hundred years of cinema history on a single machine requires a wide variety of aperture plates to provide suitable aspect ratios to match individual films. The 35mm anamorphic CinemaScope process alone has been specified in three different aspect ratios, depending upon audio format and year of release. The most common **aspect ratios** are 1.18:1 (early sound), 1.33:1 (silent), 1.37:1 ("Academy" aperture), 1.66:1 (flat widescreen), 1.85:1 (flat widescreen), and 2.39:1 (current anamorphic). *[Figure 2.5. see following page]*

2.4 – **Delrin pressure "skates" on a Kinoton Model FP 38 E 35mm/16mm film projector (Germany, ca. 2000).**

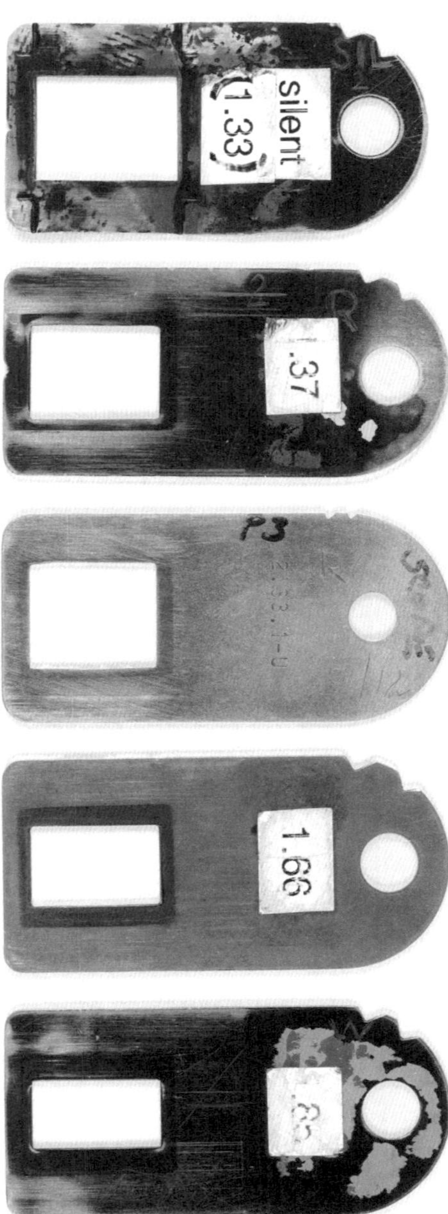
SIL
silent
(1.33)
R
1.37
P3
N.33.1-U
1.66

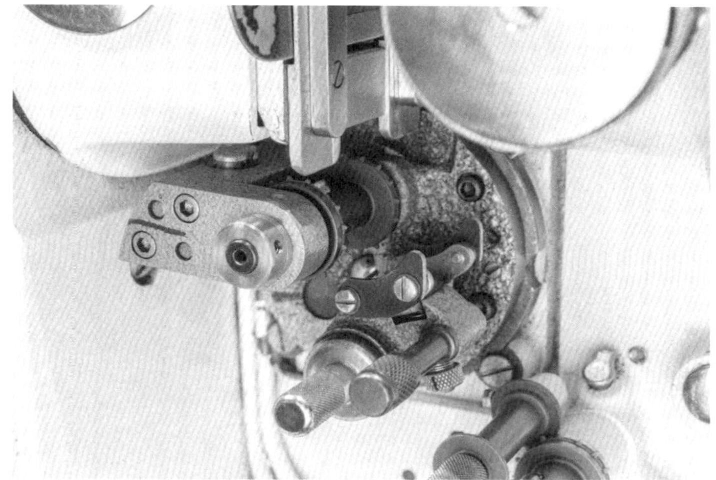

2.6 – **The intermittent sprocket and Geneva drive mechanism in a Century 35mm film projector.**

16mm projectors do not feature interchangeable aperture plates; they are manufactured with an aperture of 1.33:1, and this aperture is used regardless of whether a 16mm print has a flat or anamorphic aspect ratio (the latter requires a 2.66:1 lens).

To align the vertical position of the film frame with the aperture, both 16mm and 35mm projectors incorporate some type of mechanical or electrical framing adjustment. If the adjustment is mechanically based, make sure to center the adjustment within its range of travel before threading the projector, as this will permit adjustment in either direction.

Located just below the gate, the **intermittent drive sprocket** pulls the film through the gate, one frame at a time. *[Figure 2.6]* The **Geneva movement** of this drive sprocket converts the

2.5 – **The aperture plates of a Century 35mm film projector (from top to bottom: 1.33:1, 1.37:1, 2.39:1, 1.66:1, 1.85:1).**

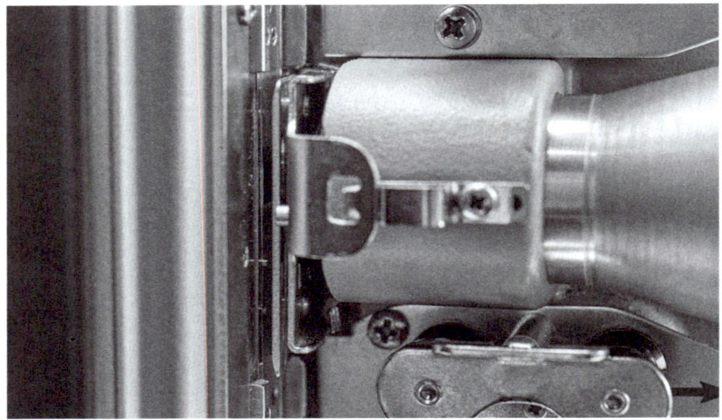

2.7 – **The claw mechanism in a Kodak Pageant 250S portable 16mm film projector (United States, ca. 1977).**

continuous motion of the motor into an intermittent rotation, holding each frame in place as light passes through the aperture. (In the early years of cinema, the name "Geneva" was adopted for this movement because the mechanism looked like those used in mechanical watches from Switzerland.)

Pressure pads hold the film against this sprocket. The pressure pads may be incorporated into the movable gate, or may be located independently. In more recent projectors, plastic film pressure skates accomplish this function as well, removing the need for separate pressure pads.

Electronic **stepper motors**, which divide a full rotation into a number of equal steps, have replaced Geneva movements in more recent 35mm film projectors.

Most portable 16mm projectors employ a **retracting claw mechanism** to engage the film perforations and pull the film intermittently through the gate, although some high-end stationary models employ intermittent sprockets. *[Figure 2.7]* After leaving the intermittent drive sprocket, the film may engage a second constant-drive sprocket before traveling into the sound head.

A **rotating shutter** works in conjunction with the intermittent drive sprocket (or claw mechanism) to produce the illusion of motion. Most projectors feature a two-blade mechanical shutter, which alternately blocks and allows light to travel from the lamphouse to the projector gate. *[Figure 2.8]* The shutter rotates in sync with the intermittent mechanism. One blade blocks the light while the intermittent mechanism pulls the film into place within the gate. As the shutter continues to rotate, the film frame is then exposed to light, blocked by the second blade, then exposed to light a second time, before being advanced while the first blade blocks the light again. A three-blade shutter can be installed in place of a two-blade shutter, considerably reducing the **"flicker"** (or strobing) effect when films are shown at less than 24 frames per second. *[Figure 2.9]* Unfortunately, this also results in a significant loss of light output (approximately 50%), and requires the projectionist to make adjustments to the lamphouse components to bring the light output up to the recommended specifications.

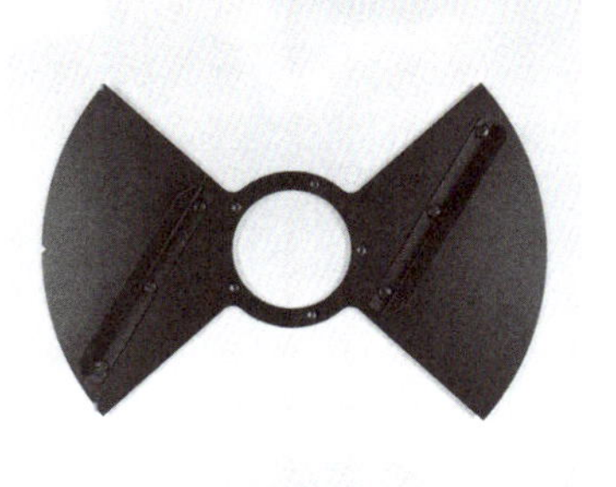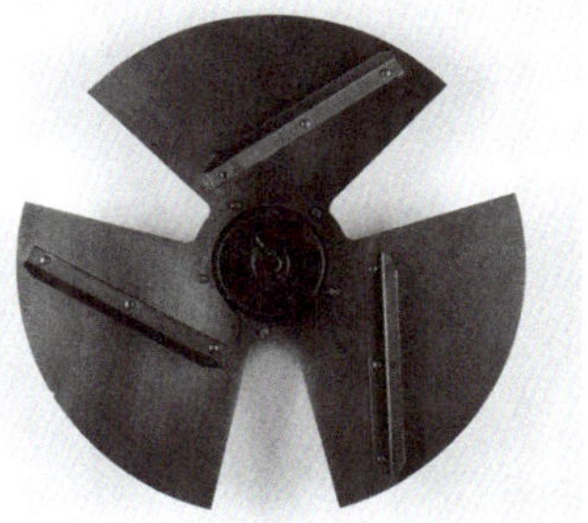

2.8 & 2.9 – **Two- and three-blade shutters for Century 35mm film projectors.**

For safety reasons, the spinning shutter is located either inside the projector mechanism behind the aperture, or in a housing located on the back of the projector mechanism, facing the lamphouse. The earliest 35mm projectors featured open spinning shutters in front of the lens. Many film projectors of more recent manufacture incorporate electronic shutters, rather than mechanical shutters. These shutters adjust to eliminate flicker when the projector is run at slower frame rates. One example of this is Kinoton's Variodrive shutter system, which increases the speed of shutter rotation as the projection speed (frame rate) decreases.

When a projector shutter becomes out of sync with the intermittent movement, it results in a **"ghosting"** effect on screen. "Ghosting" has the appearance of blurring the image near the top or bottom of the picture, depending upon which direction the shutter is out of sync. This is most easily noticed when viewing subtitles, intertitles, or white credits on a black background: the white letters will appear to "streak" upward or downward. Some 35mm projectors feature a shutter knob on the picture head, which allows for minor adjustments to the shutter timing.

The picture head of the projector mechanism also accommodates a holder and focusing mechanism for the **lens**. Lenses magnify and focus the projected image on the screen. The **focal length** of a lens, usually measured in millimeters, determines the amount of image magnification. Lenses with shorter focal lengths magnify an image greater for any given distance than those with longer focal lengths. Lenses are also rated in **f-stops** by the amount of light they transmit. Fast lenses (which have low f-stops) transmit more light, while slow lenses with high f-stops have greater depth of focus, which is advantageous for presentation.

To exhibit multiple aspect ratios while maintaining a common screen width or height (which is typical of most theater screen installations), a separate lens and aperture plate is required for each aspect ratio that is to be presented. Each projector should have its own set of lenses and plates. A sharp, well-defined picture can only result from the use of good lenses. Lenses manufactured before 1978 should be avoided when possible (with the possible exception of the Bausch & Lomb CinemaScope adapter), as lenses produced after 1978 take film "flutter" into account by providing better depth of focus.

Focus is achieved by matching the focal point of the lens with the focal plane of the film. Most projectors feature a focus knob mechanism which translates radial motion into lateral motion, allowing for fine control of the focus. The lens moves back and forth, relative to the film in the gate, until the best focus is achieved.

Projection lenses are typically secured within lens mounts, collars, or holders, designed to fit particular projectors. *[Figure 2.10]* Some lens mounts feature a collar which surrounds the lens, fitted with an adjustable stop ring, designed to horizontally position the lens within focus range when installed in the projector. Some lens holders clamp the lens inside a fixture, which is then clamped onto the projector when the lens is needed.

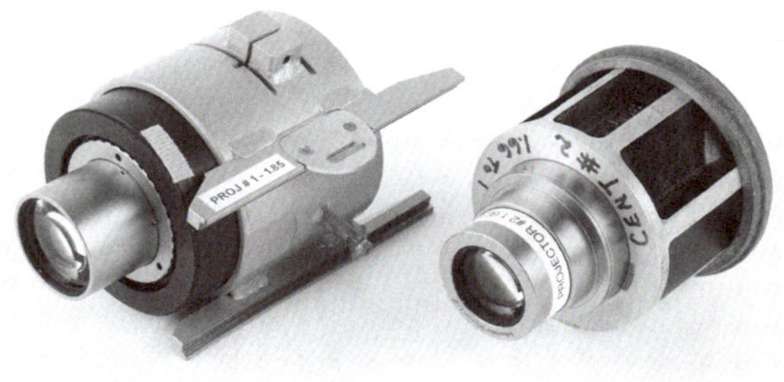

2.10 – **Projection lenses mounted within a Kinoton 35mm/16mm film projector fixture (left) and a Century 35mm film projector collar (right).**

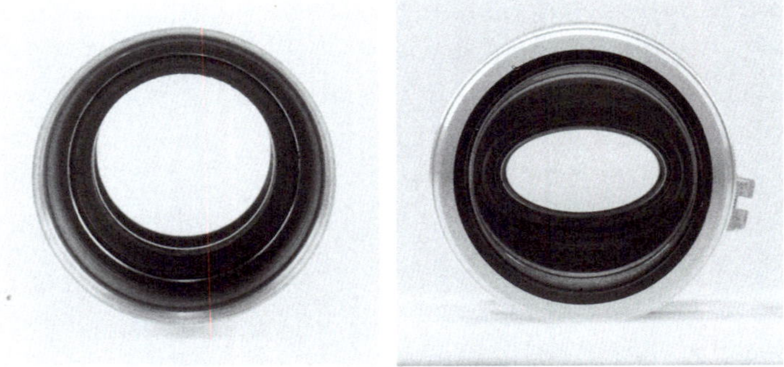

2.11 & 2.12 – **Front views of spherical or "flat" (left) and anamorphic (right) 35mm film projection lenses.**

Most projection lenses are spherical in design and construction. These **"flat" lenses** can be mounted in the projector in any radial orientation. *[Figure 2.11]* **Anamorphic lenses**, however, such as those required for CinemaScope films, are optically designed to squeeze or un-squeeze the width of an image (traditionally, by a factor of 2). *[Figure 2.12]* These lenses require radial alignment to ensure that the image is not skewed as the anamorphic lens stretches the film image. Anamorphic lens elements may be manufactured as an attachment for a prime (or non-anamorphic) lens, or incorporated within integrated anamorphic lenses, for use on film projectors. When placing an anamorphic lens assembly in the projector, the radial orientation is critical to maintain proper image orientation on the screen. For projectors without an alignment mechanism, the film can be projected during pre-focus (a brief projection test required before the show), while the projectionist rotates the anamorphic lens assembly to achieve proper alignment. (Additional information on this point is presented in Chapter 7.)

When operating a two-projector system to project multi-reel films, a **changeover mechanism** on the picture head is needed to cut off the light from one projector while simultaneously permitting light from the other, so that a continuous image is projected as the reels change. *[Figure 2.13]* The changeover mechanism is an electro-mechanically operated metal shutter that blocks the light from reaching the aperture in the projector trap. This mechanism is usually located within the projector, somewhere behind the trap, and is manually activated by a button or foot pedal. The picture changeover mechanisms on both projectors are normally wired into the same circuit, so that when one opens, the other closes automatically (they may be opened and closed manually as well). These mechanisms may be built and made available from sources other than the original manufacturer of the projector.

The **"inboard" side** of the picture head (opposite the operator's side) contains gearing or electronics to enable the synchronous function of moving parts. On projectors designed to run nitrate film, this area may also contain a mechanically activated

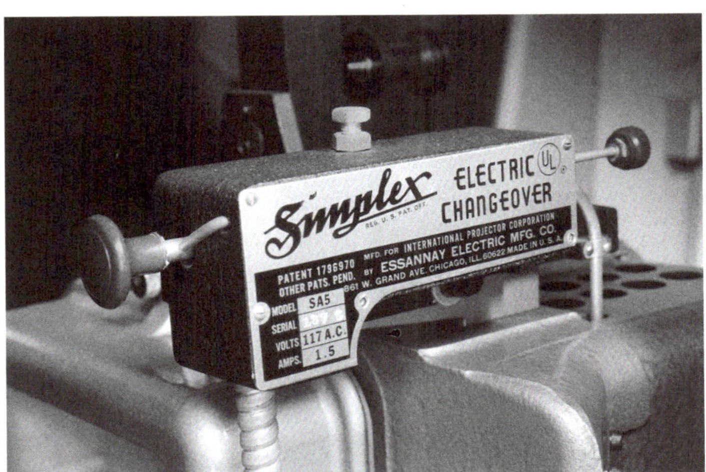

2.13 – **The picture changeover mechanism of a Strong Simplex PR-1014 35mm film projector (United States, ca. 1991).**

fire safety shutter mechanism, intended to minimize exposure of flammable nitrate film to heat. If this mechanism is present, it is good to be aware of it when troubleshooting, as it has the capacity to partially block light from reaching the aperture.

SOUND READERS

Upon exiting the bottom of the picture head, the film enters a sound head, which is enclosed on older 35mm projectors, and open on newer 35mm projectors. Since the analog optical audio track is printed a specified number of frames in advance of the image, it can be read in a continuous fashion in the sound head, while its corresponding image is simultaneously projected in an intermittent fashion in the picture head located directly above.

Prior to the advent of digital motion picture soundtracks, analog optical soundtracks were the norm (in a variety of formats). **Sound heads for analog optical tracks** contain a sound drum with tension roller(s), a sound reader (solar cell, exciter lamp, and slit lens), and a constant-drive sprocket. *[Figure 2.14, see following pages]*. To maintain a smooth and even travel past the sound reader, a sound drum is employed. Film is threaded with tension around the polished surface of the drum, with one or more rollers above and below the drum providing the tension. The sound drum is freewheeling, and attached to a weighty flywheel located on the inboard side of the projector. A constant-drive sprocket located at the bottom of the sound head pulls the film continuously through the head. Surface tension of the film on the sound drum causes the drum to turn, while the heavy flywheel keeps the drum rotating at a constant speed (the inertia of the flywheel resists changes in speed).

[Figure 2.15, see following pages] The optical soundtrack is read by a **solar cell**, which converts pulses of light to pulses of

electrical current. A DC-powered **exciter lamp** provides the light. **Direct current (DC)** is used in favor of alternating current (AC), as AC current induces a hum to the audio based on the frequency of the alternating current. The light from the exciter lamp is focused onto the soundtrack via a slit lens, which focuses and masks the light, emitting a sharp, horizontal beam of light onto the optical soundtrack portion of the film. The solar cell is located on the other side of the film, opposite the slit lens. Modulations in the variable density or variable area optical track create pulses of light, which fall upon the solar cell. (A **"variable area"** optical soundtrack is made of one or more transparent lines of varying width, running along the length of the film stock, between the perforations and the image area. In the **"variable density"** soundtrack, the width remains constant but the density changes. More information on these and other types of audio tracks may be found in the section "Soundtracks," at the end of Chapter 4.) The solar cell converts the pulsing light to weak electrical pulses, which are then pre-amplified before being processed in the audio processor. Split (stereo) solar cell readers are required to play stereo optical analog tracks. By encoding (essentially combining) a four-channel audio signal within a two-track analog optical track, Dolby Laboratories has allowed four channels of audio to be decoded: left, center, right, and surround. This type of multi-channel encoding began appearing in film audio tracks around 1977.

On 35mm film projectors, analog optical sound readers are located on the **"outboard" side** (the operator's side) of the sound drum. The soundtrack portion of the film extends outward past the edge of the sound drum in order to be read. On 16mm film projectors, analog optical sound readers are not easily visible, as they are generally located on the **"inboard" side** of the sound drum.

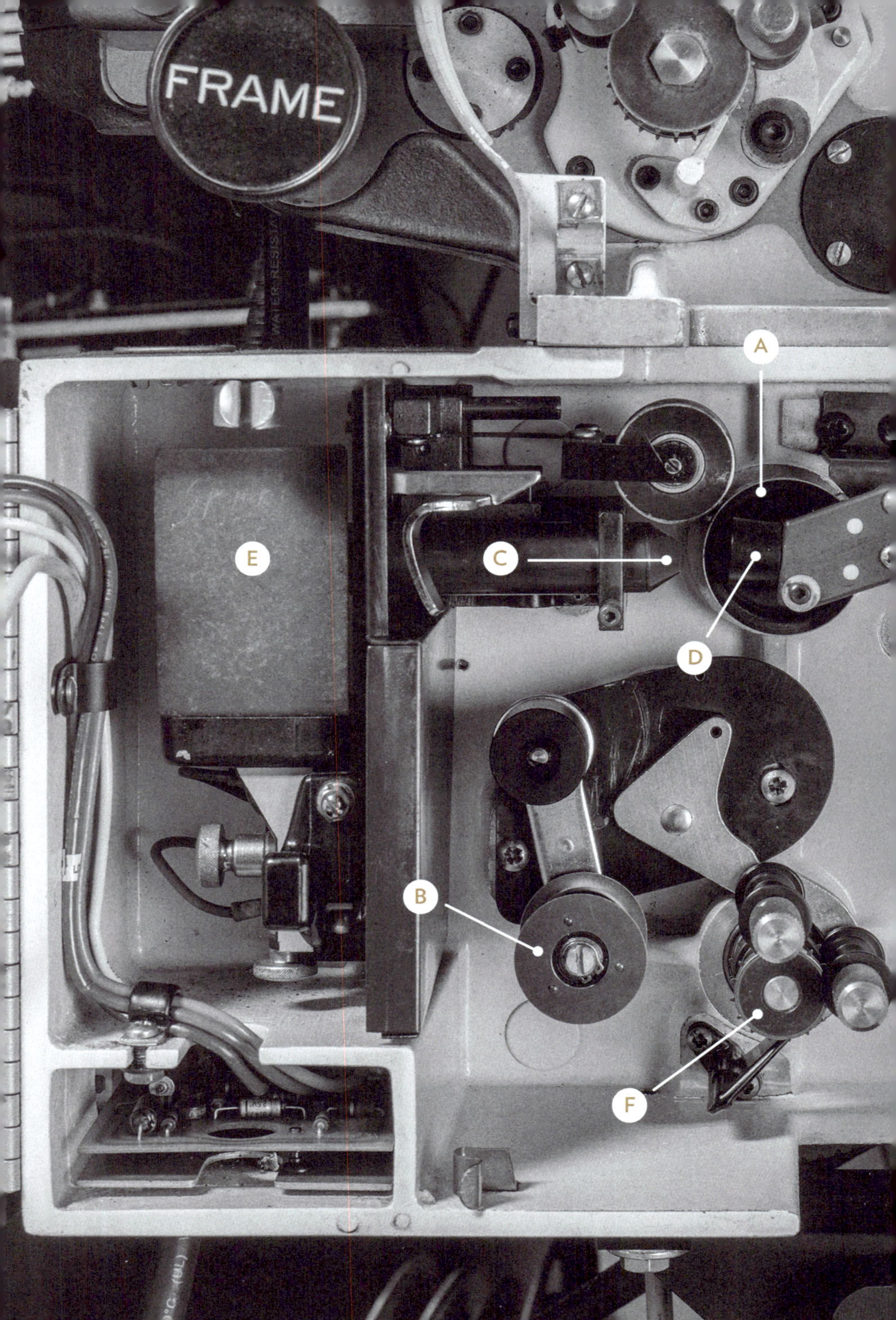

FRAME
A
B
C
D
E
F

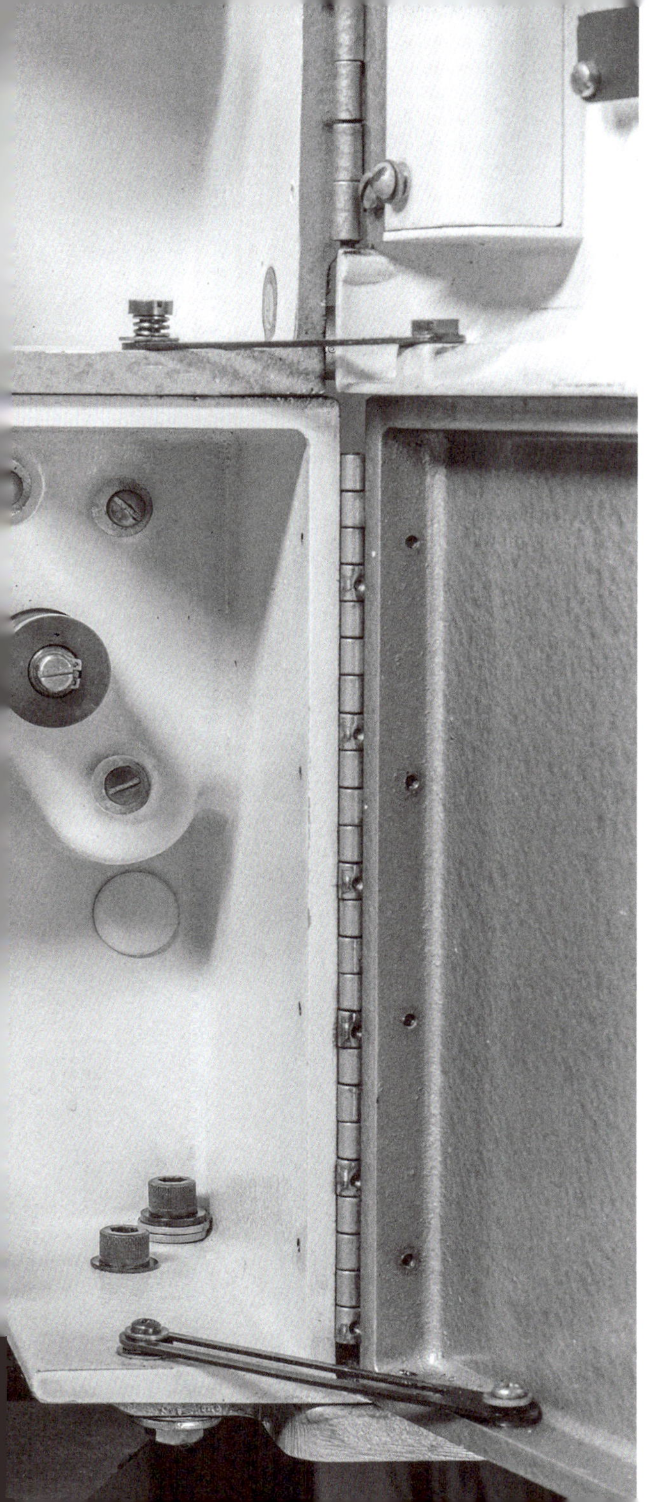

2.14 –

The main components
of a white-light optical
sound reader on a
Simplex 35mm film
projector:

A. SOUND DRUM

B. TENSION ROLLER

C. SLIT LENS

D. SOLAR CELL

E. EXCITER LAMP
(ENCLOSED)

F. DRIVE SPROCKET

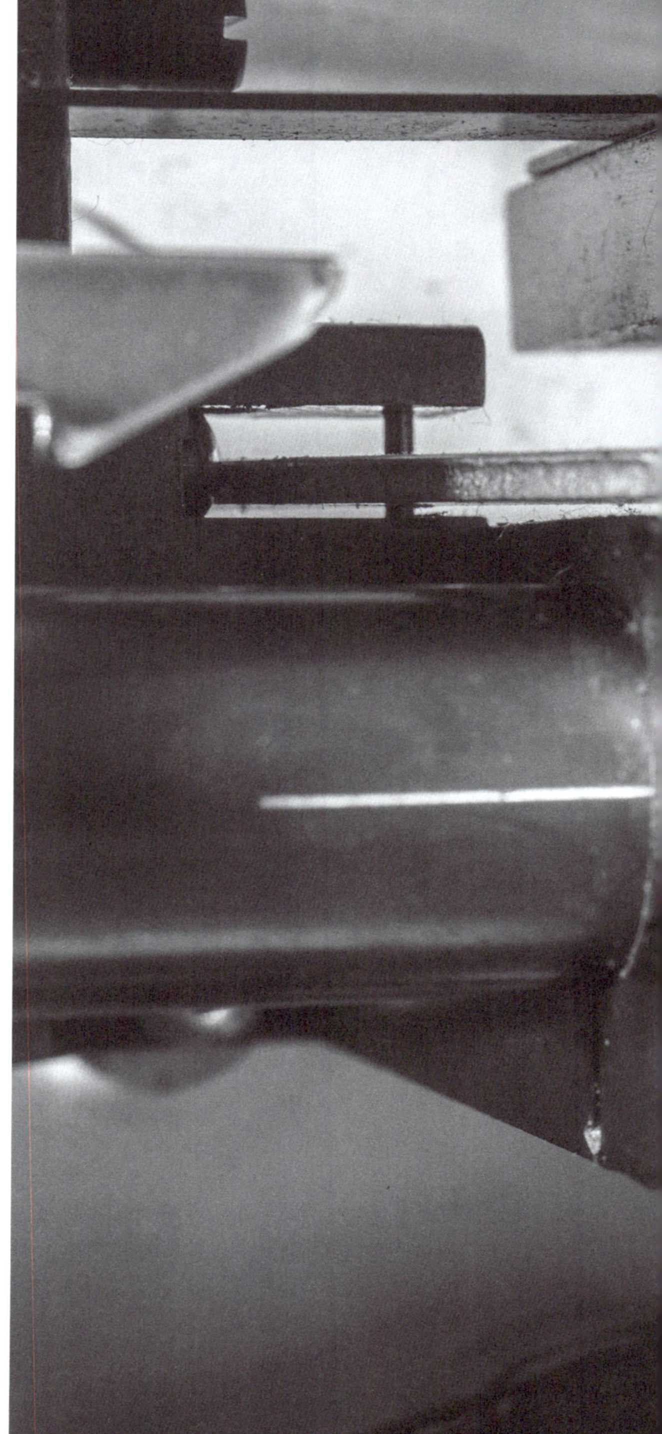

2.15 –

The white-light optical sound reader on a Simplex 35mm projector (detail):

A. SOUND DRUM

B. SLIT LENS

C. SOLAR CELL

D. SOUNDTRACK ON FILM

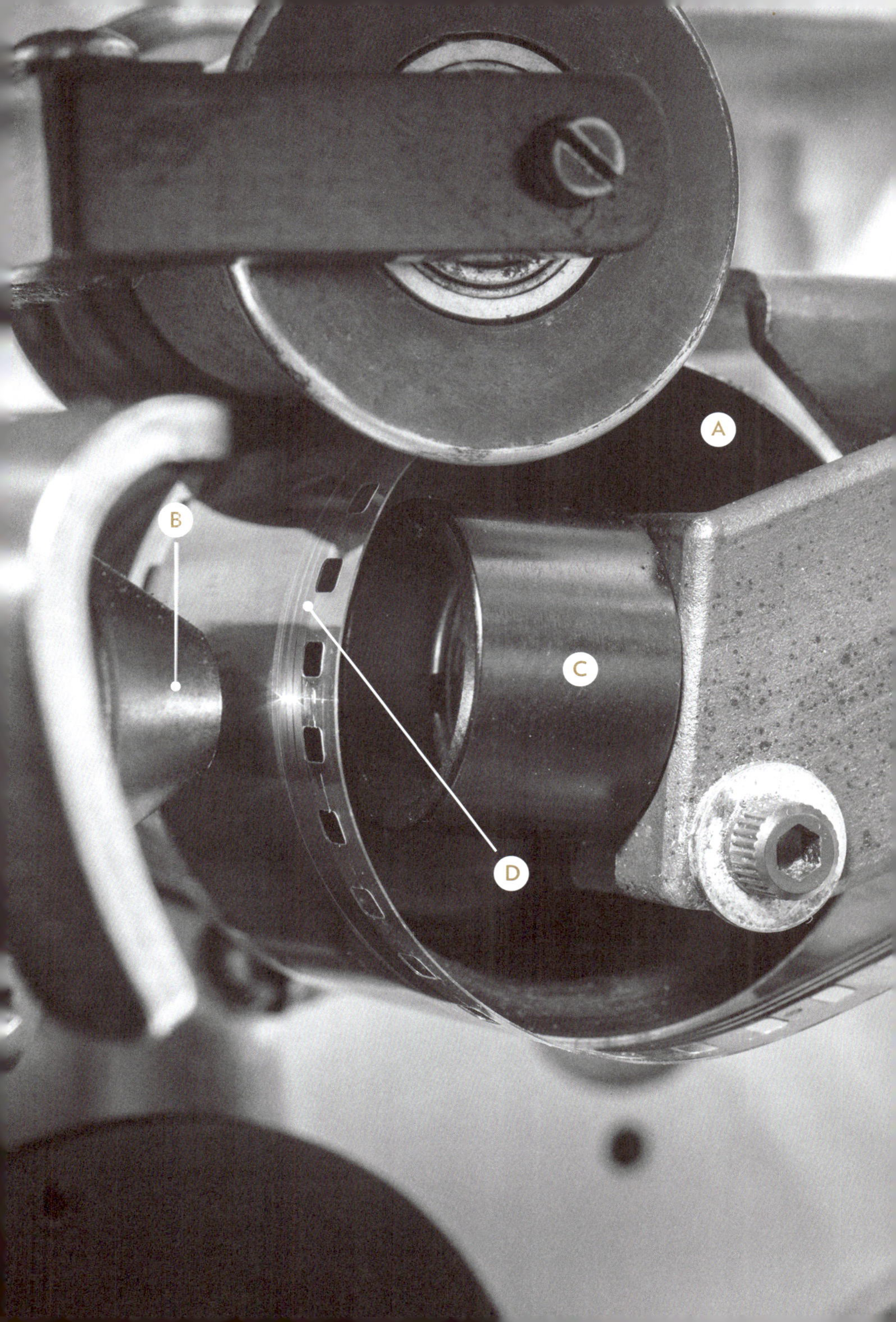
A
B
C
D

White-light tungsten exciter lamps, used to read **silver-dye optical tracks**, were the original light source for optical sound readers, and may still be found on some projectors. In recent years, alternate light sources have been developed, replacing tungsten exciter lamps. So-called IR readers, using **infrared light**, can successfully read silver-dye optical tracks, as most of the radiated energy from a tungsten exciter lamp is infrared radiation. IR (infrared) readers can also read high-magenta optical tracks. **Red LED readers** have flourished as color release prints have migrated away from silver-dye optical tracks in favor of **cyan-dye optical soundtracks**. Issues of compatibility are bound to arise for venues where motion picture films with various types of soundtracks are being exhibited. Red-light readers are not ideal (but may be used) with silver-dye optical tracks; white-light readers, however, are mostly incompatible with cyan-dye optical tracks. As such, if a venue only has the means to project films using one type of audio reader, they should opt for red LED readers, as they will permit the widest range of analog soundtracks to be played.

Projectors equipped to read 35mm magnetic soundtracks feature a **magnetic playback head** located within or above the picture head. *[Figure 2.16]* This location is due to 35mm magnetic prints having their audio tracks located 28 frames following their corresponding images. Projectors equipped to play 16mm magnetic soundtracks feature a magnetic playback head near the optical sound reader.

The advent of **digital audio** for motion picture films required additional sound readers for film projectors. **Spectral Recording Digital** (also known as **SRD** or **Dolby Digital**) is printed on the film between the perforations, with the audio signal 26 frames ahead of the picture. An SRD reader can be mounted on the projector above the picture head, with a programmed audio delay. More recent film projectors may feature a dual, red-light sound reader, below the picture head, which can read both optical analog tracks and SRD tracks. *[Figure 2.17]*

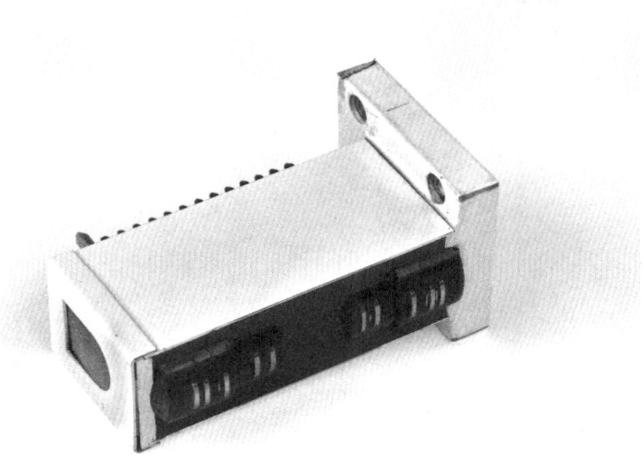

2.16 – Philips magnetic sound reader for 35mm/70mm film projectors. Object courtesy of Kodak Center Theater, Rochester, NY.

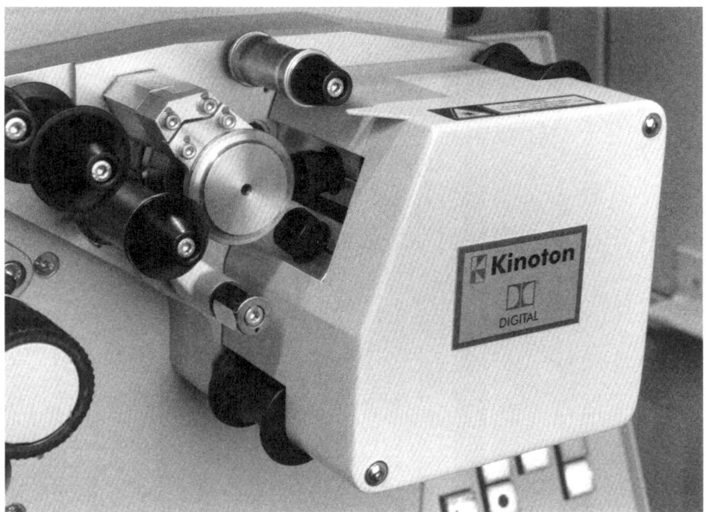

2.17 – Dolby dual red LED optical sound reader (analog and digital) on a Kinoton 35mm film projector.

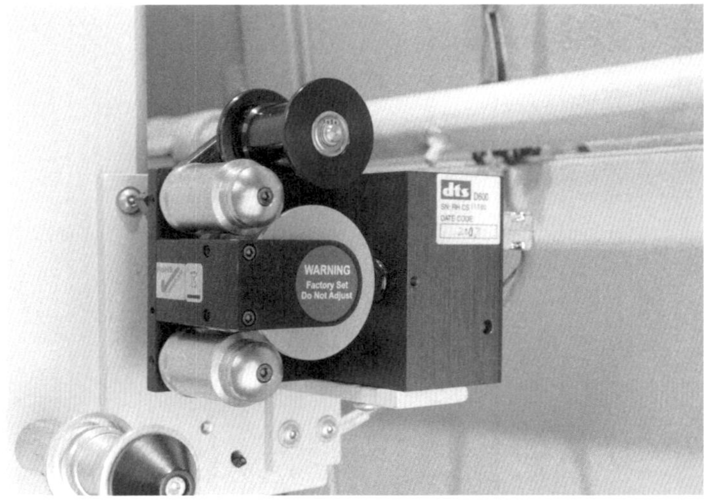

2.18 – DTS optical timecode reader, mounted on a Kinoton
35mm film projector.

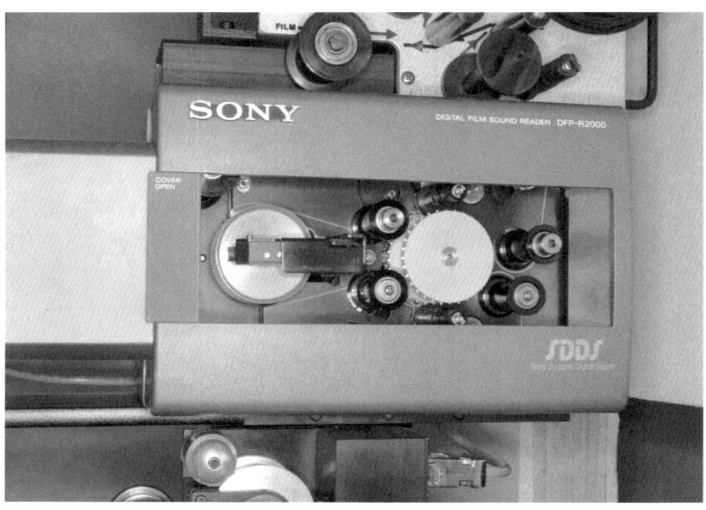

2.19 – SDDS digital optical sound reader, mounted on a
35mm film projector. Photo courtesy of Hannes Ziegenhorn.

Digital Theater Systems (**DTS**, later known as Datasat Digital Entertainment) audio employs a timecode printed on the film between the picture area and the optical track which controls playback of the soundtrack. The actual soundtrack of DTS audio is located on a CD-ROM disc, which cannot be played on a standard CD player. To play a DTS audio track, the projectionist loads the information from one or more discs to a server in advance of the screening. An optical timecode reader is mounted above the picture head on the projector, which sends the timecode information to the server, keeping the audio playback in sync with the film. *[Figure 2.18]*

Sony Dynamic Digital Stereo (SDDS) audio tracks are printed along both edges of the film. Each edge track carries four discrete channels of information, along with two back-up tracks. The SDDS reader is mounted above the picture head on the projector, with a programmed audio delay. *[Figure 2.19]* (Additional information on soundtracks appears in Chapter 4.)

Archival projection venues are challenged in their attempts to properly present the variety of soundtracks encoded on motion picture film. Film projectors have limited available room to accommodate the number of sound readers required. 16mm film prints can have optical or magnetic tracks. 35mm prints can have magnetic tracks, analog optical tracks requiring white light or red light, and digital tracks requiring separate readers. The wide variety of audio tracks available makes it nearly impossible for venues to accommodate them all.

THE PROJECTOR'S MOTOR

The motor, which operates the moving parts of the projector mechanism, is generally located either on the back or the front of older (mechanical) 35mm projectors; and inside the cabinet of 16mm and 35mm electro-mechanical projectors. In the United States, **alternating current (AC)** motors run at a single speed. They are usually employed in 35mm projectors designed to run only at 24 frames per second, and in 16mm projectors (which may use belts and pulleys to accommodate speeds of both 18 and 24 frames per second). **Direct current (DC)** variable-speed motors were employed in the 20th century for 35mm variable-speed projectors. More recently, however, variable-frequency drive AC motors (or adjustable-speed drive motors) have been adopted in projectors designed to operate at multiple speeds.

THE LAMPHOUSE

[Figure 2.20]

The lamphouse, which is responsible for transferring the film's images onto the screen, is located directly behind the projector mechanism. The main components of the lamphouse are the light source and the optical system (made of reflectors which collect and direct the light). A heat filter may be included for higher-wattage lamps. At the time of this writing, the most common source of light is the **xenon lamp**. This short-arc lamp consists of electrodes (an anode "+" and cathode "-") which are sealed in a fused quartz envelope (or bulb) filled with ionized xenon gas under high pressure. *[Figure 2.21]* Direct current arcs across the gap between the electrodes, ionizes the gas, and creates brilliant light. Xenon lamps are available in a range of

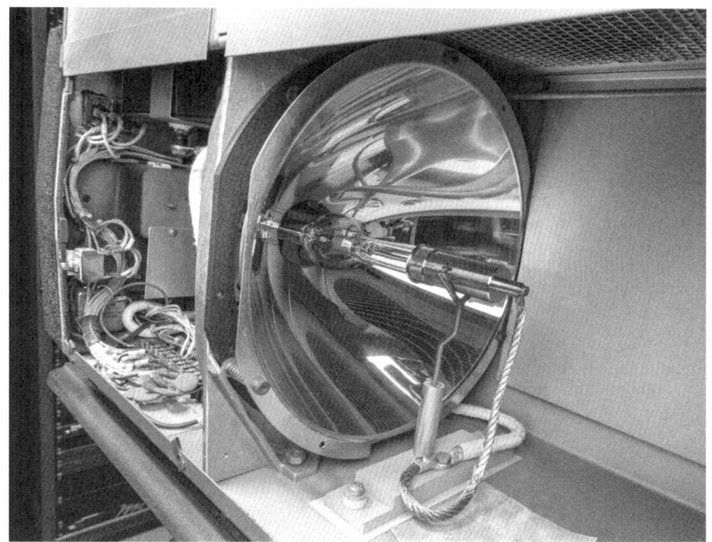

2.20 – The interior of a 35mm film projector lamphouse,
with a xenon lamp centered in the reflector.

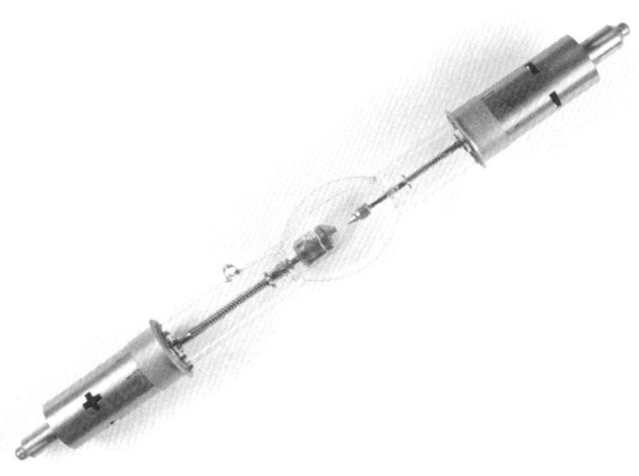

2.21 – A typical xenon lamp, showing anode + (bottom left)
and cathode – (top right).

wattage capacities from multiple manufacturers, with life spans ranging from 1,200 to 2,400 hours, depending upon wattage.

Xenon lamps (and lamphouses) are manufactured for both vertical and horizontal lamp installation, although the horizontal configuration is more common, due to its better light efficiency. Manufacturers initially recommended rotating horizontally installed xenon lamps 180 degrees at half-life in order to prevent the top of the lamp from darkening excessively, though this practice has been largely dismissed with state-of-the-art xenon lamps. However, if darkening is evident at half-life, then one may proceed with the rotation. Lamp darkening may also be indicative of insufficient exhaust strength, which does not permit the efficient removal of heat from the lamphouse. Higher-wattage lamps may require a magnet within the lamphouse to stabilize the arc.

Each lamp has an operating range of current (**amperes**, or "amps"), which may require adjustment throughout the life of the lamp in order to maintain target brightness output. Lamps should not be used longer than the time recommended by their manufacturers, as they can explode if used beyond their natural active life span. Lamphouses designed for xenon lamps feature an hour meter (active whenever the lamp is burning), allowing projectionists to monitor the life of the lamp. Xenon lamp manufacturers provide operation and installation instructions with each lamp.

Safety precautions should be followed when installing and removing the lamps, and when accessing the interior of the lamphouse, in order to protect yourself from physical injury. A face shield, chest protection, and leather gloves are highly recommended. When handling xenon lamps, avoid touching any part of the lamp with your bare skin (especially the quartz body), as any oil from your skin will etch into the quartz lamp when it becomes hot, weakening that area and greatly increasing the chance of explosion. If accidentally touched, clean the quartz with isopropyl alcohol (the purest available) and a lint-free cloth. Expired xenon lamps should be returned to their shipping cartons, and broken within the sealed box. Protective gear should also be worn during the breaking procedure. Do not discard or throw away unbroken bulbs: inexperienced handlers could be injured or blinded if a lamp were to explode.

Carbon-arc light sources, predating xenon lamps, are rarely found in modern installations. In this kind of light source, two carbon rods (a positive and a negative) are slowly moved together as direct current arcs across the gap between them, burning the ends of the carbons to create a gas ball of highly incandescent plasma, resulting in brilliant light. *[Figure 2.22]* This arc flame produces smoke, soot, and intense heat. Toxic fumes generated in this process must be vented to the atmosphere. Carbon rod diameters vary, with positive carbons having larger diameters

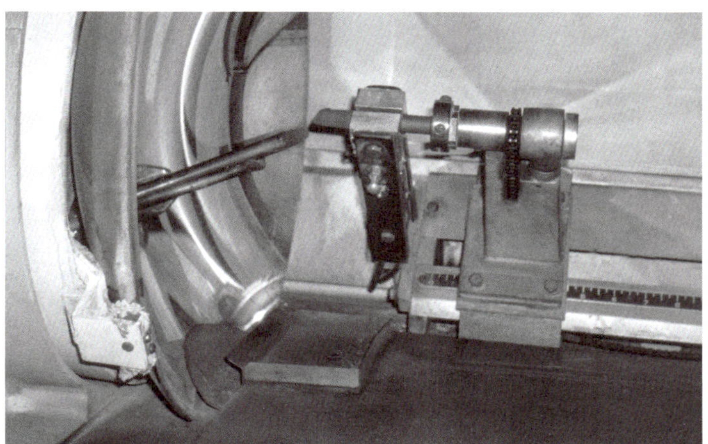

2.22 – The interior of a carbon arc lamphouse in a 35mm projector. 35mm slide courtesy of Timothy J. Wagner, The Landmark Loew's Jersey Theater, Jersey City, NJ.

than their negative carbon companions (which are typically copper-coated). In this system, since the burning carbons are slowly moved together mechanically, it is essential to keep the gas ball at a constant position in relation to the reflector. The lengths of the carbon rods determine their life span, with the longest lasting about an hour. Operating and maintaining carbon-arc light sources is labor-intensive, and sources for purchasing carbon rods are few at the time of this writing. Due to the limited capacity of carbon rods, reel size is limited, necessitating the use of two projectors for the projection of feature-length films.

Whether a lamphouse features a xenon lamp or carbon-arc light source, it contains at least one metal or glass reflector to collect light and direct it toward the film aperture. In some cases, glass reflectors may be more efficient: dichroic glass reflectors are designed to reflect visible light from the source while transmitting the infrared portion of the spectrum (heat) through the back of the mirror, minimizing transmission of heat to the film. Vertically installed xenon lamps sometimes have small auxiliary reflectors, designed to increase light level and uniformity. To direct and focus uniform light to the film aperture, adjustment of the reflector(s) or lamp is necessary. Some lamphouses accomplish this by providing horizontal pan and vertical tilt adjustments for the reflector, along with a focus adjustment to move the reflector to and from the lamp. Other lamphouse designs have adjustments to move the xenon lamp relative to a static reflector. Moving the lamp is the more common adjustment. Higher-wattage lamphouses may also feature glass heat shields, located between the light source and the douser, designed to reflect infrared light and pass visible light, minimizing transmission of heat to the film. *[Figure 2.23]* The lamphouse must be precisely aligned with the optical

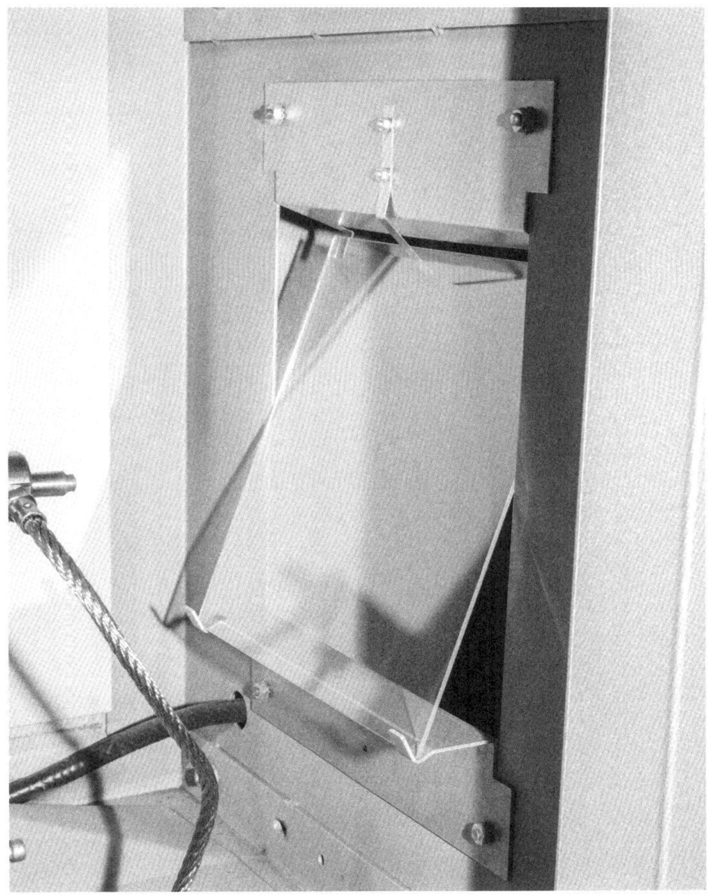

2.23 – **The heat filter inside the lamphouse of a Kinoton 35mm/16mm film projector.**

axis of the projector's aperture and lens in order to maximize light output.

To prevent intense heat from damaging the shutter, lens, and film in a projector in idle mode, lamphouses feature an internal mechanical **douser**, which is manually opened and closed by the

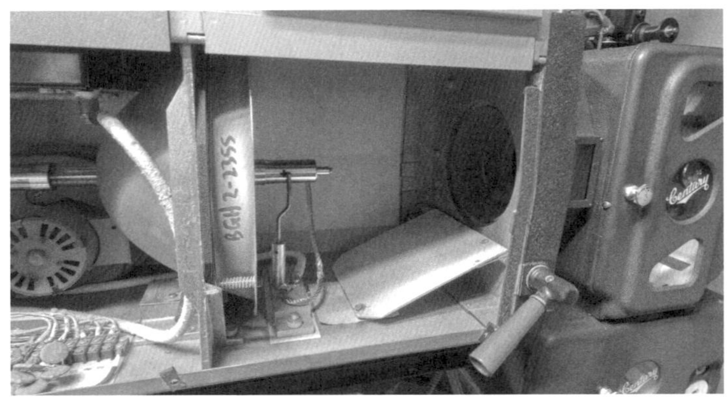

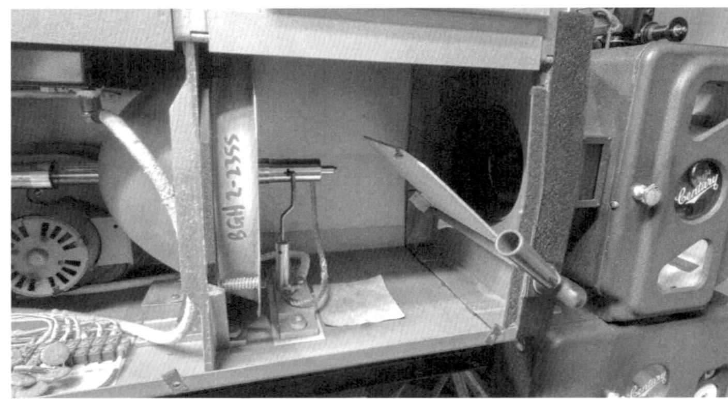

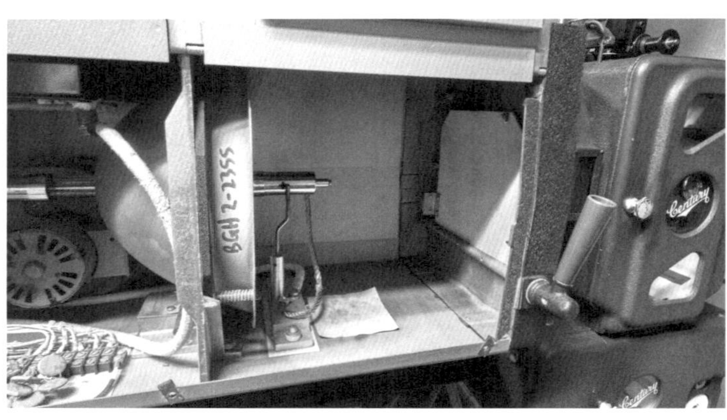

projectionist. *[Figure 2.24]* A handle which actuates the douser is present on the lamphouse exterior, near the front. A projectionist should never open the lamphouse douser until the projector is running, as the light from the lamp could overheat, melt, or (in the case of nitrate) ignite the film.

Heat and exhaust gases generated by light sources within the lamphouse need to be released. **Exhaust ports** are located on the top of lamphouses. A flexible or static duct should be attached to the lamphouse exhaust port, extending upward and connecting to the exhaust system vent in the ceiling. Equipment manufacturers supply specifications for the exhaust capacity (measured in cubic feet per minute) required for lamphouses. The ventilation system in a projection room should meet or exceed the manufacturer's requirements and any existing codes. A wall switch typically activates this system. In addition, most xenon lamphouses feature an internal cooling fan which is activated when power is supplied to the lamphouse.

A **power supply** for a projector's light source is often located on the floor, adjacent to the projector, although console-style projectors have them built in. *[Figure 2.25, see following page]* Some projection facilities feature separate rooms for their power supplies. Both xenon lamps and carbon arcs require direct current for their operation, to maintain the arc across the gap between electrodes. Power supplies, often called **rectifiers**, convert incoming alternating current (AC) power to direct current (DC) power output for the light source. Power supplies have adjustable output amperage. An amp meter to read the power output is generally located on the back of the lamphouse. The output amperage

2.24 – **The movement of a mechanical douser within a Strong Super Lume-X 35mm film projector lamphouse, from open (top) to closed (bottom). Note how the handle of the douser rotates to move the douser into place, blocking the light.**

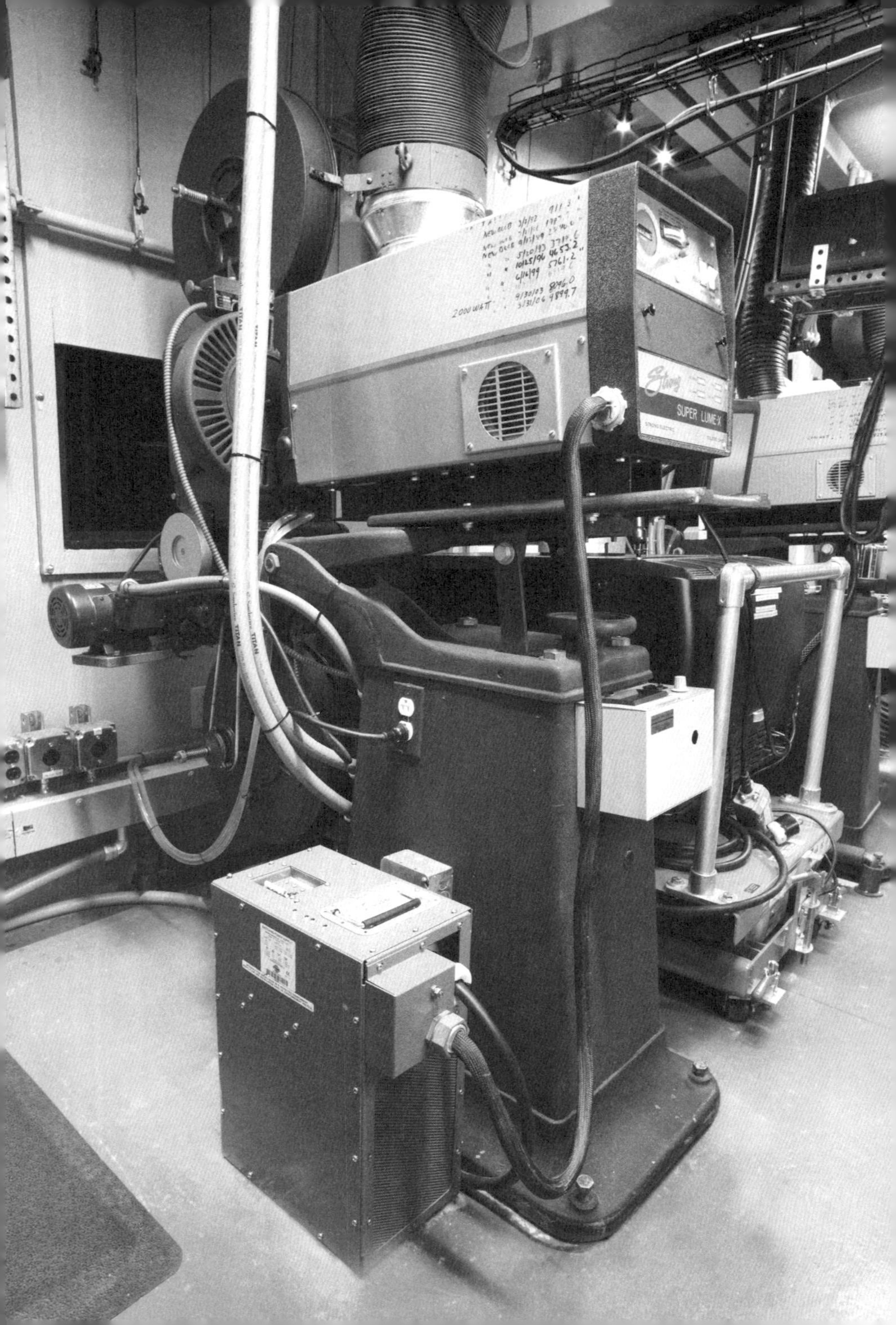

2000 WATT
NEW BULB 3/2/92 911.3
NEW BULB 9/17/99 2590.0
5/20/93 3718.6
10/25/96 4653.2
6/6/99 5761.2
9/30/03 8096.0
3/31/06 9899.7
Strong
SUPER LUME-X
STRONG ELECTRIC
TITAN

should be set within the recommended specification range of the lamp manufacturer. As lamps age, the amperage may need to be increased.

Maintaining proper screen **brightness** is important, as film laboratories are strict in their standards for processing and printing release copies according to a specific density. The ability to measure **screen luminance** is necessary for monitoring and maintaining proper brightness. The level of luminance reflected from the screen is measured in **footlamberts (fL)**. In the United States, the Society of Motion Picture and Television Engineers (SMPTE) has drafted **specifications** for screen luminance (*SMPTE Standard 196M-1995, Indoor Theater and Review Room Projection – Screen Luminance and Viewing Conditions*). The current standard offers a range of 12 to 22 fL in the center of the screen, with no more than 25% fall-off in the corners. 16fL in the screen's center is ideal. Screen luminance should be measured with a light meter that reads light reflected from the screen. (Additional information on this topic is offered in Chapter 6, "Preparing for the Show.")

2.25 – **A power supply (left) on the floor of a projection booth for an adjacent 35mm film projector lamphouse.**

DO'S AND DON'TS

ALWAYS

- Time the projector's shutter correctly, to prevent "ghosting."

- Align anamorphic lenses correctly, to avoid skewing the image.

- Wear protective clothing when handling xenon lamps.

NEVER

- Use plastic reels in 35mm film projection.

- Play cyan-dye audio tracks using white-light readers.

NOTES

79

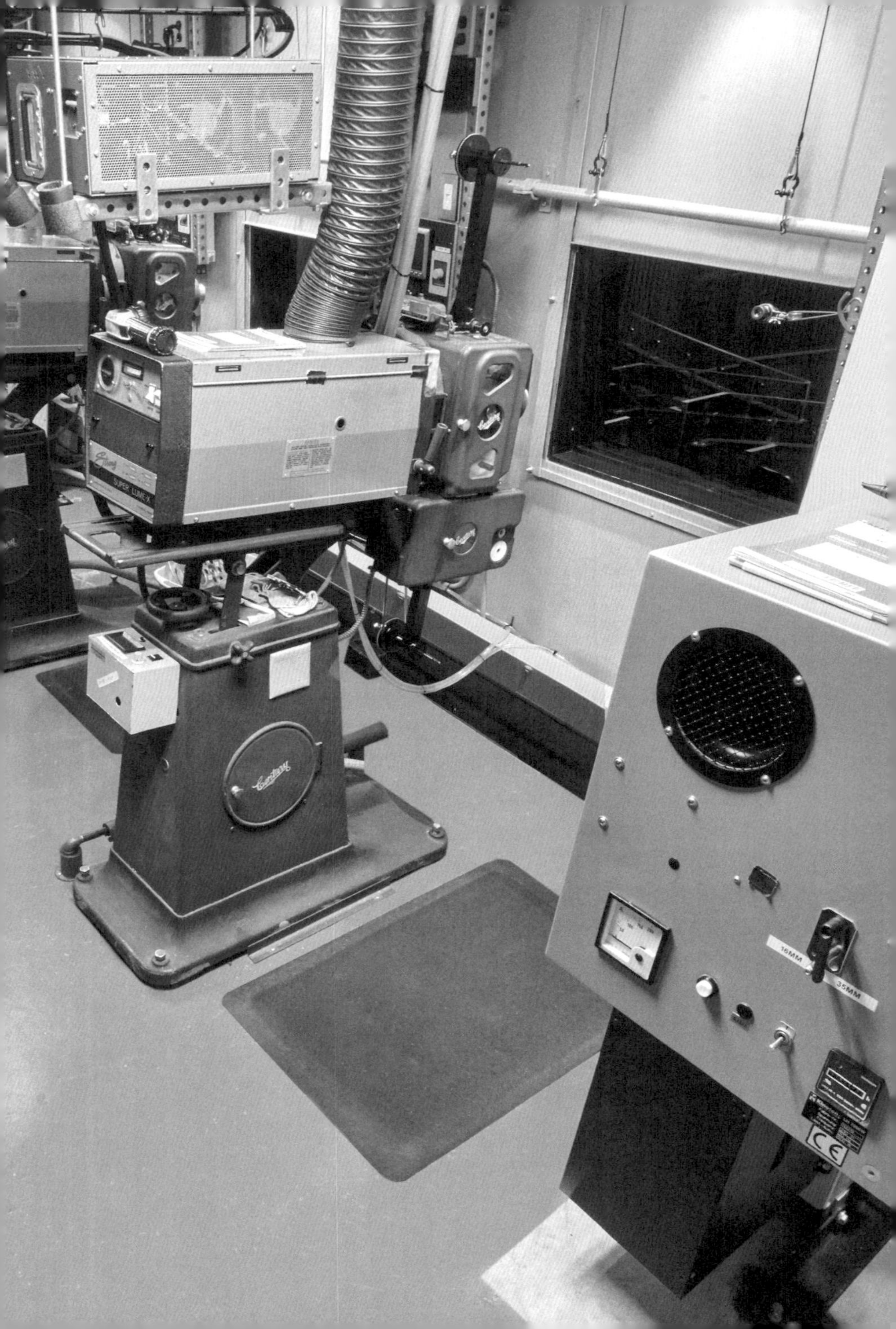

3

ENVIRONMENTS

THE RESPONSIBILITIES OF a projectionist extend far beyond the film print and the projector. The projectionist is also steward to two separate environments: one a hidden cove of machinery and technology, the other a wide-open frontier that serves as the grounds for an audience to experience fantasy, fiction, reality, humanity, and everything in between. While these environments are rarely separated by more than a thin wall and a few panes of glass, they could not be more different.

THE PROJECTION BOOTH

[Figure 3.1]

Every projection facility, whether called the projection booth or (in some countries) the "bio box," is home to a standard assembly of equipment which is necessary for the exhibition of motion picture film. As a rule, the projection booth is located in a space separate from, but adjacent to, the theater auditorium. Basic elements include 35mm and/or 16mm projectors with their accompanying equipment (lamphouses, rectifiers, and so on), an exhaust system for the lamphouses and a separate ventilation

Fig. 3.1 – **A projection booth equipped for manual changeover (or "dual") projection of 35mm and 16mm film formats.**

system for the booth, port windows to the theater or auditorium, sound processing equipment, an electrical panel, a film inspection and/or rewind table, and amplification equipment (although this equipment may be also found elsewhere).

Projection booths should be designed (or renovated) in a way that minimizes the amount of light and sound that is transferred into the audience's space. The amount of light and sound-level control required will be determined by the booth's proximity to seating in the auditorium. (Having the booth located directly behind the last row of seats in a small theater will require more stringent control of light and sound spilling from the booth than a projection booth located 15 feet above the balcony in a 3,000-seat movie palace.) The number and size of port windows, the brightness and size of the image on the screen, and the type of booth lighting are important factors in relation to the amount of light perceived by the audience as a distraction from the show.

The quality of the **port enclosures** will determine how much sound bleeds into the auditorium. Projectors (with their moving parts, exhaust fans, and rectifiers) are by their nature noisy: airtight seals on all openings between the projection booth and the auditorium are necessary to minimize the transfer of equipment and operator noise to the audience. Projection ports featuring two panes of glass (designed to deaden sound from entering the auditorium) are preferable to single-pane glass.

Dimmable task and spot track lighting by the projectors and audio equipment minimizes light spill, and should be used during projection. Low light levels in the booth allow the irises in the projectionist's eyes to open wider, enhancing their view of the screen and their ability to monitor image quality. Booths should also be equipped with bright, general overhead lighting for activity outside of show times, as well as emergency lighting in case of an electrical outage.

The ideal projection booth floor is a non-static, non-porous flooring material that can be easily cleaned. Carpeting in booths harbors dust and dirt, and can generate static electricity. Sealed concrete, heavy linoleum, and vinyl flooring are often employed in projection rooms. It is advised that booth floors be of a light neutral color (such as light gray), to make it easier to locate small parts, such as dropped screws.

Each projector should have its own **threading bin**: these bins, usually plastic, catch film leader during threading, preventing film from touching the booth floor. Dirt and debris that make their way onto the film leader can spread to the rest of the reel and accumulate on projection and inspection equipment.

Having dedicated **heating, ventilation, and air-conditioning** control (also known as **HVAC**) for the projection booth is important, not only for the comfort and safety of the staff, but also for the proper operation of the machines. Audio equipment, rectifiers, amplifiers, and lamphouses generate considerable heat (as does the near-constant movement of a film projectionist working in a booth with a changeover projection system, consisting of two or more parallel projectors), so the temperature of the booth must be carefully controlled to prevent equipment malfunction. Maintaining a humidity level of 50 – 60% in the booth is recommended to avoid static charge issues with polyester film stock. In addition to environmental control for the projection booth, a separate exhaust system leading to the outside atmosphere is required for projector lamphouses. Each lamphouse's manufacturer specifies its correct cubic feet per minute (CFM) requirement, and the exhaust system must meet this requirement.

The height of the projection booth and the projectors' lenses relative to the optical center of the screen determines the vertical angle of the projectors. Having multiple projectors in a booth results in a slight horizontal angle for each projector, relative to the center of the screen; the angle increases in proportion to the projectors' deviation from the optical center line. Vertical and horizontal **"keystoning"** of the image on the screen (when one side of the image is longer or shorter than its opposite) results from projecting off-axis from the center of the screen. The more extreme the projection angle, the greater the amount of keystoning that will occur. Keystoning also creates focus differential, making it difficult to obtain even focus from one edge of the screen to the other.

Keystoning can be addressed in a variety of ways. For theaters with a steep vertical projection angle, moving the bottom of the screen forward (toward the audience) will decrease the angle of the projected image hitting the screen, minimizing keystoning and focus differential. Equipping projectors with adjustable offset lenses may also reduce keystoning. Aperture plates can also be custom-filed at an angle by the projectionist to combat the slight trapezoidal shape of a keystoned image. Movable screen masking can also be used to cover up the edges of a keystoned image, though this is not ideal, as it will cause light to visibly spill onto the masking.

Each projector should have a port window for the lens, and an additional viewing port for the projectionist. **Projection ports** should ideally be made of high optical quality, water-white glass, with anti-reflective coatings. Standard window glass is not recommended. Projection-port glass should not be installed perpendicular to the projection beam: instead, it should be installed at an angle, in order to avoid reflecting projected light back into the lens and decreasing image contrast. **Viewing ports** should be located adjacent to the operating side of each projector to allow for monitoring of the image while making adjustments to the projector, such as focusing and framing.

Audio racks within the booth should be assembled and placed to allow for good air circulation and access to all components. Audio racks are equipped with processors, which decode the audio signals from projectors, outputting several channels of audio. This output is sent to the amplifiers, which drive the auditorium speakers. An audio monitor in the rack should allow the projectionist to monitor each channel individually. In addition to analog and digital sound processing, monitoring, and amplification equipment, audio racks may also be equipped with audio playback, recording, and mixing equipment, power supplies, and wireless microphone equipment. An electrical panel with circuit breakers is typically found in or adjacent to most projection booths. Most electrical equipment within the booth has dedicated breakers. These breakers are used to power-up and power-down the equipment at the beginning and end of projection sessions.

BEYOND THE PORT: THE THEATER

The history, economics, and culture of motion picture film exhibition has resulted in motion picture theater auditoriums of all shapes, sizes, and styles. The preferable auditorium shape for exhibiting motion pictures is narrower rather than wider, to maximize uniformity of light reflectivity throughout the auditorium and to improve sound coverage. Non-parallel walls are encouraged to prevent **"flutter echo"** (audible reverberations when the theater walls reflect audio between each other); windows are not recommended in a screening auditorium, due to light and sound transmission from the outside world. The basic components of the theater auditorium include the screen (with masking and curtain), speakers (for film sound), seating, lighting, HVAC (heating, ventilation, and air-conditioning), appropriate projection ports in the wall opposite the screen, and often a dedicated public address system. Theaters may also be endowed with accessibility equipment, such as a hearing loop and closed-captioning devices.

THE SCREEN

The shape of the screen, determined by the projection **aspect ratio** of film, has changed over time with the advent of new film technologies. During cinema's early years, a flat screen in an approximate aspect ratio of 1.33:1 (the relationship between width and height) was adequate for silent films and sound-on-disc films. The first sound-on-film presentations required a narrowing of the screen to 1.18:1 in order to accommodate space for the new audio track printed on one side of the film. Theater screens widened slightly in 1932, when an aspect ratio of 1.37:1 was adopted for exhibition of all 35mm motion pictures. After Cinerama's debut in 1952 (requiring a three-projector installation and a special, deeply curved screen) in selected venues, theater screens widened in 1953 to accommodate CinemaScope, an anamorphic film process with an initial aspect ratio of 2.55:1 (for magnetic-striped prints), later narrowed to 2.35:1 (when the optical track was added), then adjusted a few years later to 2.39:1 to better hide printed splices in the frame lines.

Beginning with the silent era, but proliferating in the 1950s, film producers and studios experimented with a variety of **widescreen aspect ratios**. This poses a challenge for screening venues trying to exhibit films encompassing the breadth of film technology throughout its history. A screen proportioned wide enough to exhibit anamorphic aspect ratios will allow proper presentation of narrow aspect ratios through the use of masking. Keep in mind, however, that not all screens are flat; some venues install (and some film processes require) curved screens. Cinerama, Todd-AO, and Dimension 150 require deeply curved screens by design. Slightly to moderately curved screens may be used for other aspect ratios.

Projector aperture plates, while defining the aspect ratio of an image, create soft outer edges on the projected image. To provide a

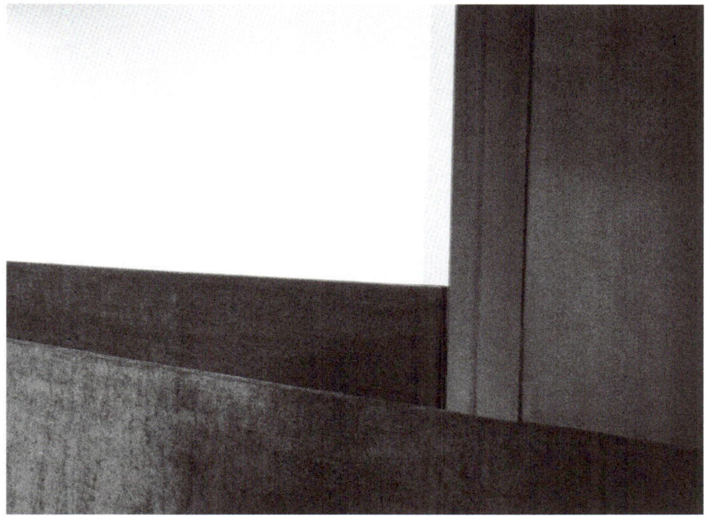

3.2 — **Movable vertical and horizontal masking system for a
motion picture screen.**

sharp edge for the image, theaters use **screen masking**, which began
as a painted black border around the silent screen. To accommodate a variety of aspect ratios, most theater auditoriums have some
type of movable screen masking in place. Black matte fabric that is
acoustically transparent is generally placed in close proximity to
the screen surface, and is recommended for masking. *[Figure 3.2]*
Fixed-height screens employ movable side-masking to vary the visible width of the screen. Fixed-width screens employ movable top
and/or bottom masking to vary the visible height of the image. In
the widescreen era, most commercial theaters in the United States
projecting 35mm film were configured to exhibit 1.85:1 and 2.39:1
aspect ratios with the aid of movable masking systems.
Screen-masking installations may be adjusted either manually or
by remote control, and may be automated. High-end installations
allow for programmable presets for a number of aspect ratios.

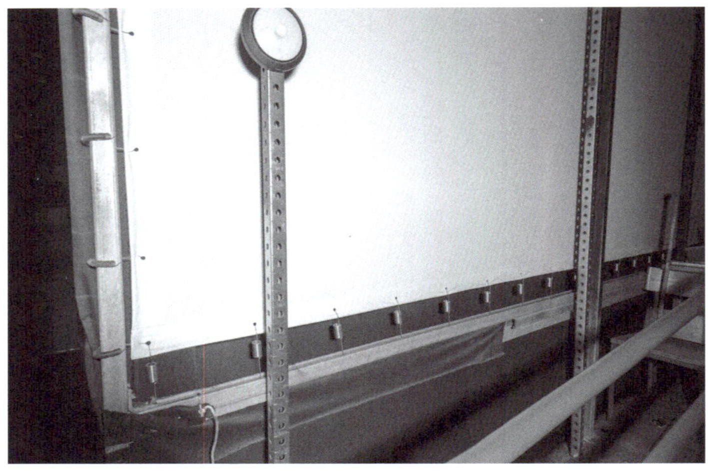

3.3 – **Rear view of a motion picture screen attached to its frame with springs. Photo courtesy of The Little Theatre, Rochester, NY.**

Cinema screens installed in public venues are usually perforated, to allow sound to pass through from speakers located behind the screen. In addition to standard **perforated screens**, micro-perforated screens are also available, designed to minimize the appearance of the tiny holes and reduce unwanted wavy *moiré* patterns from digital projectors. Screens are generally suspended across a wood or metal frame lined with hooks or eye bolts. This frame is larger than the screen itself. *[Figure 3.3]* The screen may be laced to the frame with elastic, nylon, or cotton cord, elastic bands, or springs. Screen manufacturers install grommets along all edges of the screen to provide for lacing. Non-movable masking is installed around the edges of the screen, facing the auditorium, to cover the mounting hardware.

Non-perforated screens may occasionally be encountered in film theaters. These screens tend to be wall surfaces (flat or curved) which may be coated with a special reflective paint. The location of these screens often makes them more vulnerable to contact with people and equipment. Protecting these screens with curtains when not in use is highly recommended. Speaker placement is radically altered when used in conjunction with non-perforated screens.

Different types of screens are defined by their **reflectivity,** which is measured in **gain factors**. Matte screens have a wide distribution pattern of reflected light, which is ideal for wide auditoriums, stadium seating, and theaters with balconies. **"High-gain" screens** — designed to reflect more of the light back in one direction, minimizing light spill onto walls, floor, and ceiling — work better in narrower auditoriums. Silver screens, offering a high unidirectional reflectance, are typically used for polarized 3-D projection in order to maintain separation of the polarized light from each projector. Silver and high-gain screens come with the disadvantage of the fall-off of light as one moves away from the center of the projected light beam. These screens also create a **"hot spot"** with higher brightness at the center of the image than on the corners and sides. Mounting silver and high-gain screens in a curved frame will improve brightness uniformity and reduce hot spots. Most film theater screens of the early 21st century are manufactured from polyvinyl chloride (PVC). As mentioned previously, tilting of the screen can sometimes be desirable, especially in venues with steep projection angles.

Having a front curtain in the auditorium, covering the screen when not in use, is the best way to help keep a screen clean and prevent damage. **Front curtains** come in a variety of styles: *travelers* consist of two panels that open horizontally; a *guillotine reveal* curtain rises straight up into a fly space; a *Venetian curtain* uses vertical lift lines to raise the curtain, gathering it from the bottom, whereas an *Austrian curtain*, or *Roman drape*, raised in the same fashion, features swags in the fabric, between the lift lines.

The size and shape of the screen, and its distance from the film projectors (the **"throw"**), are determining factors for the proper focal lengths of projection lenses. Theaters built at the present time are generally much smaller than the movie palaces of decades past. Accordingly, the stock of lenses available from projection lens manufacturers tends toward shorter focal lengths. This can be problematic for venues with long throws that wish to upgrade their projection lenses.

SPEAKERS

The history of film presentation technology has provided for a variety of theater speaker configurations. Prior to around 1952, speakers were located solely behind the screen. Customarily perched atop a wooden platform, the speakers were placed close to the back of the screen, at or above the midpoint. A single speaker sufficed for monophonic films. The advent of stereo audio reproduction required a 3-speaker arrangement: a center channel for dialogue, and left and right channels for stereo music and effects. The introduction of Cinerama (1952) and 70mm Todd-AO (1955) processes added two more front audio channels (from speakers located behind the screen), a left-center channel and right-center channel. The late 1970s marked the appearance of subwoofer speakers, which improve bass response. A subwoofer speaker is generally located near the bottom of the screen. *[Figure 3.4]* Current practice calls for speaker systems to be built into thin, full-coverage baffle walls behind the screen, concealing the speakers from view while providing greater clarity and bass response by minimizing reflected audio.

The debut of Cinerama (1952) and CinemaScope (1953) introduced audiences to **"surround sound,"** requiring the

3.4 – **A loudspeaker system behind a motion picture screen.**

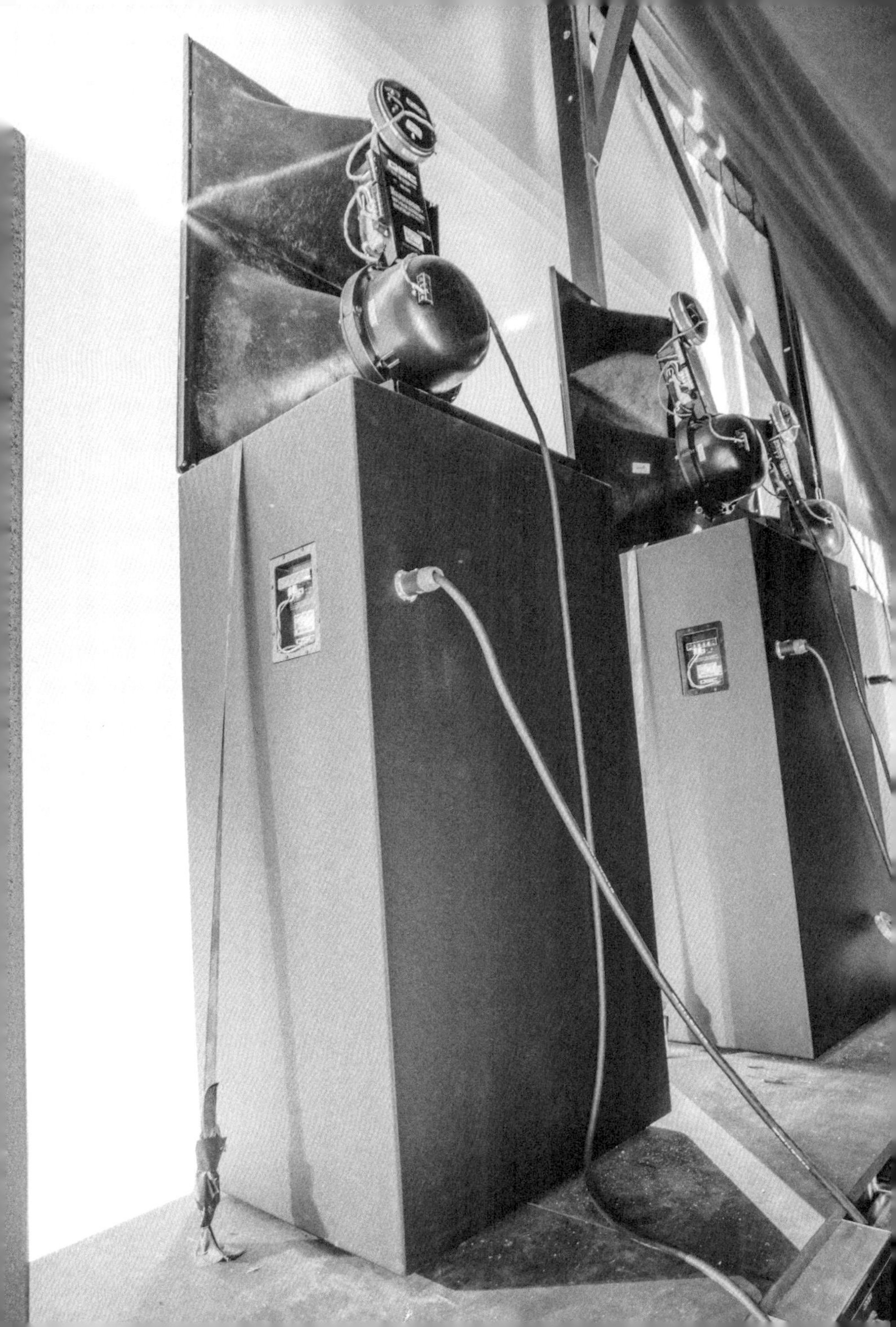

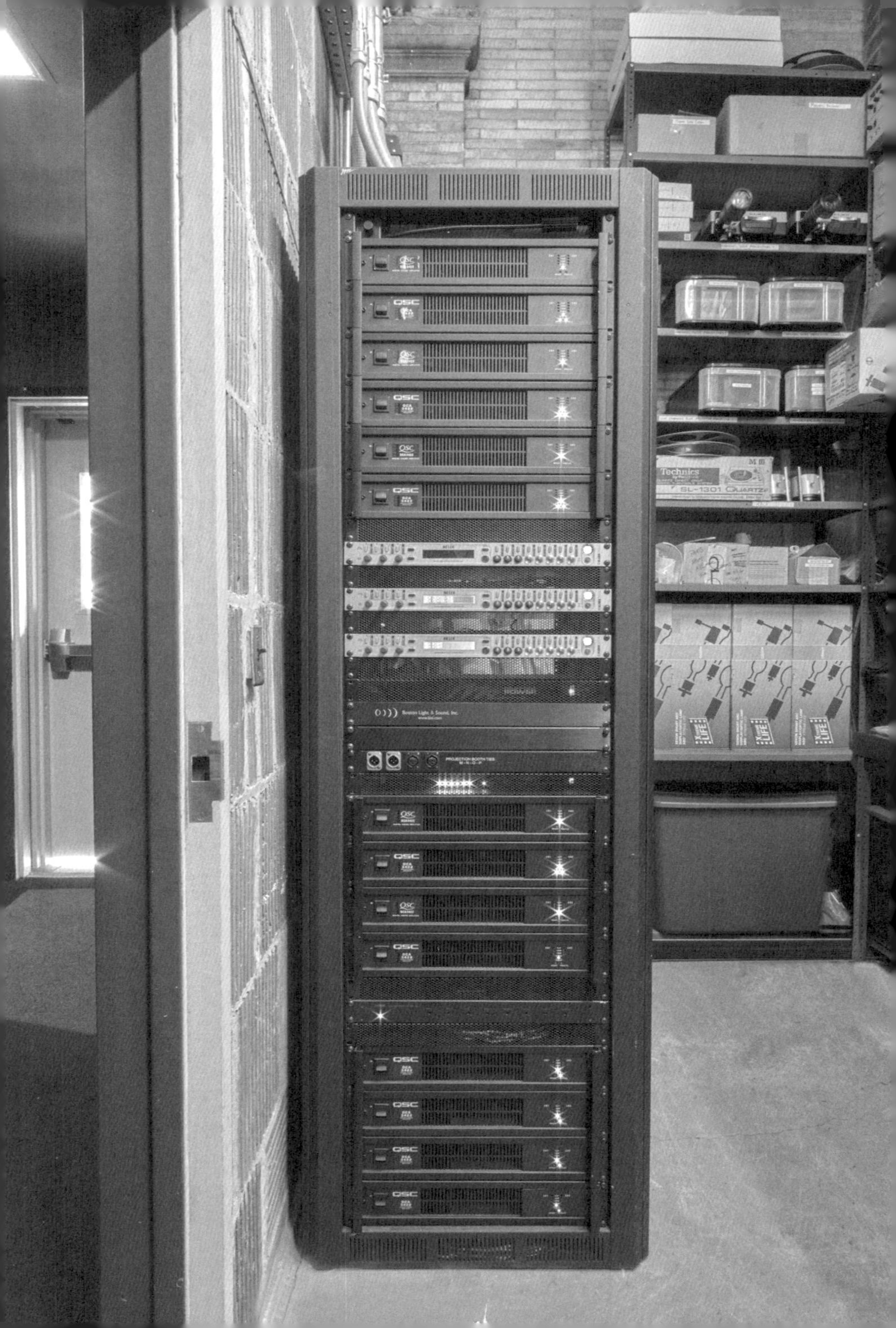

installation of speakers along the walls of the auditorium. Cinerama aside, early surround-sound processes utilized a single mono-surround channel. Stereo-surround (with separate audio channels for left- and right-surround speakers) was reintroduced in the late 1970s. "Extended surround," introduced in 1999, provides a third, separate audio channel for rear surround speakers.

Common audio formats and output channels include:
- **Mono** – single channel
- **Stereo** – left, center, and right channels
- **Dolby Stereo A / Dolby Stereo SR** (Spectral Recording) – left, center, right, and surround channels
- **SRD** (Dolby Digital) and **DTS** (Digital Theater Systems, now Datasat Digital Entertainment) – left, center, right, subwoofer, left-surround, and right-surround channels
- **SDDS** (Sony Dynamic Digital Sound) – left, center, right, left-center, right-center, subwoofer, left-surround, and right-surround channels

The multiple-audio signal output from the audio processor is not strong enough to drive the speakers; powered amplifiers are thus required to boost the signal. Amplifiers may be located behind the screen, in an adjacent space, or in the projection booth. *[Figure 3.5]*

THEATER SOUND

Regardless of the size, shape, and acoustics of the venue, choosing the appropriate sound level will depend on the number of people seated in the auditorium. The presence of more patrons causes greater absorption of sound, requiring more volume. It may be

3.5 – **Audio amplifiers and processors for multi-channel sound playback.**

advantageous to set the volume slightly on the loud side (without "blasting" the audio), in order to better accommodate patrons who are hard of hearing. If you preset the volume in an empty auditorium during pre-focus, the theater manager and staff should be mindful to monitor the audio during the screening and advise the projectionist to increase the volume when necessary.

Installing a **public address system** in theater auditoriums provides obvious opportunities for additional use, such as public interviews and live performances. It is important that the system, whether using separate speakers or incorporating speakers used for film projection, is designed to prevent the occurrence of audio feedback. The simplest way of avoiding feedback is to place the speakers in front of the microphone(s), rather than behind them. The supporting audio equipment is generally installed in the projection booth. Wireless microphones, with the receivers in or near the booth, eliminate the need for audio cables within the auditorium. Any exposed cables within the auditorium should be carefully placed and secured to avoid tripping hazards.

COMFORT

The most well-projected film will not impress an audience that is uncomfortable or distracted. Lighting, seating, and HVAC (heating, ventilation, and air-conditioning) must work in concert to provide a safe and comfortable viewing environment. A successfully functioning auditorium allows the audience to focus solely on the screen.

Well-maintained seating is important to provide comfort and minimize distraction. Seats oriented in a curve benefit the viewing comfort of patrons sitting off-axis. Aisles along side walls are recommended, in order to avoid having seats located next to a wall, which many patrons find uncomfortable. While a center aisle from the front of the house to the back may be

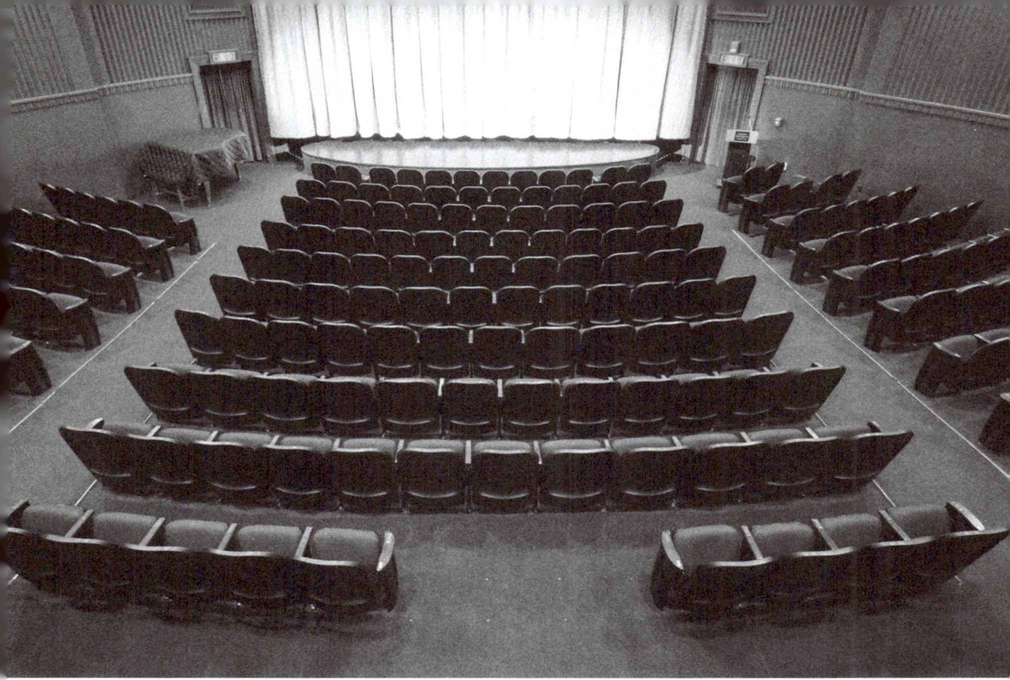

convenient, it takes away space for the best seats in the venue. If
the auditorium's width requires the seating area to be divided, a
three-section division will maintain ideal center seating. *[Figure
3.6]* The minimum recommended distance from the front row of
seats to the screen can be calculated by multiplying the screen's
width at its widest aspect ratio by a 0.6 factor.

Appropriate light levels within the auditorium are necessary
to provide safe entry and exit before, after, and during the screening. Aisle lights allow patrons to walk safely in a darkened auditorium. If the auditorium contains a podium or stage, focused
lighting for this area will enable its use for public presentations.
Separate work lights may exist to provide bright illumination for
cleaning purposes. Light spill onto the screen during projection

(most commonly caused by exit lights adjacent to the screen) should be avoided. Control of auditorium lighting is often located in the projection booth or in the theater manager's office.

Lighting protocols should be formally established and communicated to projection and theater staff. Raising auditorium lights during film credits should be avoided, as it encourages patrons to exit the auditorium and distracts those who wish to view the entire film.

The size and location of projection ports on the back wall of the auditorium should also be taken into consideration when addressing theater light levels. Projection ports located close to seating areas can leak distracting light from the projection booth onto adjacent seating, walls, or ceiling within the auditorium. Care should also be taken to minimize light spill from the projection booth.

Unseen by the audience, but affecting all, are room temperature, humidity, and air exchange systems. Well-maintained and properly functioning HVAC equipment is essential to provide a comfortable and safe viewing environment. An auditorium full of patrons generates a considerable amount of heat, humidity, and carbon dioxide. Frequent air exchange with proper heating/cooling and humidity control is very important to human comfort; moreover, excessive heat, cold, and humidity are often distracting to the viewing experience. HVAC vents placed near the screen or near the image path can result in visible heat waves obstructing the image on screen during projection. In addition, proper installation and sound dampening of the air-handling components minimizes noise and distraction from the HVAC system itself. Frequent variations in the number of patrons in the theater auditorium, from zero to many in a short amount of time, can be taxing to an HVAC system working to maintain a consistent environment. The importance of proper maintenance of the equipment and monitoring of the auditorium cannot be overstated.

DO'S AND DON'TS

ALWAYS

- Clean both sides of the projection booth port windows on a regular basis.

- Project film in dim booth lighting and avoid spilling light into the auditorium.

- Strive to maintain a comfortable level of temperature, humidity, and air exchange in the auditorium.

- Keep the projection booth as clean and orderly as possible.

NEVER

- Let loose film fall to the projection booth floor and accumulate dust, dirt, and debris.

- Neglect to keep clean your working environment and film equipment.

NOTES

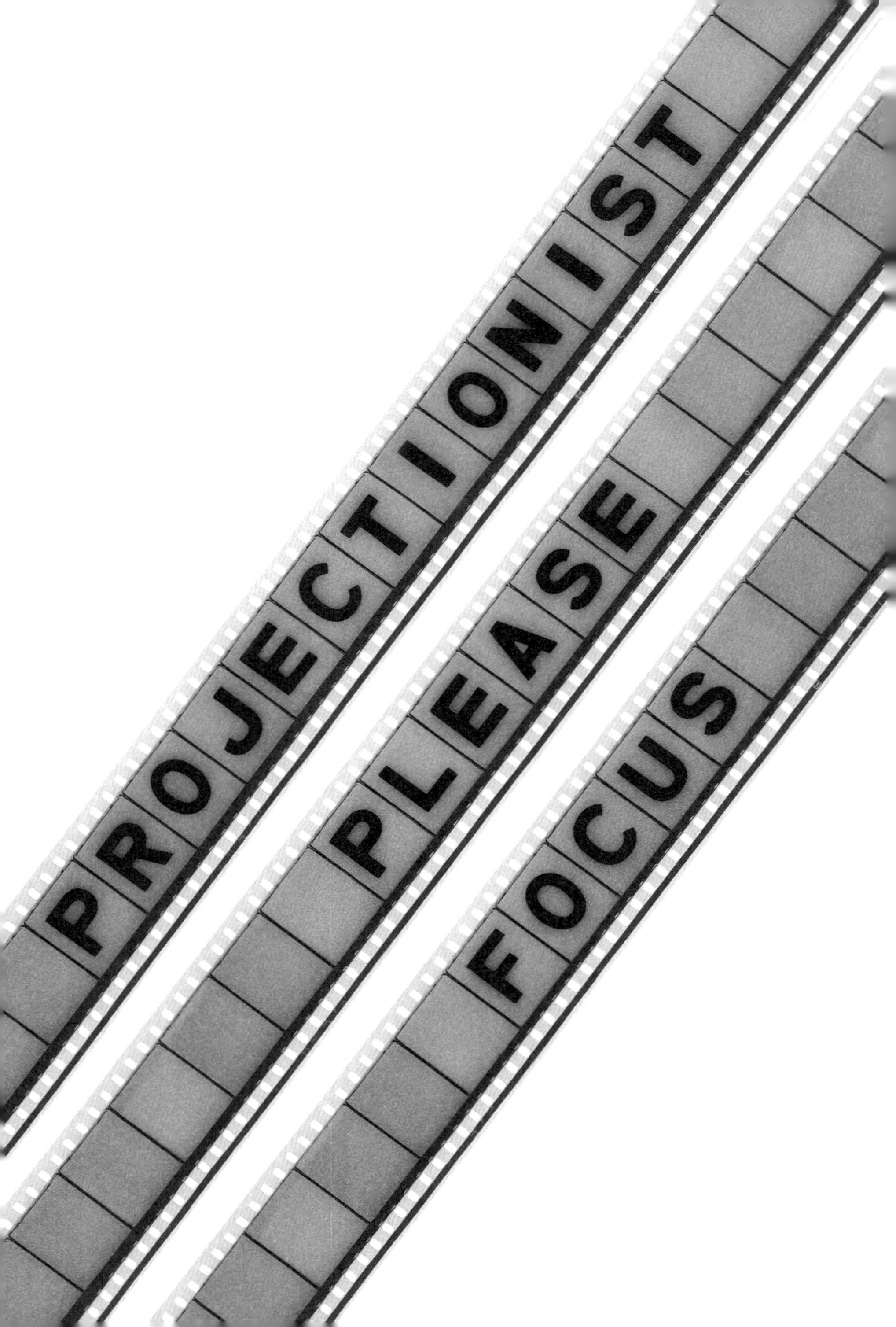

PROJECTIONIST
PLEASE
FOCUS

4

FILM IDENTIFICATION

FILM INSPECTION BEFORE** projection is a necessity.** A projectionist should never blindly trust that a print is in projectable condition. Although some commercial distributors ship film prints with "Quality Inspected" stickers, these stickers must not be interpreted as proof that the reels are ready to be projected. Prints may contain a variety of unaddressed conditions, such as one-sided tape splices (sometimes employing masking tape or other inappropriate substitutes), incomplete countdown leaders, inaccurate cue marks, and unrepaired damage.

Starting in the 1970s, with the advent of the multiplex, most commercial theaters began to employ **platter** technology for film exhibition. This method utilizes a single film projector, along with a multi-tiered platter mechanism to store and transport the film to and from the projector. The entire multi-reel film print is spliced together and wound onto large horizontal rotating platters. *[Figure 4.2]* The projectionist removes the head and tail leaders from each reel in order to splice the entire film together.

Fig. 4.1 – **The physical characteristics of a film print provide valuable information on how it may be optimally presented.**

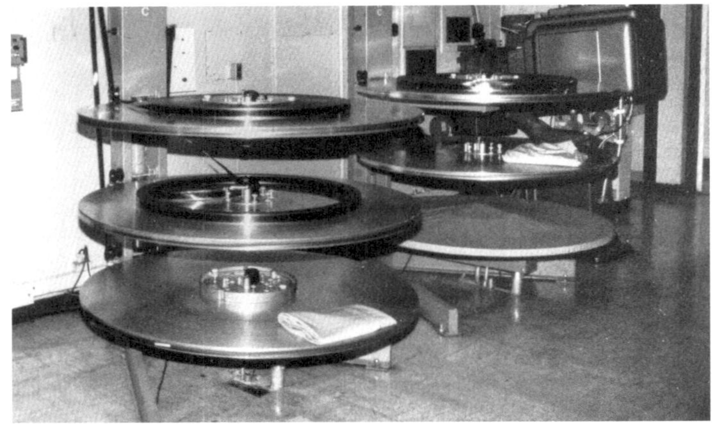

4.2 – **A 3-tiered platter film projection system in a multiplex cinema at the Boulevard Cinema II in Amherst, NY (July 1991). 35mm slide courtesy of Timothy J. Wagner.**

Countdown leaders (and cue marks) are not used in platter projection. Some theaters incorporate other film handling technologies whereby film reels are spliced together, such as 6,000-foot reels on each of two projectors, towers, and double MUTs (Make-Up Tables). These systems, now virtually superseded by digital technology in commercial cinemas, allowed automated projector operation for each screening, enabling one projectionist to operate an entire multiplex of theaters.

Head and tail splices, countdown leaders, and properly spaced cue marks are not the archival projectionist's only concerns. Many projection prints, especially those coming from commercial distributors, have seen a great deal of service. Older acetate prints frequently contain perforation and edge damage that needs to be repaired before projection. One of the principal causes of edge damage is poor winding. An uneven wind will leave film edges exposed and susceptible to damage from film reels or cans during handling and transport. Mind your wind!

This chapter focuses on **preparing films for projection** utilizing a two-projector, manual changeover operation, employing multiple reels, which is widely considered best practice in a museum or archival venue. The inclusion and completeness of leaders, countdown, and cue marks on each reel are necessary to perform this type of projection successfully. The information presented here applies to 16mm, 35mm, and 70mm film exhibition.

THE INSPECTION REPORT

One of the most important tools in the projection booth is the film inspection report. The purpose of this document is to provide the projectionist with all the information necessary to perform a flawless presentation. Information on the inspection report should include the film's title, screening date, number of reels, frame rate, format/gauge, condition, aspect ratio, sound format, cue marks, descriptions of the opening and closing shots, information for return shipping, and space for notes. Since the projectionist is using this information to set the equipment parameters for each screening, it is vital that all the information is reproduced with the utmost accuracy. By inspecting and repairing the film and correctly interpreting and documenting its parameters, the film inspector contributes as much expertise to a screening as the projectionist. See Appendix A for a Sample Inspection Report.

RECEIVING FILM PRINTS

Film prints may be obtained from a variety of sources, including distributors, studios, archives, museums, and private collectors. Film prints arrive at screening venues wound on reels or cores. Prints on reels are often shipped in hexagon-shaped metal or plastic containers, commonly referred to as **"Goldbergs"** (for the manufacturing company Goldberg Brothers, Inc.), or ICC cans (for the U.S. Interstate Commerce Commission), or in plastic film shipping cartons. Cored films are generally shipped inside film cans, packed within boxes. Most archives store and deliver their films on cores within cans, while distributors and studios tend to store and ship their films on reels. Since storage and shipping methods vary, the archival projectionist should expect to receive prints that are wound either heads or tails out, with emulsion wound inward or outward.

Once a film has been received, it's a good idea to verify immediately that it is the correct and complete film, especially if you aren't planning to inspect it for several days. Despite the labeling on film cans, shipping containers, or paper bands (wrapped around reels), reels of film do occasionally get mixed up. Open the shipping container(s) and count the number of reels or cans to determine if you have received the correct amount. Then check the leaders of each reel to verify the title, and that you have all of the reels. If splices appear between the leaders and the body of each reel, this indicates that the film has likely been "plattered," "built up," or combined onto larger reels. If this is the case, you must verify that the leaders match the reels to make sure you have received a complete print. Hopefully, there will be one or two frames of image attached to each head and tail leader, which match up with the body of the film. When projectionists in venues equipped with platter systems remove head and tail leaders in order to assemble the film, they often make the splice one or two frames into the body of each reel, so that some images of the film remain attached to the leaders. *[Figure 4.3]*

4.3 – Tail splice from a "plattered" 35mm print (*Azaan*, Prashant Chadha, India 2011), showing a reference frame. The last frame has been kept attached to the tail leader in order to assist the projectionist in matching up all film leaders to their appropriate reels when breaking down the print at the end of the film's theatrical run.

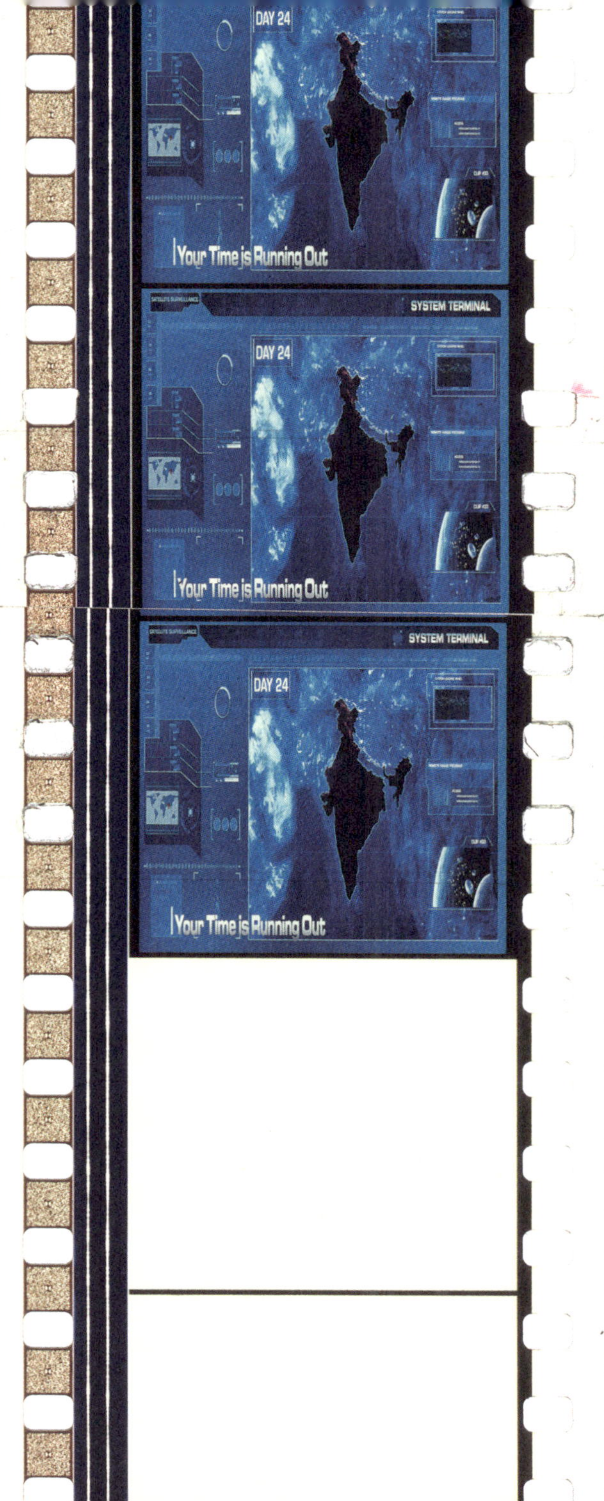

DAY 24
Your Time is Running Out
SATELLITE SURVEILLANCE
SYSTEM TERMINAL
DAY 24
Your Time is Running Out
SATELLITE SURVEILLANCE
SYSTEM TERMINAL
DAY 24
Your Time is Running Out

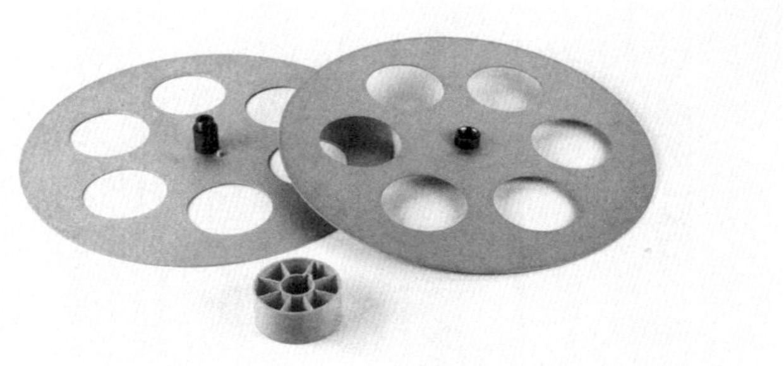

4.4 – **A 2,000-foot "split reel" for 35mm film. The film is wound around the 3-inch plastic core shown at the center.**

When breaking the films down after their run, the image frames on the leaders are matched to the body of each reel, thus allowing projectionists to correctly attach the proper head and tail leaders. When inspecting a previously plattered film, be sure to verify that any image frames on the leaders match the images on the body of the film. This will prove the reel's identity. It is not uncommon to find leaders spliced incorrectly, so checking this during every inspection will ensure that reels are projected in the correct order.

Film prints received from archives are usually wound on cores, necessitating the use of a split reel to properly handle the cored rolls of film. At least one 16mm and one 35mm split reel, in good condition, should be available in the film inspection area. A split reel features a brass core with aluminum flanges which screw together to sandwich the cored roll of film. *[Figure 4.4]* Avoid over-tightening split reels, as this may damage the core's threads. As with projection reels, all split reels need to be in excellent condition to prevent any damage to the film. Due to preservation and care, archival prints tend to be in better condition than your average distribution print. However, you may sometimes receive an original release print from an archive, with all the wear and tear that it has endured.

TYPES OF FILM PRINTS

During the heyday of film projection, there were many, subtly different, kinds of prints that an operator might encounter. Although such prints were, in many cases, quite similar (in terms of aspect ratio, soundtrack, etc.), they also had unique characteristics that reflected their intended use. A true archival projectionist must acquire an appreciation of *why* certain prints possess the characteristics that they do.

Release prints are the most common type of print. They are produced to accommodate multiple bookings during theatrical runs. Regardless of any presence of wear and tear, or damage from improper handling and projection, original release prints represent a good baseline for intended contrast and density.

Answer prints are test prints produced by a laboratory. Labs will produce as many answer prints as necessary until the client (e.g., the studio or the filmmaker) is satisfied. Although rejected answer prints should never be distributed, some do manage to get into collections or circulation. If your print displays distracting fluctuations in tone or color, it may be a print that was never intended for distribution and should be contextualized as such.

Preview prints are rare, as they represent intermediate versions of the film before all editorial decisions are locked in. As such, they may possess slight variations in scenes or even lack entire sequences. These prints may lack some or all main and final credits.

Show prints (premiere prints) are high-quality copies intended for a high-profile screening (e.g., a premiere or festival). These prints are often struck directly from the original camera negative, thereby exceeding the quality offered by conventional release prints, which are struck from intermediate material. Show prints may lack conventional motor start and changeover cues.

Compilation prints (colloquially referred to as "Franken-prints") combine footage from two or more damaged prints to produce a complete, projectable copy. These prints may possess very noticeable differences in color and density, but they are a cheap alternative to striking new prints. A projectionist may need to adjust focus and framing frequently during projection, as the film stocks and their printing may differ.

Television prints are prepared for television broadcast. This may mean that the print has been censored for language or content, or that the original cinematography has been "panned and scanned" to accommodate television's 4:3 aspect ratio. To avoid disappointment, it's a good idea to acknowledge the limitations of the print to the audience before the start of the screening.

A **fine grain master** is an intermediate positive that looks, in many respects, like a conventional release print. As an intermediate duplicating element, fine grain masters are printed on negative perforation, short-pitch stock (see the section "Perforations" in Chapter 1), with lower contrast. These preservation elements should *never* be projected. However, some are mistakenly identified as projection prints, and find their way into distribution channels or private film collections. Short-pitch stock can be damaged by projectors which cannot accommodate shrunken film.

FILM STOCKS

Motion picture film is or was created by several manufacturers: Agfa (or Agfa-Gevaert), DuPont, Eastman Kodak, Ferrania, Fuji, Ilford, Lucky Film, 3M, Orwo, Pathé, and many others. Most film stocks feature information printed along the edge of the film (edge codes) which indicates the manufacturer.

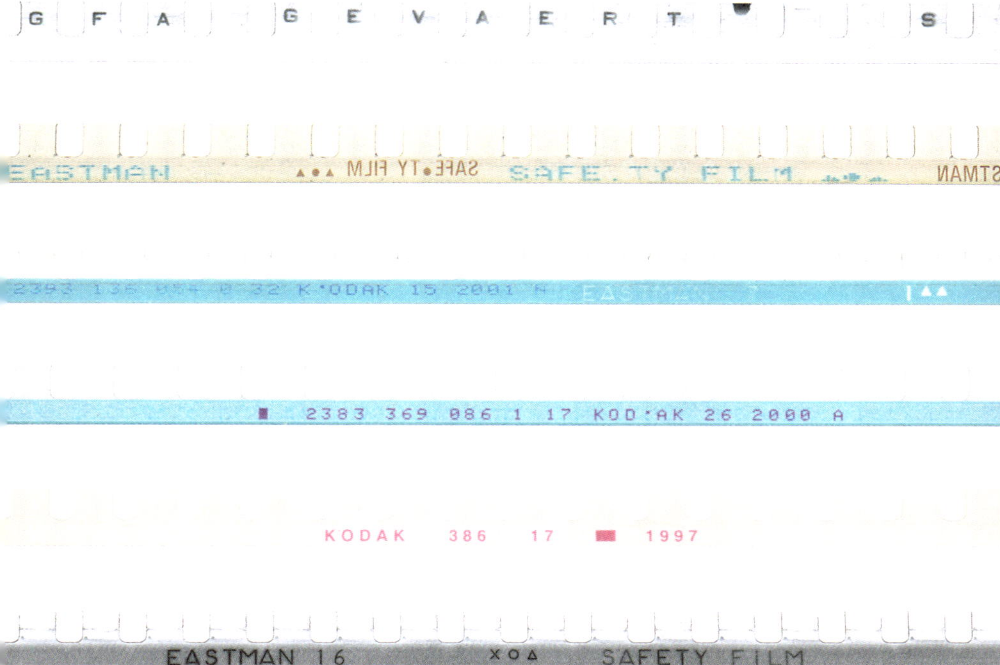

4.5 – Some examples of edge codes, printed on one or both sides of
35mm motion picture film.

Edge codes may also indicate the type of film stock, and, in
the case of Eastman Kodak, the year of manufacture (via numbers
or geometric codes). *[Figure 4.5]* Be aware that edge codes can be
printed-through onto subsequent generations of film in the duplicating process. Original edge codes are typically black text (sometimes cyan) appearing sharp in definition, with print-through
edge codes from negatives generally appearing as white text and
slightly blurred. Black-text edge codes from a previous positive
generation tend to be softer in their appearance. Film prints may
contain several generations of print-through edge codes.

16mm reversal film stock, which is a positive created directly within the camera at the time of shooting, can be encountered if you are projecting 16mm film. Reversal film normally has black or dark margins, and shows Kodachrome I, II, or Anscochrome edge codes. By and large, Kodachrome stock tends to retain most of its color, while the earlier Anscochrome stock is likely to to fade over time. While reversal stock has been infrequently used for duplication for cost-saving purposes, most films shot with reversal stock are camera originals, and should be treated accordingly.

Eastman Kodak's color print stock manufactured before 1979 (often referred to as **Eastmancolor** film) has a reputation for **color fading**, or "turning pink." The cyan and yellow dyes tend to disappear, leaving the more stable magenta dye. As a result, the image color is pinkish, reddish, or brownish in hue. The era of Kodak **low-fade print stocks** began in 1979. Things began to change in 1982, when Kodak introduced its low-fade stock carrying the "LPP" (Lowfade Positive Print) edge code. By the 1990s, the LPP edge code was dropped, even though the manufactured film continued to be a low-fade stock.

Projectionists have been known to use **color filters** in front of the projector lens when showing color-faded prints, in their efforts to balance the color. This method, however, has proven ineffective, as it only addresses one portion of the color spectrum and generates an inaccurate and arbitrary chromatic experience.

Projection prints produced in the **Technicolor** dye-transfer process are best at retaining their chromatic balance. The Technicolor Corporation employed a color imbibition printing process for 16mm and 35mm release prints, which ended in 1975 in the United States and in 1977 in Great Britain. Technicolor release prints may have some damage, as they are surely older, vintage prints, but if they are in good enough physical condition to project, then the audience can expect to see color at its most vibrant. Some

Technicolor prints have an **"IB Tech"** edge code. Others can be identified by a silver-dye soundtrack, gray frame lines, and sometimes slight color registration overlaps or fringes, appearing out-of-frame in the corners. The emulsion side of the film also exhibits a high-relief pattern in the image resulting from the dye-transfer process.

ASPECT RATIOS

The shape of a moving image projected onto the screen is determined by its **aspect ratio**: the ratio between the height of the image (always stated as 1) and the width of the image (e.g., 1:1.85). In practice, however, the width measurement is almost always listed first (e.g., 1.85:1), and often the width is the only measurement stated (1.85). Technological advancements, aesthetic choices, and financial implications have provided motion picture film exhibition with a variety of aspect ratios. Determining the proper, intended aspect ratio of a film is an important part of the film identification process.

35mm motion picture film projectors utilize metal **aperture plates** to define the different aspect ratios on the screen. As mentioned in Chapter 2, these aperture plates may be purchased in multiple aspect ratios, as well as "undercut" (meaning that they won't show the "full" printed image, in accordance with the aspect ratio) or blank, to allow custom filing by the projectionist for each installation. The exact dimensions for aspect ratios are determined by industry agencies such as the **Society of Motion Picture and Television Engineers (SMPTE)**.

16mm film projectors are designed and manufactured with a native aspect ratio of 1.33:1. They do not use interchangeable aperture plates, unless in those projectors that are fitted for a quick conversion from one gauge to another, such as 35mm/16mm.

35mm films with aspect ratios from 1.18:1 to 1.85:1 are photographed and projected using **spherical lenses**. Spherical lenses do not alter the image that is printed on the film stock. 35mm **CinemaScope** films (2.35:1, 2.39:1, 2.55:1), along with some other wide aspect ratios, require **anamorphic lenses** during cinematography and projection. Anamorphic camera lenses impart a **horizontal squeeze** to the image, which is captured on film. Upon projection, an anamorphic lens mounted on the projector will "unsqueeze" the image. When looking at the film print, the images appear compressed (everyone and everything in the frame appears stretched from top to bottom, and looks thin).

35mm film prints come in a wide range of aspect ratios, including 1.18:1, 1.33:1, 1.37:1, 1.66:1, 1.75:1, 1.78:1, 1.85:1, 2:1, 2.35:1, 2.39:1, and 2.55:1. Determining the proper aspect ratio for projection can be difficult, as not every film is printed at the aspect ratio intended for projection. **Non-anamorphic widescreen** films, which debuted in 1953, provide the greatest challenge, as they are often *printed* at 1.37:1, though intended for *projection* at 1.66:1, 1.75:1, or 1.85:1. Knowledge of film history (studio production, exhibition and projection practices, in particular) is a valuable tool here. Information regarding the following aspect ratios pertains to 35mm film only.

1.33:1 is the aspect ratio for films without printed audio tracks **(silent films) and sound-on-disc films**. *[Figure 4.6]* The image fills nearly the entire width of the film, from perforation to perforation, and is 4 perforations in height. The frame line is often pencil-thin, maximizing the use of space. The 1926 introduction of sound films by the Vitaphone Corporation did not affect the image area, because the sound was recorded on separate discs.

1.18:1 is the aspect ratio for **early sound-on-film** prints. *[Figure 4.7]* The 1927 introduction of Movietone sound films narrowed the image area by placing an optical soundtrack alongside it, resulting in a nearly square image. Though sound-on-film became standard, many exhibitors disliked this aspect ratio.

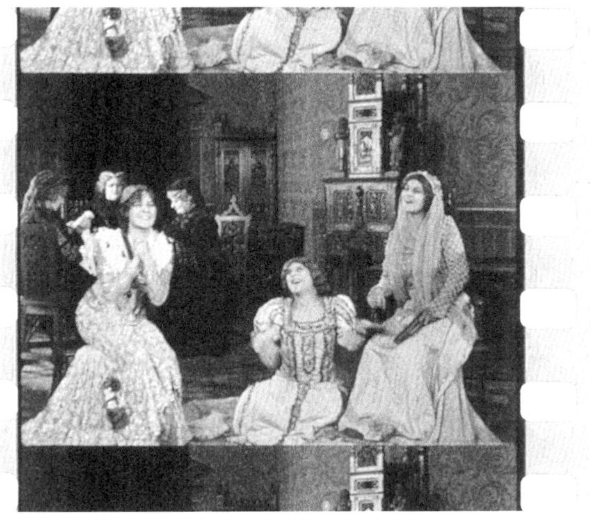

4.6 – **35mm film with 1.33:1 aspect ratio**
(*La Fille du margrave*, Louis Feuillade, France 1912).

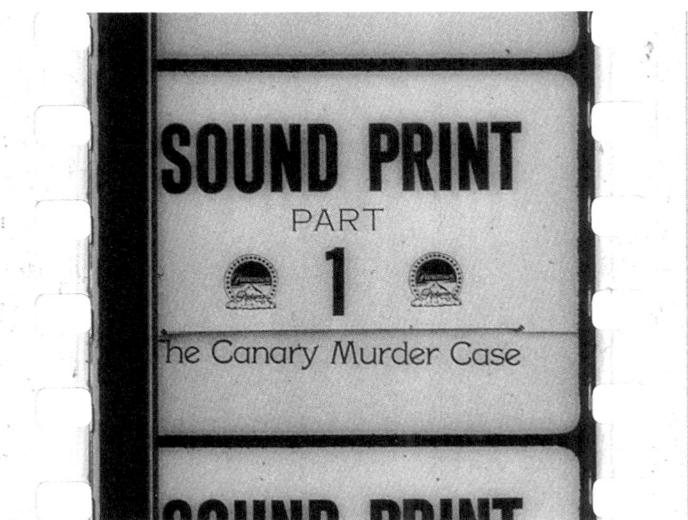

4.7 – **35mm film with 1.18:1 aspect ratio**
(*The Canary Murder Case*, Malcolm St. Clair, US 1929).

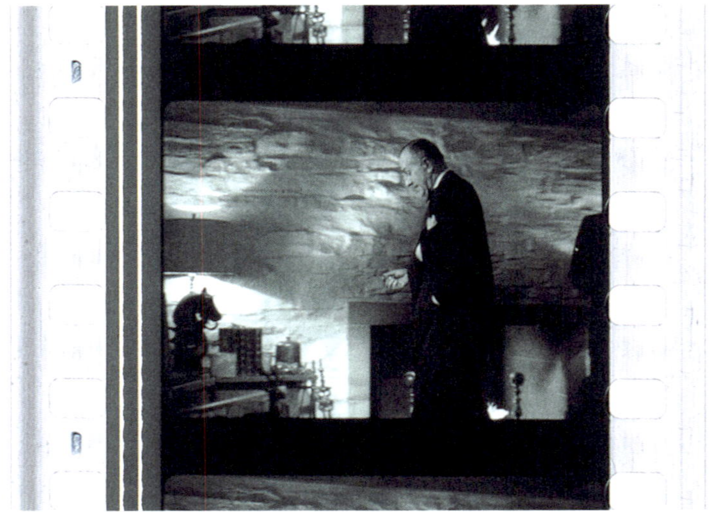

4.8 – **35mm film with 1.37:1 aspect ratio**
(*The Asphalt Jungle*, John Huston, US 1950).

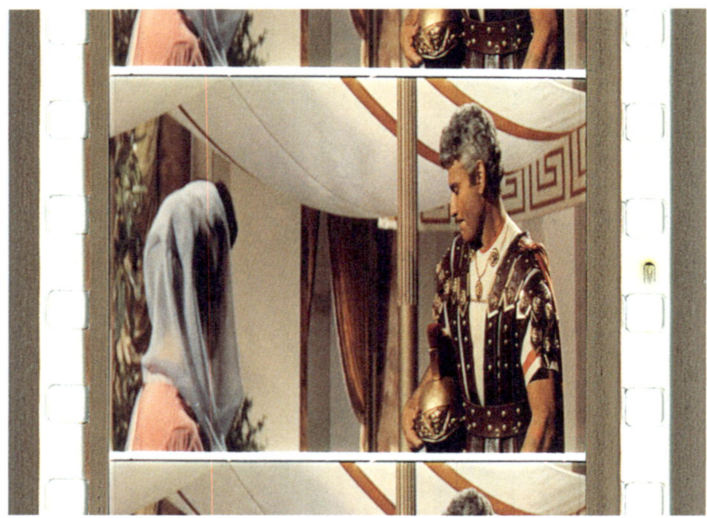

4.9 – **35mm film with 2.55:1 (anamorphic) aspect ratio and magnetic
audio track** (*Sign of the Pagan*, Douglas Sirk, US 1954).

1.37:1 was adopted as the aspect ratio for **sound films** in 1931, when major film studios in the United States reached a consensus to widen the shape of the image. *[Figure 4.8]* This aspect ratio was achieved by thickening the frame lines while maintaining the image width, resulting in a shorter, wider image. This aspect ratio, often referred to as **"Academy" aperture**, remained unchanged until the advent of widescreen formats in 1953.

In response to declining theater attendance after 1946, the impact of television, and the 1952 debut of Cinerama (an impressive three-projector film process wowing audiences with its wide, deeply curved screen), Hollywood film studios began to devise their own widescreen film processes and push for larger screens in theaters.

In 1953, 20th Century-Fox debuted **CinemaScope** in Henry Koster's *The Robe*, employing anamorphic lenses (in production and projection) to achieve their widescreen process. 20th Century-Fox also had a special 35mm print stock manufactured, with very narrow perforations (known as "Fox Hole" perforations), to accommodate the addition of four magnetic soundtracks on their release prints (three channels of audio behind the screen, and a fourth surround-sound channel). Containing **no optical soundtrack**, early CinemaScope prints featured a projected aspect ratio of **2.55:1**. *[Figure 4.9]* The projected aspect ratio was later narrowed to **2.35:1** in order to fit an optical track, along with the magnetic audio track. The expense involved in upgrading theaters across the country to accommodate the special multi-channel magnetic audio print stock prevented its exhibition in most theaters. The studio adopted standard perforation stock and a mono optical track on most CinemaScope release prints, retaining a projected aspect ratio of **2.35:1**. This aspect ratio changed to **2.39:1** in 1971, when the image height was slightly reduced to better hide laboratory splices during

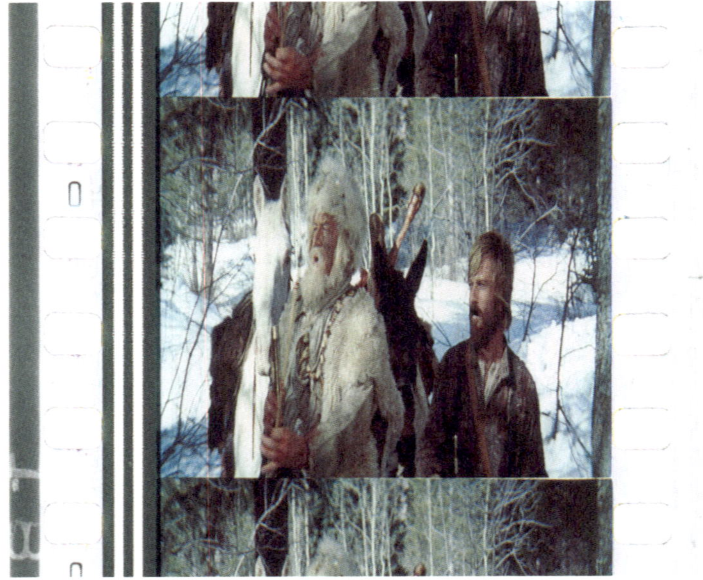

4.10 – **35mm film with 2.35:1 (anamorphic) aspect ratio**
(***Jeremiah Johnson***, Sydney Pollack, US 1972).

projection. *[Figure 4.10]* Projector **aperture plates** for 2.35 / 2.39 presentation allow the transmission of the most amount of light (and image information) for any 35mm sound film aperture.

After 20th Century-Fox launched its CinemaScope process, the format was made available to other studios via licensing fees. Aside from some high-profile films shot in CinemaScope, most other studios ventured into widescreen presentation by simply trimming the existing image. Paramount Pictures and RKO adopted a **1.66:1** aspect ratio *[Figure 4.11]* by cropping the top and

4.11 – **35mm film with hard-matted 1.66:1 and 1.85:1 aspect ratios.**
Top: ***Barry Lyndon*** (Stanley Kubrick, UK / US 1975);
Bottom: ***Who Framed Roger Rabbit*** (Robert Zemeckis, US 1988).

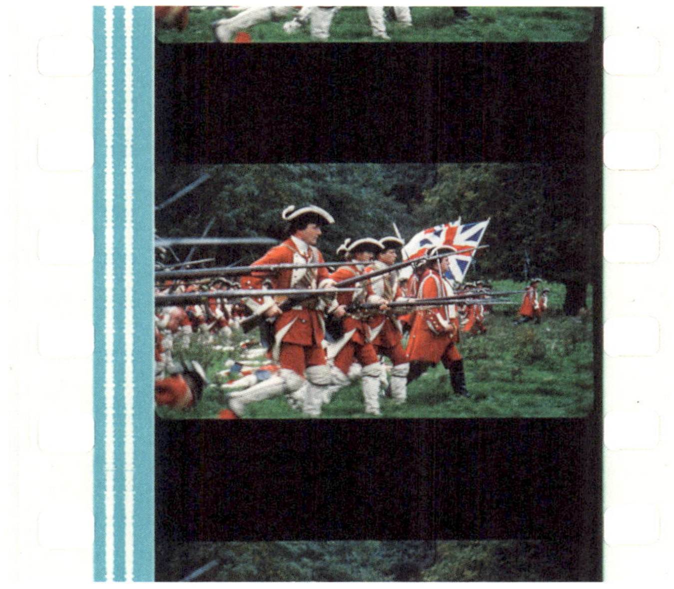

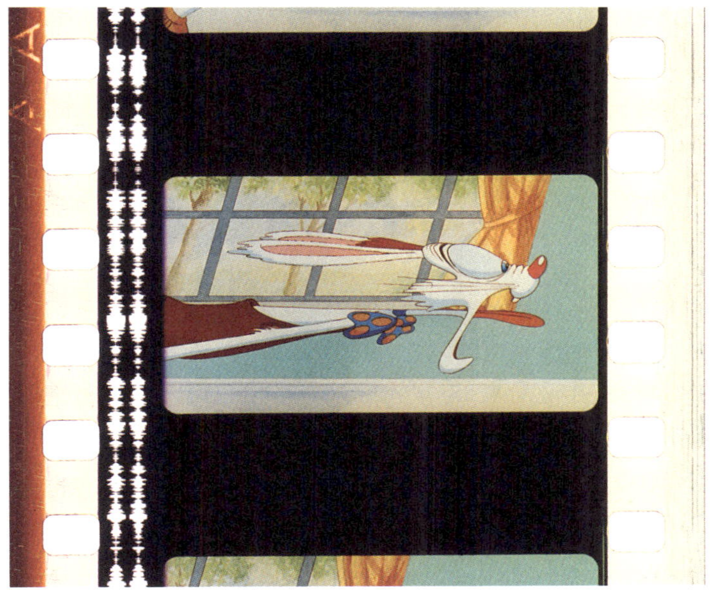

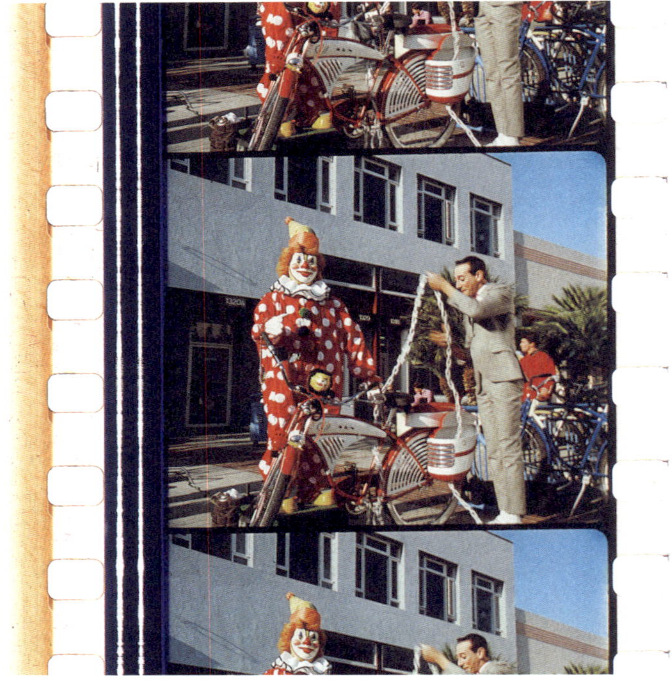

4.12 – Open-matte 1.85:1 aspect ratio on 35mm film. Note the extra space at the top and bottom of the frame, intended to be cropped by the projector aperture plate (*Pee-wee's Big Adventure*, Tim Burton, US 1985).

bottom of the 1.37:1 image, while Metro-Goldwyn-Mayer and Walt Disney Productions cropped the frame to a **1.75:1** aspect ratio. A **1.85:1** aspect ratio (via more cropping) was adopted by both Columbia Pictures and Universal-International Pictures. While most projection prints from these studios continued to be printed at 1.37:1, their composition and projection were intended for cropped, widescreen presentation. *[Figure 4.12]* These non-anamorphic, widescreen ratios are sometimes referred to as "**flat widescreen**." Disadvantages of the flat widescreen process include loss of light on the screen (aperture plates with smaller openings), with enlarged film grain and print damage becoming more apparent on the screen (due to the magnification of a smaller image to fill a larger screen).

Many **other film formats and processes** were developed for widescreen presentation, such as VistaVision, Superscope, Todd-AO, and Grandeur 70. A wealth of information on widescreen film exhibition processes is available (as of the time of this book's publication) on Martin B. Hart's American WideScreen Museum website, widescreenmuseum.com.

As mentioned earlier, determining aspect ratio is an important part of the film inspection process, and identifying the proper aspect ratio for flat (non-anamorphic) widescreen films can be a challenge. Fortunately, there are several tools that can help with this.

Some **flat widescreen** film prints are hard-matted, utilizing black borders at the top and bottom of the image to present it on the film stock at the intended aspect ratio. Unfortunately, many flat widescreen films are printed at 1.37:1, requiring the film inspector, projectionist, and/or curator of film exhibitions to determine the intended aspect ratio for projection. In this case, it is useful to know that despite the variety of flat widescreen aspect ratios initially adopted by studios over many years, film exhibitors in North America adopted the **1.85:1** aspect ratio as the **flat widescreen standard**, while European exhibitors adopted the **1.66:1** aspect ratio. By the end of the 20th century, most European exhibitors had migrated to **1.85:1**, as well.

In North America, from the 1960s onward, most commercial theaters projected two aspect ratios only: 1.85:1 (often referred to as "flat") and 2.39:1 (usually referred to as "Scope"). Projectionists screening flat widescreen films from before 1960 should generally follow the studio policies toward aspect ratio as outlined above.

Projector aperture plates can be useful tools in determining aspect ratios. Laying an aperture plate atop a film frame on the

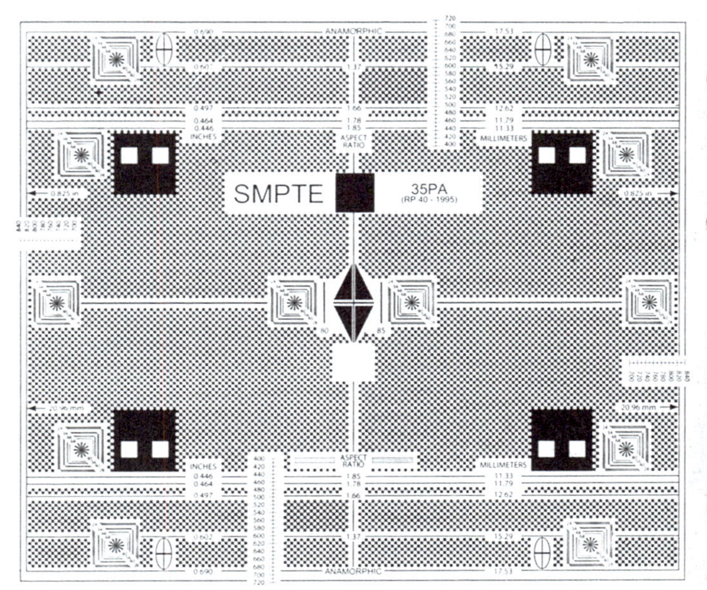

4.13 – Multiple aspect ratios are delineated on each frame
of 35mm *SMPTE RP 40 Projector Alignment and
Image Quality Test Film.* © SMPTE

light box of an inspection bench will illustrate the image area
that the audience will see for any given aspect ratio.

Another tool is a frame or two of the **SMPTE RP 40 Projector Alignment and Image Quality Test Film**, which has multiple
aspect-ratio delineations printed on each frame. *[Figure 4.13]*
Overlaying this on a projection print allows us to see the image
appearance at several aspect ratios. Sometimes the size and disposition of a film's opening credits can be of guidance in choosing the correct aspect ratio.

Projecting a non-anamorphic film made after 1953 at the
1.37:1 "Academy" aspect ratio would most likely be incorrect, as

the audience would see more than the filmmakers wanted to show. This could include boom microphones at the top of the frame, and gaffer's tape or equipment at the bottom of the frame. Projecting film in an incorrect aspect ratio does not preserve the *mise-en-scène* intended by the filmmakers. The objective is emphatically *not* to show as much image as possible; it is to **present films as they were *meant* to be seen**.

In the twilight of commercial film distribution, **independent filmmakers often recorded on videotape, but still needed 35mm film prints for distribution** purposes. In transferring the video works to film, laboratories often produced copies with a 1.78:1 frame, although it was expected that the theater would mask the print to 1.85:1, as very few exhibitors felt the need to invest in new aperture plates and lenses to accommodate this modest difference in aspect ratio.

Despite the fact that most **16mm** film prints are intended for 1.33:1 presentation, there are **exceptions** to be taken into consideration. Some 16mm films are anamorphically printed, requiring an anamorphic lens for the projector. Some 16mm films are printed with hard-matting, creating an aspect ratio chosen by the director or studio. Like 16mm anamorphic films, hard-matted 16mm prints are somewhat rare.

SOUNDTRACKS

Technological developments and competition throughout the history of cinema have provided motion picture film exhibition with a variety of audio formats. Determining the proper sound format of a film is an important part of the film inspection process. Projecting a film using the wrong audio format compromises the filmmakers' intentions and greatly reduces the quality of the audience's sonic experience. The ways in which film audio tracks are read during projection is addressed in the "Sound Readers" section of Chapter 2.

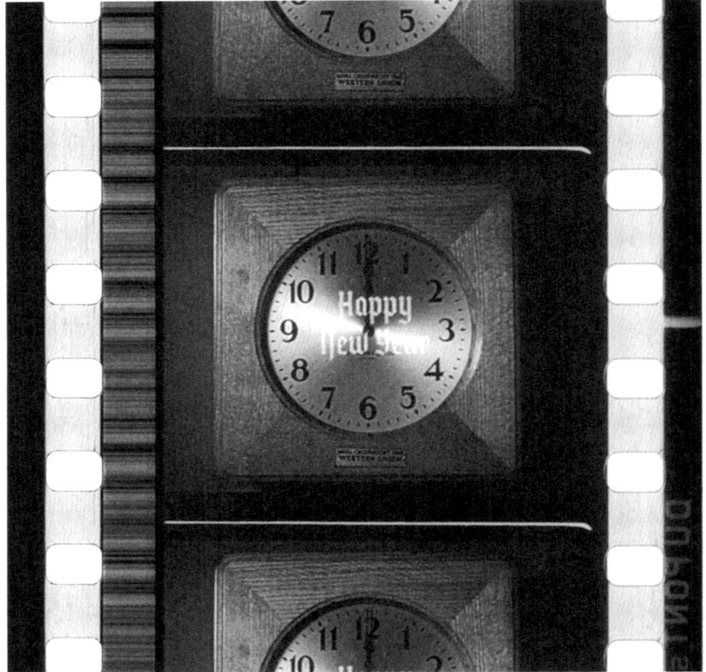

4.14 – Variable density optical soundtrack on 35mm film
(*Daughter of Diogenes*, Michael Luciano, US 1938).

OPTICAL SOUND

The most common soundtrack found on 35mm and 16mm film prints is the **analog optical track**, whereby the audio for the film is represented optically and printed alongside the image.

There are **two basic types of analog optical soundtracks: variable density and variable area.**

The entire soundtrack area of **variable density** optical tracks varies in density (or transparency). *[Figure 4.14]* The density relates to the audio track's volume, and the width of the bands to the pitch. Originally, the **"Western Electric"** soundtrack — a variable density track — looks similar in appearance to a bar-code, and offers a slightly better frequency response than a variable area track, though it has a higher noise level. Variable density tracks are **mono**, and are found mostly on older prints. Film prints with multiple variable density tracks also exist, featuring several narrow, identical, variable density tracks in the same area normally occupied by a single variable density track. Film prints with this kind of soundtrack are quite rare.

Far more common than variable density is the variable area optical track. This track area is located next to the picture, and is opaque (usually black), with a narrow, clear track or two in the center (in most prints), which varies in width according to variations in the sound. The width of the modulations relates to the soundtrack's loudness, while the frequency relates to the pitch.

Variable area optical tracks come in many varieties, with some of the most common being the following *(see following pages)*:

- **Unilateral** — one clear track with only one edge modulating. Mono. *[Figure 4.15]*
- **Bilateral** — one clear track with both edges modulating. Mono. *[Figure 4.16]*
- **Dual Unilateral** — two clear tracks with one edge of each track modulating. Mono. *[Figure 4.17]*
- **Dual Bilateral** — two clear tracks with both edges of each track modulating. Mono or Stereo. *[Figure 4.18]* If both tracks on a film print are completely identical throughout, the print is monaural. If one track appears different from the other, then stereo information is present. Playback of stereo optical tracks requires a split solar cell in the projector.
- **Multiple Variable Area** — four or more clear tracks with one or both edges modulating. Mono. *[Figure 4.19. see page 128]*

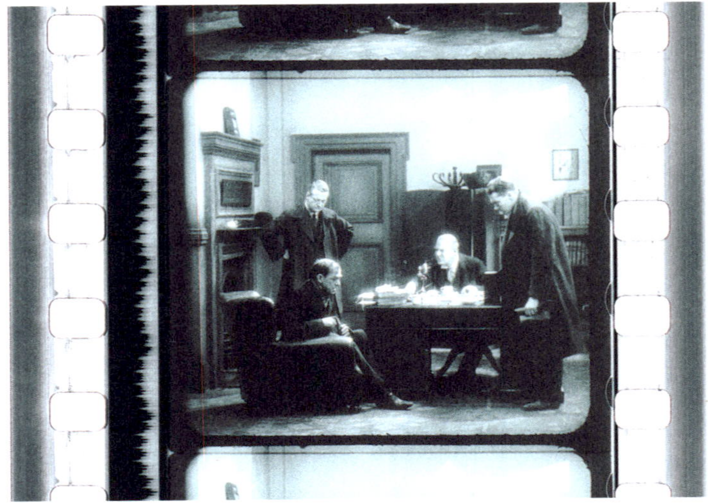

4.15 – Unilateral variable area optical soundtrack on 35mm film
(*Blackmail*, Alfred Hitchcock, UK 1929).

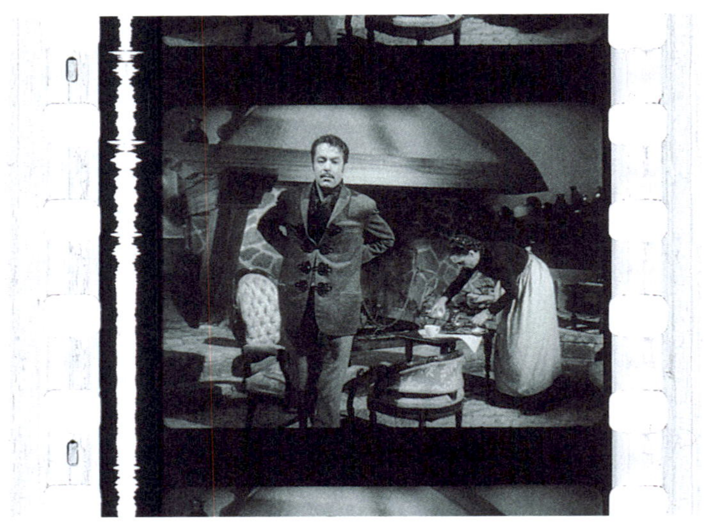

4.16 – Bilateral variable area optical soundtrack on 35mm film
(*Abismos de pasión [Wuthering Heights]*, Luis Buñuel, Mexico 1954).

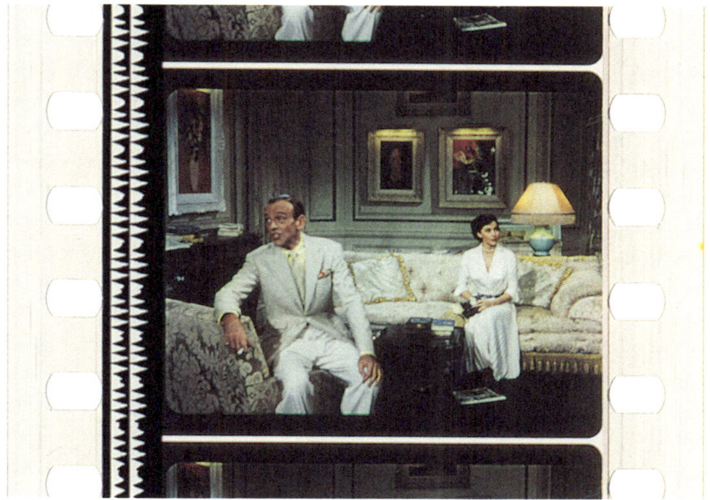

4.17 – Dual unilateral variable area optical soundtrack on 35mm film
(*The Band Wagon*, Vincente Minnelli, US 1953).

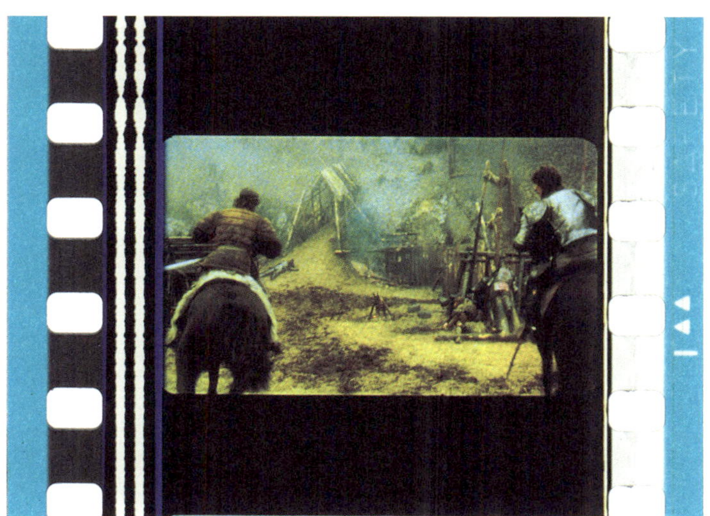

4.18 – Dual bilateral variable area optical soundtrack on 35mm film
(*Excalibur*, John Boorman, US 1981).

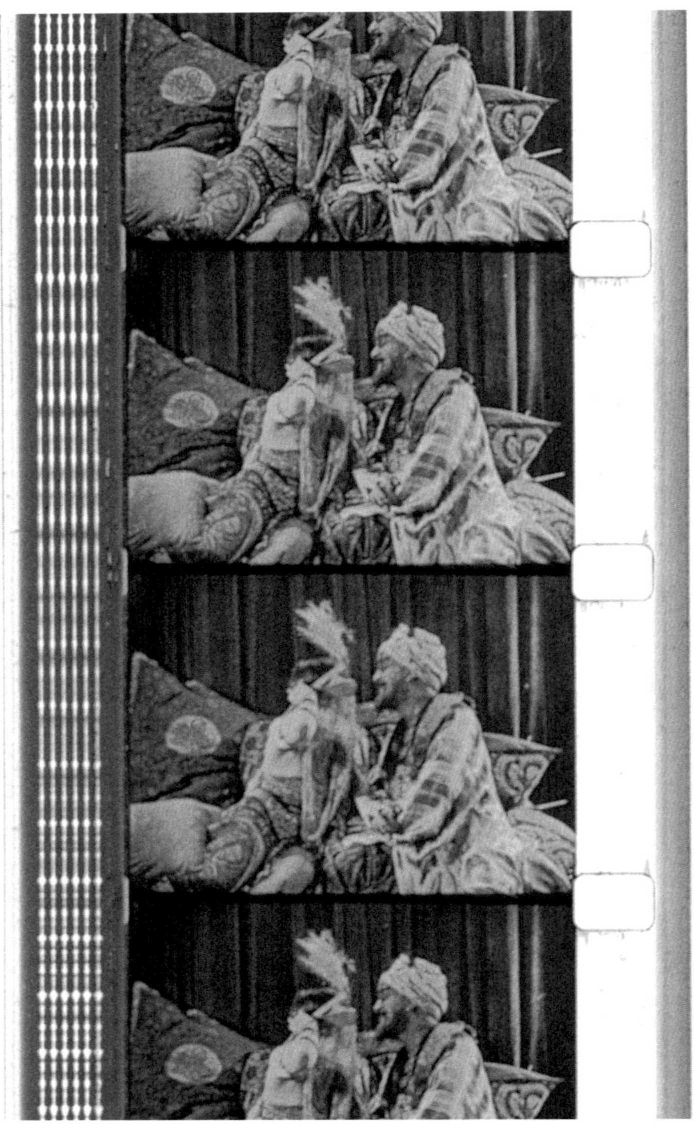

4.19 – Mutliple variable area optical soundtrack on 16mm film
(a reissue print of *How John Came Home*, Sidney Drew, US 1915).

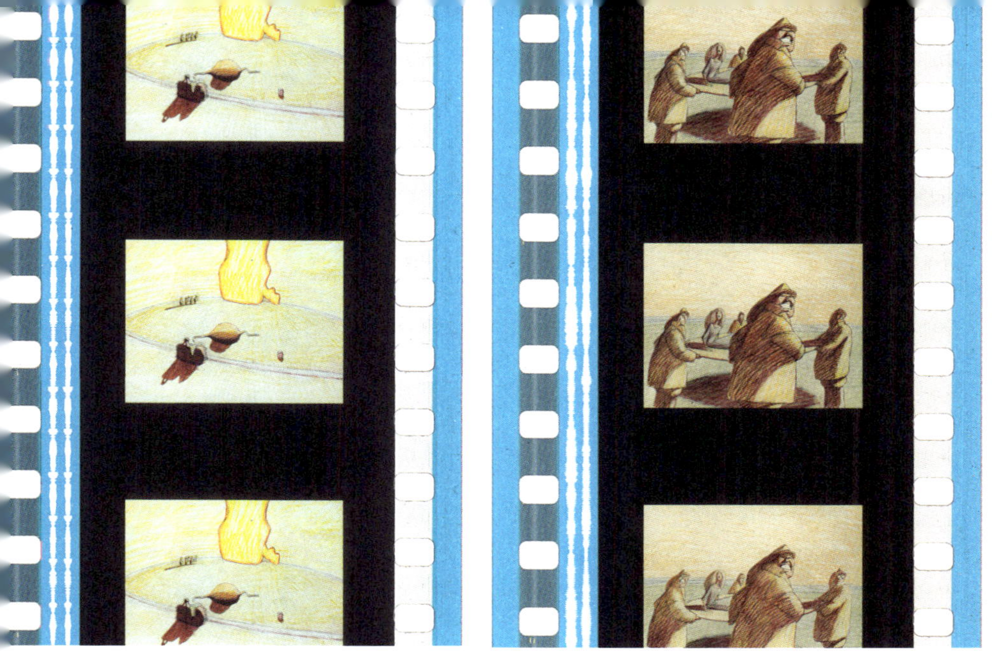

4.20 – **Dual bilateral variable area optical soundtrack on 35mm film exhibiting similar mono information (left) and dynamic stereo information (right) in** *Hot Dog* **(Bill Plympton, US 2008).**

Commercial 35mm optical stereo film prints debuted in the early 1970s though experimental stereo sound films had been in existence for decades. Dolby Laboratories, utilizing matrix technology, actually encoded four channels of audio, with Dolby A noise reduction within the dual bilateral optical tracks. Named "**Dolby Stereo**," the process provides four audio channels (left, center, right, and surround).

While prints encoded in stereo may be identified as such somewhere in the head leader (likely in the optical soundtrack area), this is not definitive proof of the type of audio track actually present on the print.

Stereo prints can be identified by looking at the soundtrack. The two clear audio tracks on the film print look different from each other when stereo information is present. *[Figure 4.20]* Unfortunately, this is rarely identifiable from a single glance at the film. Determining the sound mix of a print on the basis of a single scene or a few feet of film can be misleading. A stereo film print contains many scenes (usually dialogue-heavy) with little or no stereo information. The audio tracks for these scenes looks identical, indicating a mono mix, and the film inspector or projectionist might incorrectly judge the entire print based on this section. It is best to examine the opening and closing credits of a film, which are likely to carry stereo information (such as music).

Due to licensing costs, some distributors have chosen to release prints with non-Dolby stereo sound. Competing stereo systems, such as Kintek Stereo and Ultra Stereo, can be run satisfactorily with Dolby audio processing equipment.

If properly calibrated, the optical sound reader in the projector can read variable density and variable area tracks interchangeably, without the need for any particular adjustment. Any dirt or scratches within the optical track area of a film print will be read as noise, and heard as such by the audience. To minimize this, optical noise-reduction processes for variable density and variable area tracks were implemented since the 1930s. For scenes containing low levels of audio, the track area containing the audio information is narrowed (i.e., the opaque area of the soundtrack is increased), thereby reducing the readable area that may contain dirt and scratches. This type of noise reduction is visible upon print inspection. *[Figure 4.21]*

In the 1970s, Dolby Laboratories applied an **electronic noise reduction** system (developed for professional recording studios), **Dolby A**, to matrixed stereo optical tracks on 35mm film prints. The first feature film to use Dolby noise reduction was Stanley Kubrick's *A Clockwork Orange* in 1971. An improved system, **Dolby SR** (Spectral Recording) was introduced in 1986, offering a greater dynamic range.

These noise reduction systems cannot be determined simply by looking at the audio track. Prints encoded with Dolby A or

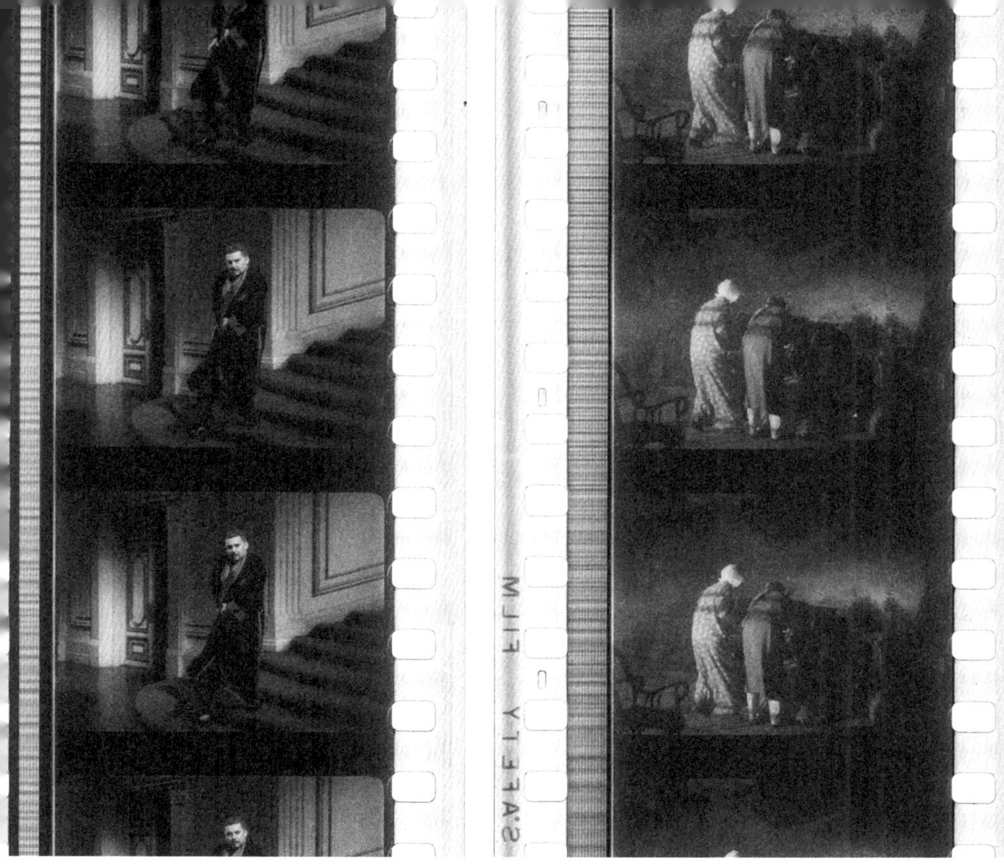

4.21 – **35mm optical soundtrack with printed noise reduction (left) and without (right) (*Mark of the Vampire*, Tod Browning, US 1935).**

SR may be identified somewhere in the head leader as such, and are generally printed in the optical soundtrack portion. Dolby A prints are usually marked as "Stereo" by the laboratory, while Dolby SR prints are identified as "Dolby" or "SR."

If the leaders are missing, or lack this information, other resources can be used to determine the proper noise reduction scheme encoded, if any. The closing credits of a film frequently carry a logo for the Dolby system in question. Dolby A prints show the "Dolby Stereo" graphic, while SR prints read "Dolby Stereo SR" or "Spectral Recording."

The inspector may also use the print's edge code to determine what the audio track may be. Prints made from 1977 to 1987 which exhibit analog stereo activity are Dolby A, while prints made from 1992 through the present are Dolby SR. Prints made from 1987 to 1992 can be either Dolby A or Dolby SR. If a film was originally released with a Dolby A track, but the print was made after 1992, then the print's audio track is most likely Dolby SR. A test run of the film can also help; if the audio processor is set to Dolby SR for a Dolby A print, the resulting sound is likely to be rather flat and unpleasant.

It is important to remember that the Dolby A and SR markings not only indicate a method of noise reduction, but also refer to Dolby Stereo (also known as Dolby Surround), which, via matrixing, provides four audio channels on the two optical tracks (left, center, right, and surround audio channels).

Cyan-dye optical tracks appeared at the end of the 20th century. Until then, optical soundtracks on film prints contained silver dyes, which were necessary to obtain the opaque density of the soundtrack area. Black & white film stocks featured silver-dye soundtracks as a matter of course. The introduction of color film created complications for the soundtrack, as the silver halide crystals are removed during color film processing. To maintain the opaque density necessary for the soundtrack area, silver has to be added back to the soundtrack dye image on the film. This is accomplished by re-developing the optical soundtrack area, a complex and expensive step.

In 1995, Kodak and several labs began working together to develop an alternative that would eliminate the re-development step for release prints. Their solution was the cyan-dye soundtrack, based on a red LED illumination source. *[Figure 4.22]* The necessary dye imagery is located only in the cyan layer of the print film, which is red-light sensitive. The cyan track is safer and simpler to produce. It reduces the use of water and chemicals in the developing process, and eliminates the need for re-development.

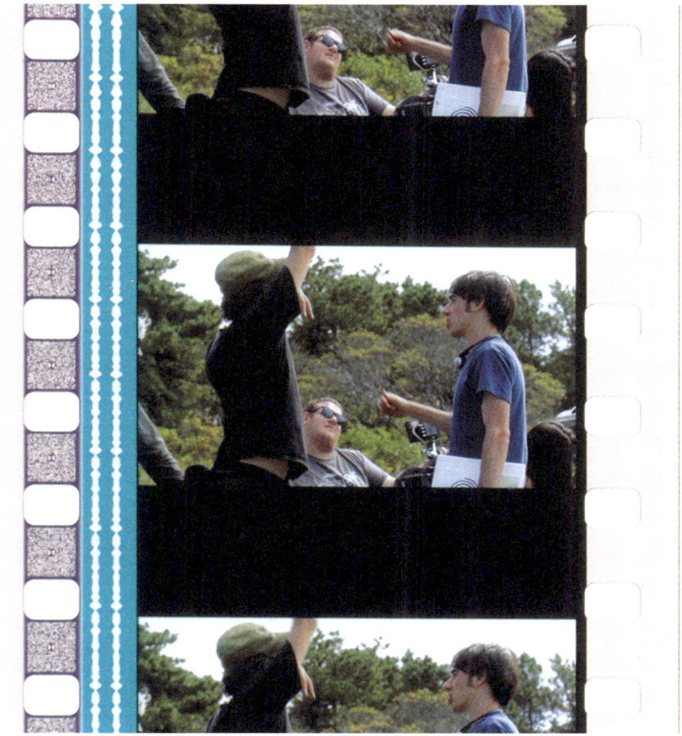

4.22 – **Cyan dye optical soundtrack on 35mm film**
(*Side by Side*, **Christopher Kenneally, US 2012**).

Cyan-dye optical tracks first appeared in mainstream cinemas in test runs of a limited number of prints of Tommy O'Haver's *Get Over It* and Kevin Smith's *Jay and Silent Bob Strike Back*, both released in 2001. Cyan-dye tracks were then applied to all 1,200 prints of Woody Allen's *Anything Else* in 2003.

It is important to keep in mind that cyan-dye tracks are designed to be read with a red LED light source. Reading a cyan track with white light results in a very weak signal with poor signal-to-noise ratio.

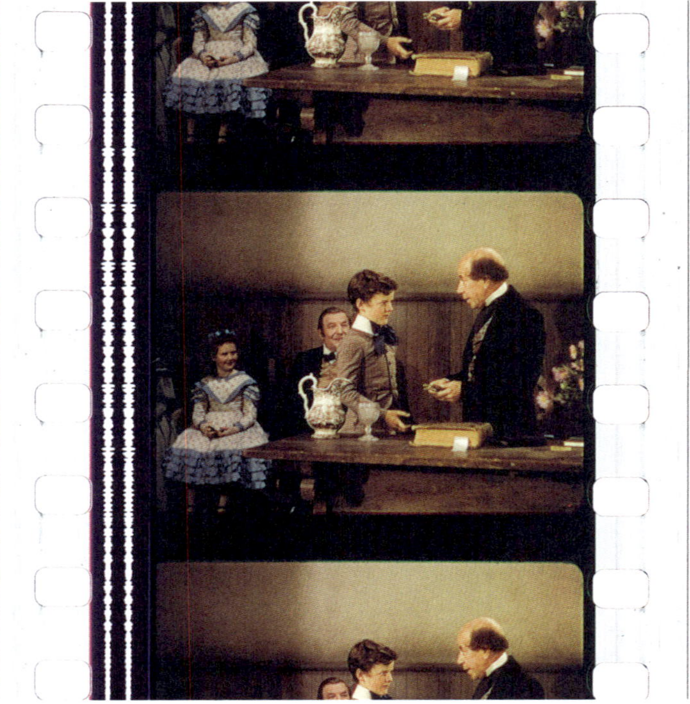

4.23 – High magenta optical soundtrack on 35mm film
(*The Adventures of Tom Sawyer*, Norman Taurog, US 1938).

High-magenta optical tracks, made up of silver and dye, were part of the planned transition from silver tracks to cyan-dye soundtracks as theaters converted from white-light to red-light readers on their projectors. *[Figure 4.23]* High-magenta tracks can be read successfully with either light source. High-magenta tracks were first introduced to audiences in April 1998, with a test run of 150 prints of Brad Silberling's *City of Angels*, and included on all 3,000 prints of Nora Ephron's *You've Got Mail* in December that same year. By 2005, the majority of cinemas had converted to red-light readers.

MAGNETIC SOUND

The debut of CinemaScope in 1953 introduced **magnetic audio tracks** to commercial cinema. CinemaScope incorporated multiple magnetic tracks within its 35mm release prints. 20th Century-Fox had special 35mm print stock made up, with very narrow perforations, to allow for the addition of four discrete magnetic soundtracks (in the same Left / Center / Right / Surround configuration as the later Dolby Stereo process). *[Figure 4.9, see page 116]* The sound quality was excellent, provided that the magnetic tracks were in good condition. Multi-channel magnetic audio on 35mm film prints offered crisp, uncompressed stereo sound at a time when optical tracks were confined to mono. Magnetic audio can be found on 16mm films as well.

As with optical tracks, there is a displacement between the picture and sound on films with magnetic audio tracks. Per SMPTE specifications, the magnetic audio on 35mm film is recorded 28 frames (+/- ½ frame) *behind* its corresponding picture, and the magnetic audio on 16mm film is printed 28 frames (+/- ½ frame) *in advance* of its corresponding picture.

Magnetic tracks require a separate "striping" step after the picture is printed, making it more expensive to manufacture than optical track prints.

A drawback with this system is that, unlike optical sound, information recorded on magnetic tracks is not a permanent part of the film, and could be accidentally erased. Placing a reel too close to magnetic fields, like those found in rewind motors, could be hazardous. Even reels and cans can become magnetized, sometimes erasing all or part of the magnetic track. This required re-dubbing, which was costly. Also, the magnetic sound heads required frequent cleaning in order to maintain peak audio quality.

To play magnetic soundtracks, the film projector must be equipped with a **magnetic reader**. Magnetic readers installed on 16mm projectors are located in the vicinity of the optical reader. Magnetic readers for 35mm projectors are generally located above the picture head; they are thus often referred to as "penthouse readers."

Magnetic tracks worked reasonably well, and were used through the 1970s on 35mm prints, and later on 70mm prints. Factors such as the added expense and effort associated with magnetic release prints, as well as the development of matrixed stereo optical tracks with 4-channel output, caused magnetic sound to fall into disuse. However, before the rise of digital sound, special release prints continued to be made with magnetic tracks for showing in selected theaters for "special engagements" and the like.

DIGITAL SOUND

Introduced in the 1990s, digital soundtracks are printed optically on the film, representing sound with a series of consecutive "samples" of the sound, rather than by a continuous waveform (as with a variable area track). In practice, digital film soundtracks usually sound cleaner and brighter than analog optical tracks, and are capable of greater dynamic range. A scratch or a splice on a digital soundtrack is less likely to produce audible disruptions than analog optical tracks, unless the damage is so severe that it disrupts (or prevents altogether) playback of the track.

Three commercial, non-compatible digital audio systems were developed for motion picture soundtracks. Each system requires a special decoder on the projector, along with dedicated processing equipment in the sound racks of the projection booth. Each digital soundtrack occupies a separate area on 35mm film prints, along with an optical track. Film prints may contain one, two, or all three digital tracks, in addition to the optical track. *[Figure 4.24]*

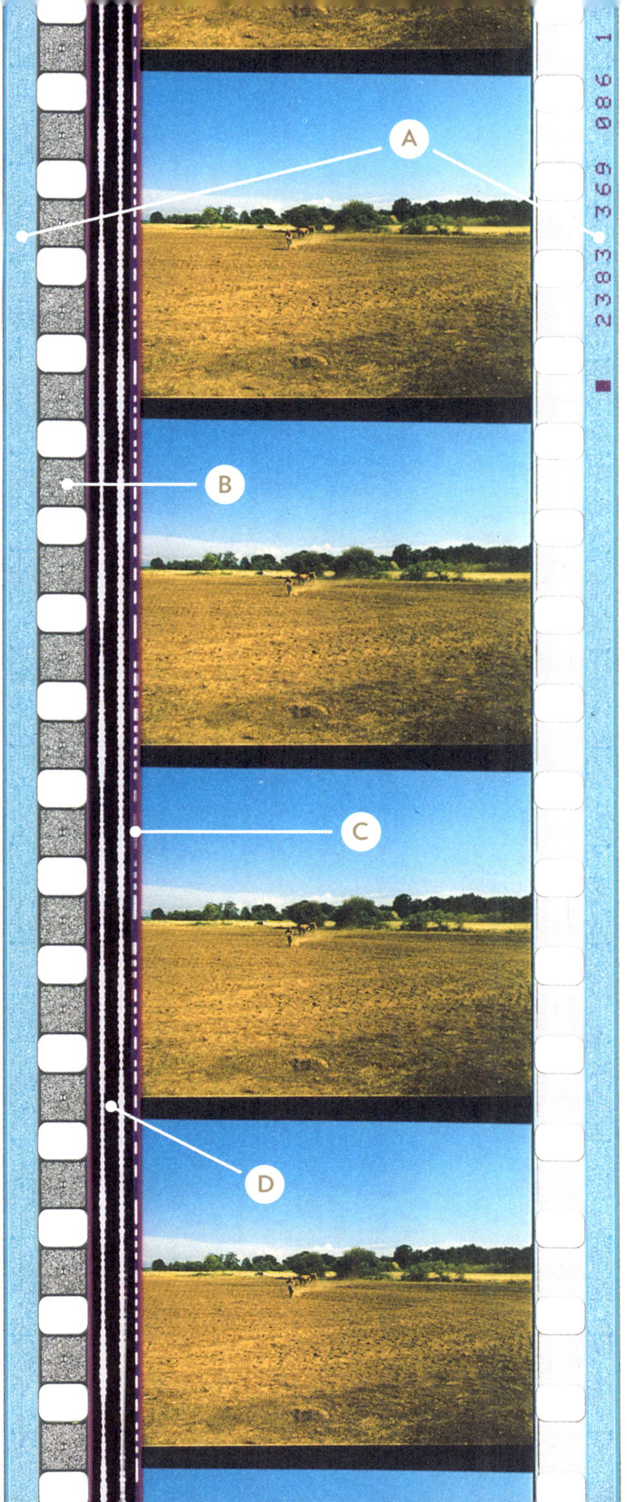

4.24 –

35mm film with SDDS, SRD, and DTS digital soundtracks, along with Dolby SR optical track (*Men of Honor*, George Tillman Jr., US 2000):

A. SDDS SOUNDTRACK

B. SRD SOUNDTRACK

C. DTS DIGITAL SOUNDTRACK

D. ANALOG DOLBY SR OPTICAL TRACK

Dolby SRD: Dolby Laboratories introduced the first commercially viable digital soundtrack in 1992 (*Batman Returns*, directed by Tim Burton). The digital information for **Spectral Recording Digital** — also known as SRD and Dolby Digital — is printed on the film in the spaces between perforations (also called "interperforations"), and runs 26 frames *ahead* of the picture. The reader is placed before the picture head, or in some installations, within the projector sound head. The reader works much like a video camera, capturing images of the track.

Dolby SRD is capable of reproducing six tracks (left, center, right, left-surround, right-surround, and subwoofer), and features the highest level of compression of the three digital audio systems.

As with analog optical tracks, splices can create small "pops." Due to the audio track's location between the perforations, SRD tracks are particularly susceptible to damage, as this area frequently comes into contact with the mechanisms of the projector.

Dolby Digital processors read SRD tracks from a level of 0 to 8, with 0 being perfect and 8 being the worst quality. It is extremely rare for SRD tracks to read at levels below 3, even on brand-new prints coming straight from the laboratories. Above level 8, the read fails, and the processor reverts to the analog optical track (usually Dolby SR). After a short period, the system will then make another attempt to read the SRD track, and if it fails, will again revert to the analog optical track. This process continues throughout the show, although the time elapsing between attempts to read the SRD track grows after each failure.

Projectionists are advised to pay close attention to the processor readout during pre-focus. If the SRD track is repeatedly failing, it may be best to play the entire feature using the analog optical track, as a repeated switch between digital and analog tracks is audible and quite jarring to the audience.

DTS – Digital Theater Systems, also known as DTS (or Data-sat Digital Entertainment from 2009), made its debut in 1993 (*Jurassic Park*, directed by Steven Spielberg). The DTS system uses a timecode printed on the film and a separate audio CD-ROM which contains the digital audio soundtrack. The timecode is located between the picture area and the optical track on the film. It is read by an optical reader on the projector, located a variable number of frames *ahead* of the picture head. The timecode is fed to a computer, which reads compressed soundtracks from a CD-ROM disk (its audio has been transferred to a media player unit), keeping the sound in sync with the film. The compression factor is the least of the three digital sound systems.

The DTS system reproduces left, center, right, left-surround, and right-surround tracks, plus the subwoofer (though the subwoofer information is not encoded as a separate track). DTS systems have multiple CD-ROM drives. The computer is capable of accommodating splices within the film, and adjusting the soundtrack to match.

Because the soundtrack is not on the film, no "popping" noise is heard during splices or changeovers. Should the timecode be unreadable for more than 40 frames, the system reverts back to the optical analog track.

Receiving the audio disc(s) along with the film print, and in an undamaged state, is a concern with this double-system sound format.

DTS audio has been applied to 70mm prints as well, replacing the magnetic tracks.

SDDS – Sony Dynamic Digital Stereo, also known as SDDS, premiered in 1993 (*Last Action Hero*, directed by John McTiernan). SDDS tracks are found along both edges of the film, with each track carrying four main channels and two back-up tracks. One edge track (called the P-track) is in sync with the picture, while the other (the S-track) is 17.8 frames behind. If one of the tracks cannot be read, the SDDS system will use the back-up tracks. Like its digital counterparts, this system requires a separate reader on the projector and processor in the sound rack.

SDDS reproduces left, left-center, center, right-center, right, left-surround, and right-surround tracks, plus the subwoofer. Of course, this requires that theaters install additional speakers behind the screen in order to take advantage of the format.

SDDS uses a mid-level of compression among the three digital systems. Splices are accommodated without difficulty. Similar to SRD tracks, SDDS tracks are prone to damage, due to their location along the edges of the film.

DO'S AND DON'TS

ALWAYS

- Project films on "changeover" projection systems.

- Wind film evenly, without exposing the edges.

- Project films in their intended aspect ratios, even if that means cropping part of the printed image (e.g., a film printed open-matte at 1.37:1, but intended to be viewed at 1.85:1).

- For the sake of film prints and of your fellow projectionists, be accurate in reading and especially in filling out inspection reports.

NEVER

- Project a museum or archival print on a "platter" projection system.

- Cut or separate the head and tail leaders from a film, even when a print's heads and tails have already been cut and re-spliced: removing the splicing tape and applying it again for the purposes of platter projection increases the chances of further damaging the film.

- Project a print designated as "fine grain master."

- Expose prints with magnetic audio tracks to magnets, as this may damage or erase the soundtracks!

NOTES

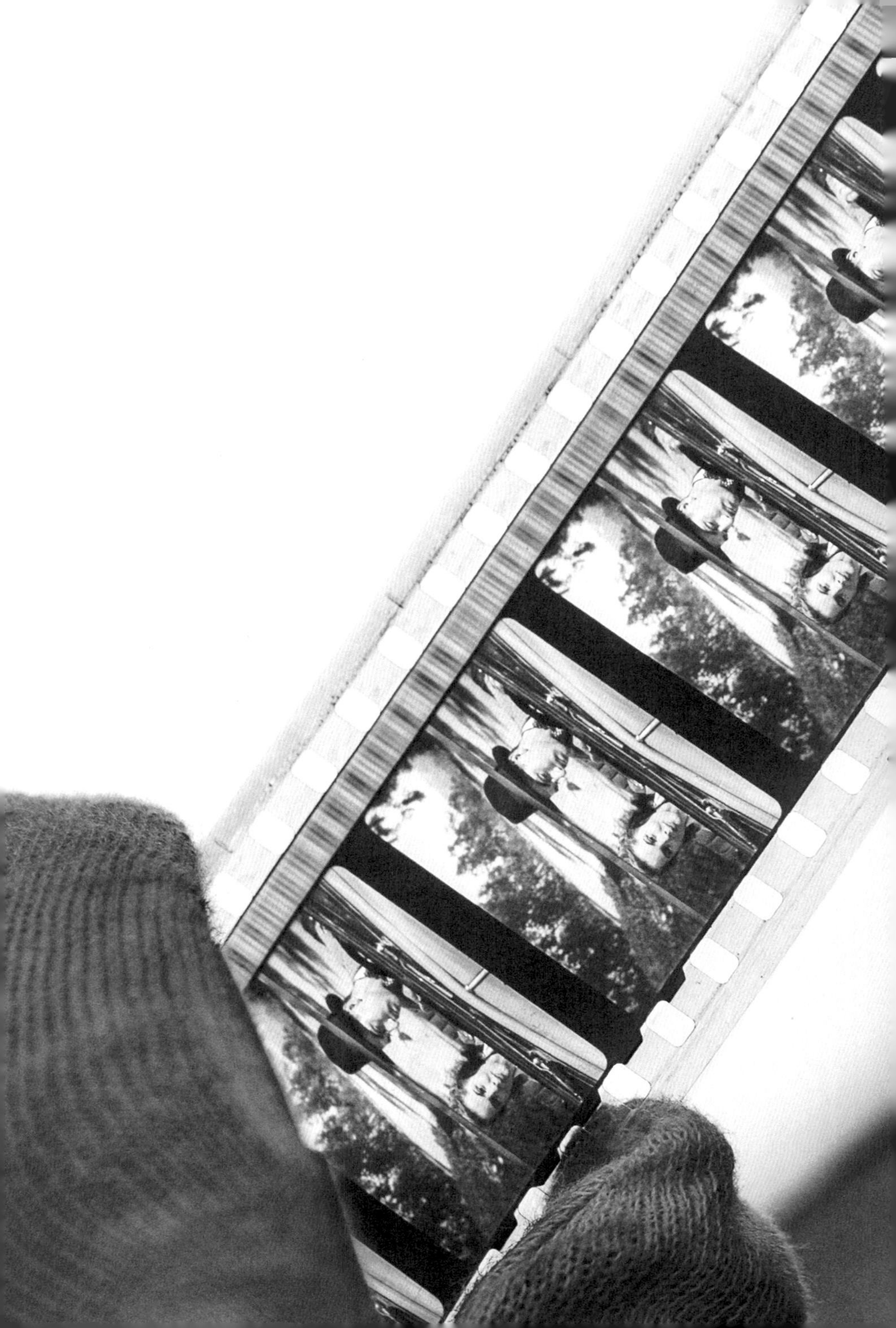

5

FILM INSPECTION

FROM THE MOMENT film prints arrive at your venue, until the time they ship out, you are responsible for their physical condition and security. As expensive assets to distributors, film archives, and museums, your venue is financially responsible for all film prints while in your care.

Many prints you encounter will require at least some amount of repair before they can be projected responsibly. In addition to the resources invested in inspecting and projecting a print, it is important to assure its safety while in your possession. Limiting access to film prints, tracking their location at all times, and providing secured, climate-controlled storage for them is recommended best practice. Properly caring for motion picture film prints will develop a good reputation for your venue, thereby increasing the possibility of borrowing prints from distributors and collecting institutions.

Fig. 5.1 – **35mm film being carefully inspected by hand on a motorized vertical rewind bench** (*Rebecca*, **Alfred Hitchcock, US 1940**).

EQUIPMENT AND TOOLS

An **inspection or rewind bench** must be fitted with the proper tools and supplies for film inspection and repair.

Suggested basic equipment includes:
- Split reels and metal house reels for projection, with straight, unbent flanges
- Shrinkage measurement devices to accommodate all film gauges used in projection
- Archival tape splicer(s) with adjustable pins (to accommodate shrunken film)
- One or more film counters
- Perforation repair tape
- Splice tape for the appropriate splicer(s) and film gauge(s)
- Audio blooping tape
- Trichloroethylene film cleaner (such as ECCO 1500) and cotton swabs
- A light box and magnifying lens
- Cotton gloves
- Tweezers, scissors, precision knife, grease pencil, low-tack adhesive tape ("artist tape")
- Cotton wipes and isopropyl alcohol

Film cleaner should be used to clean any damaged film areas before repair. Repair tape will not adhere to dirty surfaces.

Perforation repair tape is available in 16mm and 35mm gauges. *[Figure 5.2]* Manufactured for non-shrunken film, perforation repair tape (or Perf-Fix) can be used successfully with shrunken film by employing multiple shorter pieces instead of a single continuous strip. While the Perf-Fix brand is no longer active at the time of this writing, it may be possible to purchase

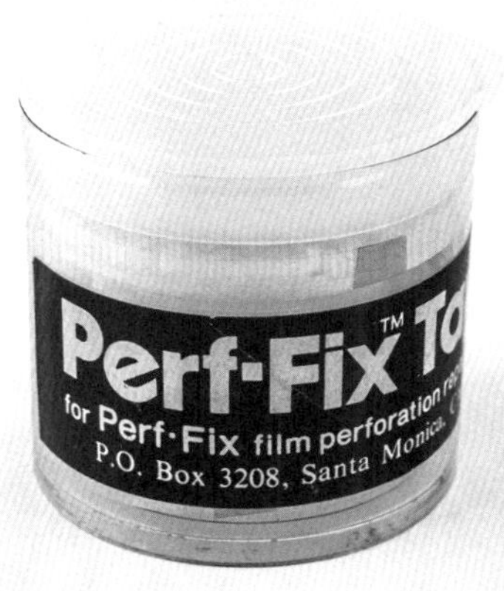

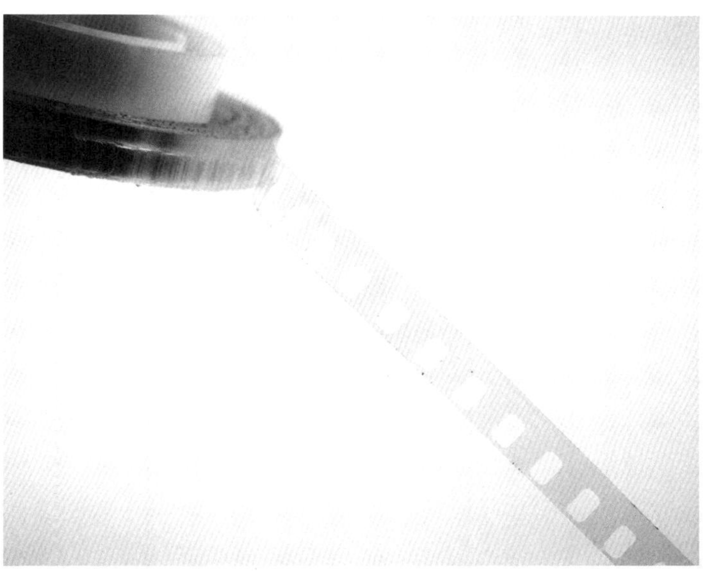

5.2 – **A container and an individual roll of 35mm Perf-Fix repair tape.**

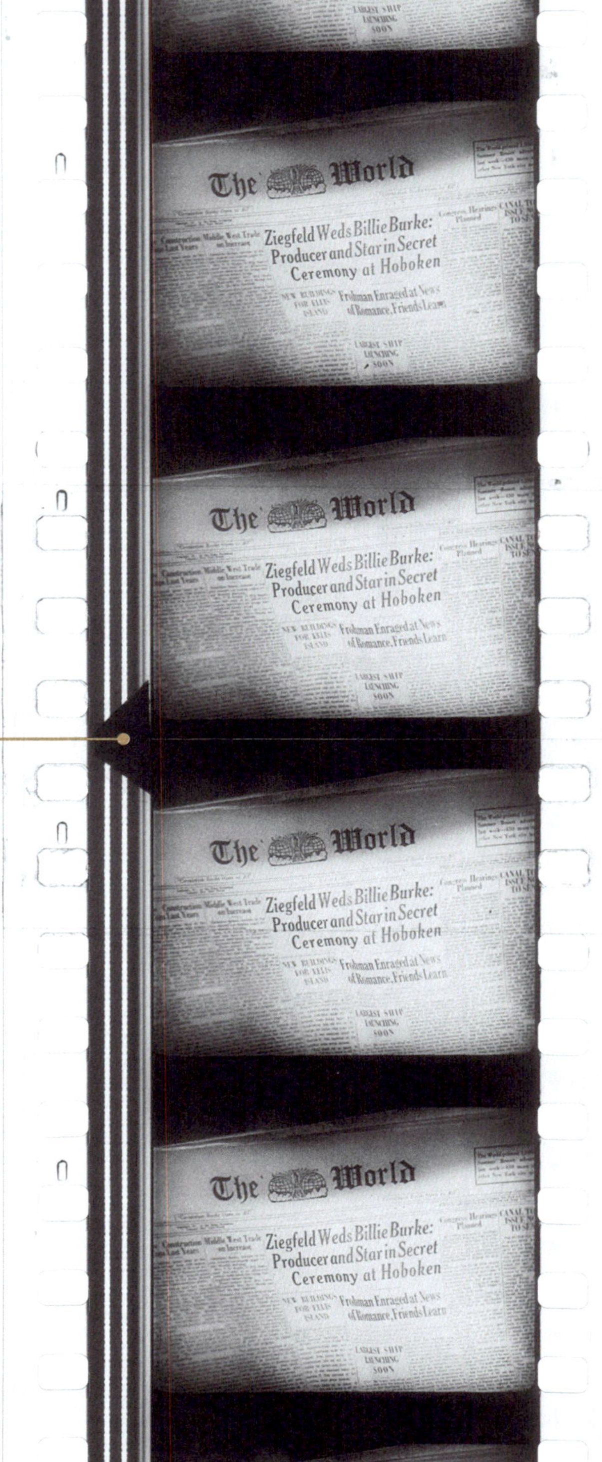
The World
Ziegfeld Weds Billie Burke:
Producer and Star in Secret
Ceremony at Hoboken
Frohman Enraged at News
of Romance, Friends Learn
LARGEST SHIP LAUNCHING SOON

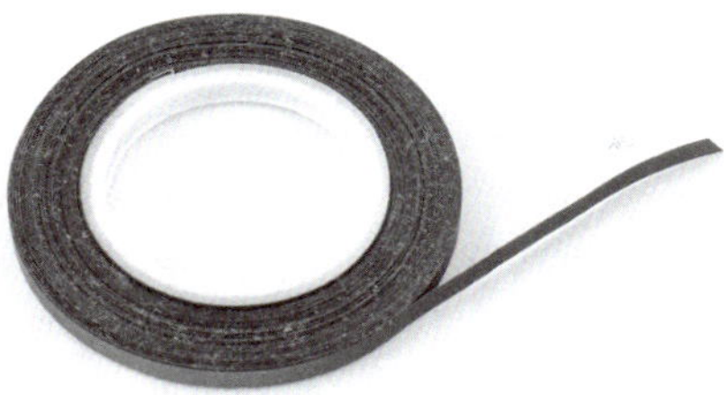

5.4 – **Audio blooping tape.**

this type of tape through archival suppliers. As with tape splices, perforation repair tape should be applied to both sides of the film to mend any perforation or edge damage. Although applicator machines are available to facilitate the operation, it is common for this type of repair to be done by hand (tweezers are recommended). When applying perforation repair tape, be sure that the tape aligns with both the perforations and the edge of the film. Trim any overhanging edges with scissors.

In addition to its use for splicing, **clear splice tape** (manufactured in several widths) is an excellent tool for repairing tears as well as for reinforcing creases and cement splices.

When making tape splices, adding a small triangular piece of **audio blooping tape** atop the optical soundtrack, centered on the splice, will eliminate the popping sound that is heard when this area passes through the sound reader. *[Figure 5.3]* Audio blooping tape is a narrow black opaque tape intended to block audio on optical soundtracks. *[Figure 5.4]* Made for both 16mm and 35mm film, it is manually applied to the optical soundtrack area. When using audio blooping tape to silence a splice, it is best to insert the small triangular piece to the film

5.3 – **Audio bloop included in a tape splice**
(*The Great Ziegfeld*, **Robert Z. Leonard, US 1936).**

before applying the splice tape. This way, the blooping tape will be encased within the splice tape, preventing its adhesive from spreading.

Placing damaged film atop a **light box** makes repairs — especially those requiring alignment — much easier to see and perform.

Wearing **cotton gloves** minimizes fingerprints on the film.

After inspecting a film, the surfaces of the film inspection bench should be wiped down with alcohol and cotton wipes to **keep the work area clean**.

INSPECTING FILM FOR PROJECTION: AN OVERVIEW

There are many things to take into consideration when inspecting film for projection. We shall begin with an overview, before delving into specific aspects of the process.

The main purposes of inspection for projection are:
1. To repair the print to protect it from further damage.
2. To prepare the print for projection.
3. To document the print's characteristics and its physical condition to aid the projectionist at the time of screening.

These objectives are accomplished concurrently as you inspect a print. Inspection should occur as far in advance of a screening as possible to allow for print replacement if the print proves to be incomplete or unprojectable.

Knowledge of film history can be valuable, especially when dealing with older films. A familiarity with timeframes for technical advances in film production and distribution can also assist with the identification of many technical parameters of great importance in the context of film exhibition.

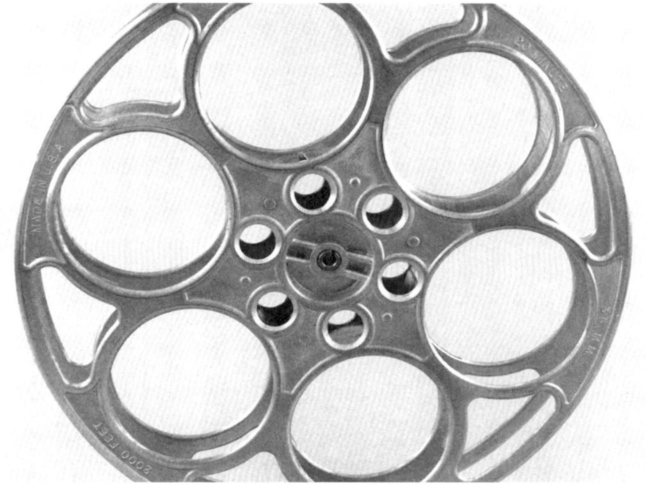

5.5 — **Goldberg Bros. cast aluminum 35mm film reel.**

USE IN-HOUSE REELS

Regardless of how film prints arrive at a screening venue, they should be mounted on in-house projection reels after inspection. Reels used for shipping are often damaged and should not be used for projection, as they may cause damage to the print. It is recommended that every film screening venue is equipped with several house reels in excellent condition (35mm and/or 16mm, where applicable) for use at every screening. Keeping these reels exclusively for both feed and take-up in film projection will prevent or at least minimize any damage caused to prints by warped, bent, or cracked shipping reels. For 35mm film, cast aluminum Goldberg Bros. 15-inch-diameter flange projection reels are recommended. [Figure 5.5] At the time of this writing, research and testing are under way at the George Eastman Museum for the adoption and use of improved museum-quality shipping containers.

INSPECT REELS IN SEQUENTIAL ORDER

Whether a print arrives heads-out or tails-out, on reels or cores, it is recommended that you inspect the print in sequential order, beginning with Reel 1. Inspect each reel from the head or tail, whichever way it arrives, before winding it further, to avoid the possibility of damaging the print by winding it while in need of repair. Have the inspection form handy to fill in as you go along, as well as all the proper equipment, supplies, and tools.

PACE OF INSPECTION

Whether working on a vertical or horizontal bench, manual wind or motorized, your pace of inspection should never jeopardize the safety of the print. When using a vertical bench to inspect films, split reels are necessary for mounting film delivered on cores.

REEL ORIENTATION AND IDENTIFICATION

If the film arrives tails out, you may wish to wind the film onto projection reels as you inspect it to minimize film handling, as it will be ready to go after one wind. Remember: **A smooth wind is important**.

To wind films for projection after their inspection, you need to **know the proper orientation of film on reels for projection**.

For **35mm** film, projectionists traditionally wind the film so that it comes off of the feed reel in a counterclockwise direction, head-out, with the soundtrack oriented toward the "outboard" side of the projector (that is, the operator's side, away from the projector).

For **16mm** film, the feed reel should be wound so that the film comes off the reel clockwise, head-out, soundtrack on the "inboard" side (that is, toward the projector), with the perforations on the outboard side. With 16mm reels, however, you need to check the center hub of the reel before mounting film on it. Unlike 35mm film reels, 16mm reels may not have the same-shaped hole on both sides of the reel hub. Some 16mm reels feature a square hole on one side and a round hole on the other. *[Figure 5.6]* The side with the square hole should face the projector (inboard), with the round side facing outboard. The spindle design on most 16mm projectors will not allow the round side of a reel hub to face inboard (toward the projector). Be mindful of this factor when mounting 16mm film on a reel for projection.

When working with **double-perforation, silent 16mm** film prints, there is no soundtrack to help in orienting the film. Therefore, it is important to double-check the film orientation to avoid projecting a film with the titles and images reversed. The image should be upside-down and backwards (as you face the screen) in the gate of the projector. Title cards are particularly useful for determining the correct orientation of 16mm silent prints.

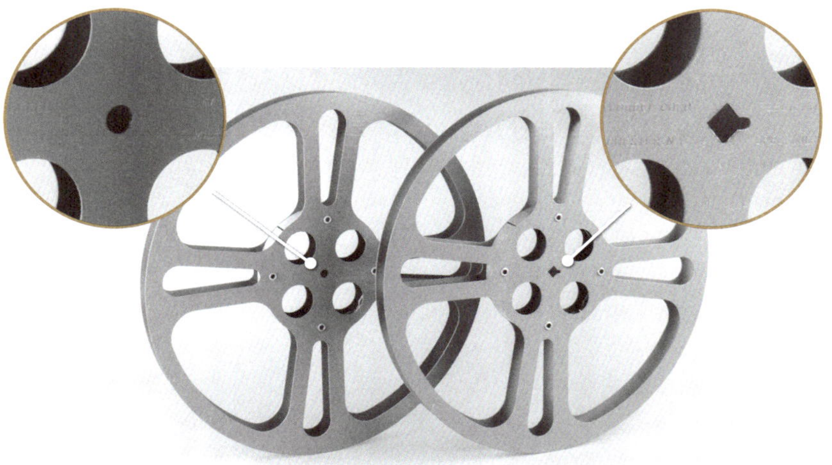

5.6 — **16mm film reels with round and square hubs.**

You will receive films both heads-out and tails-out, and they can be properly inspected from either orientation. For the sake of clarity and logic in this section, we shall address film inspection beginning at the head of a reel.

Begin by **confirming the identity of the reel**, so that you can inspect (and exhibit) the reels in the correct order. Is the reel of film, labeled as Reel 1, actually Reel 1 of that particular title? As mentioned earlier, it is important to always check the leader of each reel, which typically contains the title, reel number, and an indication of head or tail. If the head or tail leader has not been spliced to the body of the reel, you can most likely trust the identification printed on the leader. If, however, splices do appear between the leader and the body of the reel, you must verify that the leader matches the reel to assure its identity. Hopefully, you will find one or two frames of image attached to the head or tail leader, matching up with the body of the film. When referring to "leader" here, we are referring to the laboratory leader that is printed with the film, as opposed to any additional leaders that may be added by other entities, such as film archives or museums. Information on the leader that is written by hand, either directly on the stock or on white tape, should be judged cautiously, as it may contain errors.

While addressing the head leader of the film, look for information printed on the leader that can help you in completing the inspection report.

Information about the soundtrack is often included, and usually printed in the soundtrack area of the leader. If the soundtrack is encoded with Dolby noise reduction, the leader may indicate whether it is Dolby A or Dolby SR. The leader may also provide information about digital soundtracks included on the print.

Versions of a film — domestic, foreign, television, and so on — may be indicated on the leader as well. *[Figure 5.7]*

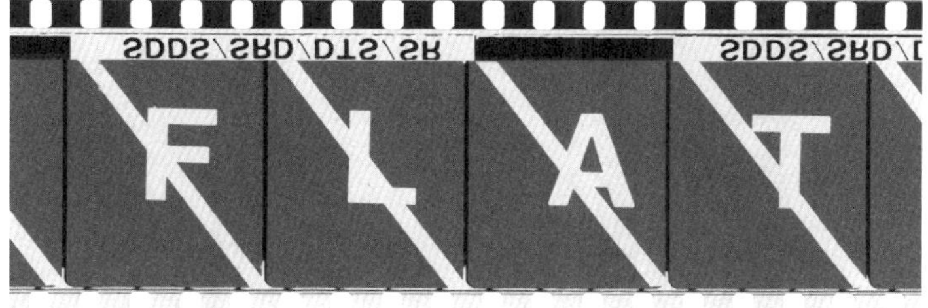

5.7 – Information printed on the tail leader of a 35mm trailer, indicating aspect ratio ("FLAT" = 1.85:1) in the picture area, and audio formats (SDDS / SRD / DTS / SR) in the soundtrack area.

When you come across films made in the 1950s or before, you may find reel-numbering information on the head and tail leaders that appears confusing. For example, the head leader on Reel 1 may read, "Reel 1, Head," while the tail leader reads, "Reel 2, Tail."

This kind of labeling indicates a change in the history of film exhibition practice. Prior to the advent of 35mm safety (acetate) film stock in 1951, **nitrate film stock** was the norm. Nitrate projection prints were stored, shipped, and projected on 1,000-foot (or 300-meter) reels. In the latter years of nitrate projection, it became more common to double up these reels, creating 2,000-foot (or 600-meter) reels, for ease of projection. The result is that former Reels 1 and 2 became Reel 1; former Reels 3 and 4 became Reel 2; former Reels 5 and 6 became Reel 3; and so on.

When 35mm film production shifted to **safety film**, release prints were standardized at 2,000-foot reels, while negatives continued to be on 1,000-foot rolls. To accommodate this change, the labeling of negative reels was modified as well. Negatives for the first (2,000-foot) reel were labeled 1A and 1B; negatives for the second (2,000-foot) reel were labeled 2A and 2B; and so on. Since this information is printed through in the leaders of projection prints, it is necessary to interpret it properly. This is but one example of **the importance of knowing film history**.

PHYSICAL INSPECTION

To inspect film for projection, it is recommended that you **wind each reel of film through your hand**, running the edges between thumb and forefinger, with a very slight amount of pressure on the film from your fingers. This method allows you to identify and check all splices, and locate and address any edge damage in need of repair. **Wearing cotton gloves** for this process is recommended, both to protect the film, and to make it easier to feel any damage along the edges and perforations of the film.

COUNTDOWN LEADERS

Once you have captured all the relevant information from the leader, you must inspect the countdown for completeness and damage. A complete countdown is necessary on every reel of film for projection with a two-projector system. The projectionist threads the film in each projector using the countdown, aligning a certain point on the countdown (usually the 9-foot or 8-foot mark) with the aperture in the gate. This registration, made in coordination with properly spaced cues on the tail of the previous reel, allows for a smooth manual changeover projection with a two-projector system. If no countdown is present, a new one will need to be added. If a countdown is incomplete, an appropriate number of frames must be added to make it complete.

There are **two types of countdown** commonly found on projection prints: **Academy and SMPTE**. Either of these countdowns can appear on 16mm, 35mm, and 70mm prints. *[Figure 5.8]*

5.8 – **35mm countdown leader in the Academy format (left) and SMPTE format (right).**

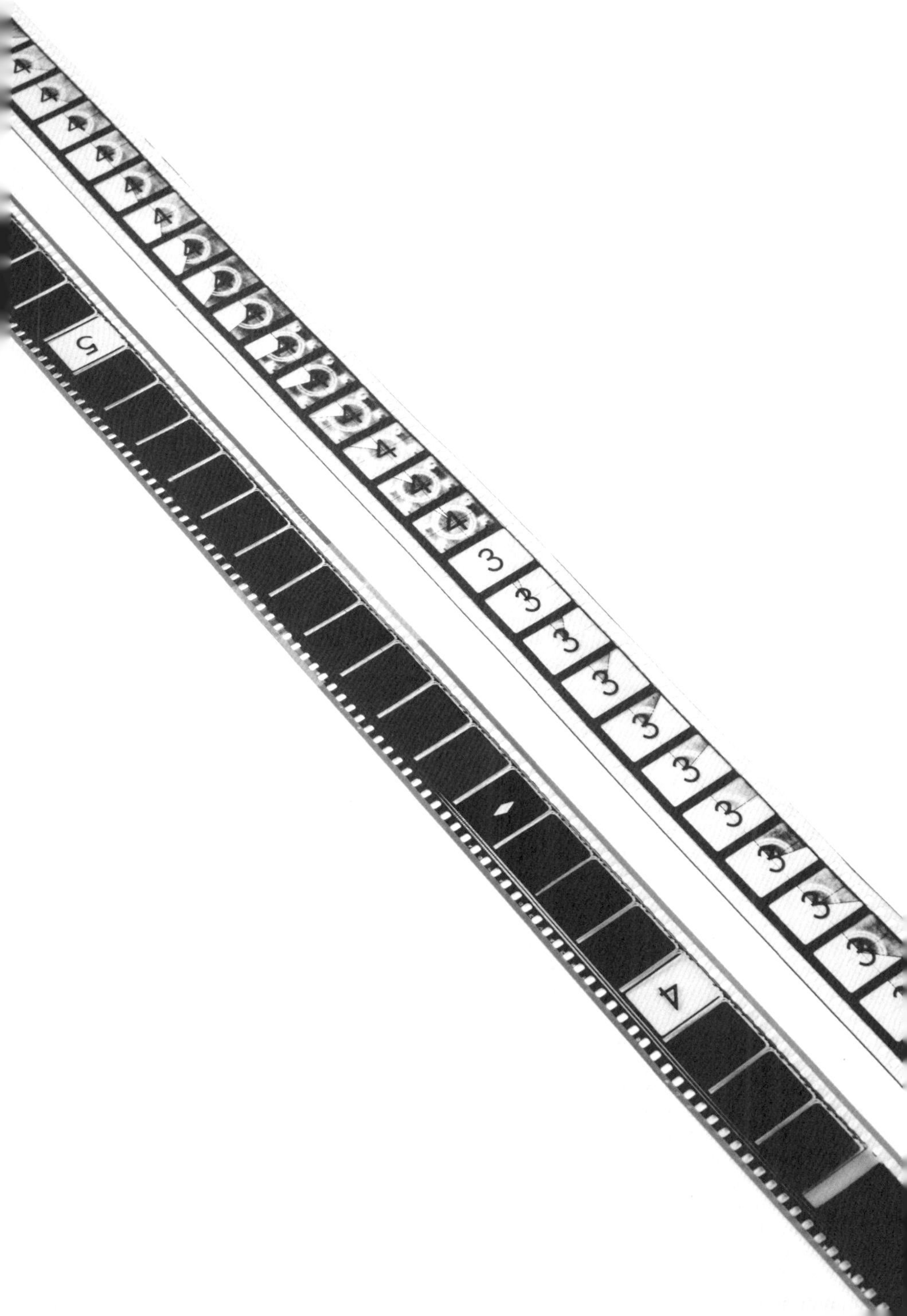

5
4
4
4
4
4
4
4
4
3
3
3
3
3
3
3
3
3

ACADEMY COUNTDOWN

Developed in the late silent era of 35mm film, the Academy countdown is measured in feet. Numerals appearing on Academy countdown begin with "11," and count down to "3," in a descending sequence every 16 frames. Usually, there is just one frame of number printed, followed by 15 frames of black, followed by the next number, and so on. The last numeral printed is "3," indicating this point is 3 feet from the head of the reel. A complete Academy countdown contains 47 frames of black following the "3," before the reel begins.

SMPTE COUNTDOWN

Developed by the Society of Motion Picture and Television Engineers, the SMPTE countdown measures time in seconds. It is standardized for sound film speed at 24 fps. Numerals appearing on SMPTE countdown begin with "8," and count down to "2," in a descending sequence every 24 frames. As a rule, each numeral appears on 24 consecutive frames. The last numeral printed is "2," meaning that this point is 2 seconds from the head of the reel. A complete SMPTE countdown has 47 frames of black following the "2," before the reel begins.

While the Academy and the SMPTE countdown are measured according to different parameters (feet and seconds), it is convenient to remember that there should always be **47 frames of black after the last number of either countdown** ("3" on an Academy countdown, and "2" on a SMPTE countdown).

SPLICES AND INCOMPLETE FRAMES

If any splices appear within the countdown, make sure that the frames adjacent to the splice or encompassing the splice are complete. If an incomplete frame is advanced into the aperture of the projector, it will project part of the adjacent frame as well, revealing a frame line on the screen thereafter. If more than a few frames are missing within the countdown, they should be replaced (with black leader, for example) in order to make the countdown complete. This is important to attain accurate timing of changeovers during projection.

SPLICES, DAMAGE, AND SHRINKAGE

With the countdown inspected, it is time to inspect the main body of the reel. The focus here is to identify and check all splices, and to locate and repair any damage. Running the entire reel of film between your fingers (while wearing cotton gloves, a recommended practice during film inspection) enables you to feel the splices and most damage, allowing you to stop and inspect and repair them. Unchecked splices may come apart during projection, or may put the film out of frame. Unrepaired damage can provoke an interruption of the screening, cause further damage to the print, and possibly damage the projector.

If the print you are inspecting has been plattered or built into larger reels on several occasions, it is common to find multiple layers of tape at the head and tail of each reel. Other than clear splicing tape, it is common to find yellow-striped tape (referred to as "zebra tape") or opaque yellow or white tape. The purpose of these tapes, which are more visible than clear tape, is to help projectionists find reel joins more easily when breaking a film down from a platter or from built-up reels.

Furthermore, it is not uncommon to find **white shoe polish** along the edge of a film, at heads and tails, on prints that have been plattered. As with colored tape, the purpose of the shoe polish is to help projectionists find reel-to-reel joins and splices more easily when breaking down a plattered print into individual reels after a screening engagement. Without marking the edge of the film with shoe polish, it is much more difficult to find the beginning and end of each reel when the entire film is spliced together on a platter. When possible, the shoe polish should be removed with film cleaner, especially if it is applied in a sloppy manner, running into the soundtrack or picture area. Also, multiple layers of splice tape should be removed, and replaced with a well-made splice with clear splicing tape.

SPLICES

A projectionist can expect to come across tape, "cement" (referring to a special type of glue used for film splicing), or ultrasonic splices when inspecting a film print. Tape splices can be found on nitrate, acetate, and polyester prints. Most common is a thin, clear adhesive tape, applied to both sides of the film. It is important to use a tape designed specifically for splicing film. Other kinds of tapes are likely to degrade the film stock over time. Tape splicers are made by a number of manufacturers. It is recommended to procure an archival tape splicer, with movable registration pins (such as one manufactured by CIR), which can accommodate shrunken film. *[Figure 5.9]* Most tape splicers are manufactured to work on new, unshrunken film stock; they can damage perforations if used with film that has some degree of shrinkage.

When splicing shrunken film in a tape splicer with movable registration pins, it is important to adjust the spacing of the pins to match the shrinkage of the film *before* making the splice. This can be accomplished by first moving the pins closer together and placing a length of the film (without cuts) into the splicer, registering the perforations onto the pins. There will likely be an overlap of film in the center if the pins are too close to each other.

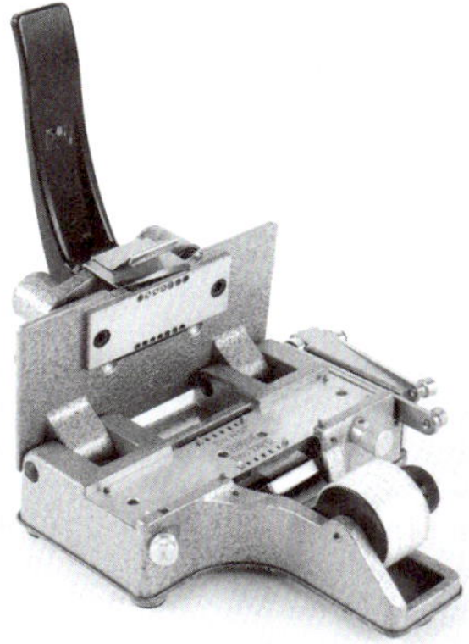

5.9 — **35mm tape splicer (CIR, Italy) with movable registration pins.**

Adjust the movable pins slowly apart until the film lays flat in the splicer, without stressing the perforations in the film. The splicer is now calibrated to match the shrinkage of the film. Failure to be proficient in this technique may result in damage to perforations when splicing shrunken film. Proper tape splices should be two-sided (always apply splice tape on both base *and* emulsion), with both pieces in alignment.

Cement splices are generally made at the laboratory where the film was printed. You can find them in either nitrate or acetate prints. Polyester prints cannot be spliced with cement. When made properly, cement splices are very sturdy and can hold for decades. It is important to note that cement splices require an overlap of the film stock, which results in the loss of a frame or two. At the overlap join, the emulsion is scraped away so that the cement bonds the two pieces of film together. Cement splices are usually made at the frame line, between frames, but they can occur within a frame as well.

Ultrasonic splices are only found in polyester prints. An ultrasonic signal in the splicer melts the film together. Like cement splices, they are most often made at the film laboratory. Unlike a tape splice, where the clear tape covers a portion of the image frame, cement and ultrasonic splices take up very little space on the film's frame. When made on a frame line, they are less likely to be detected by the audience than a tape splice.

Every splice in the film should be checked for strength and flexibility. To check a splice, flex the film into a U shape, with the splice at the apex. By moving your hands, run the splice through the U, observing its strength and flexibility. Repeat this with the U in the opposite orientation. Then, holding the film on either side of the splice, gently twist the film a bit, applying some torque to the spliced area. The purpose of this test is to find out if the ends of the splice (near the film's edges) are beginning to come loose. If the ends of a cement or ultrasonic splice have lost some of their adherence, reinforce the join with a tape splice.

When checking tape splices, make sure there is tape on *both* sides of the film (base and emulsion). Trim any tape that extends beyond the edges of the film, as this can cause added tension when going through a projector. Remove any tape chads which remain in the perforations. Built-up or plattered prints may feature one-sided splices at the heads and tails of reels; replace these with proper, two-sided splices. Alternatively, prints which have been built-up or plattered multiple times may feature multiple layers of splices at the head and tail, which should be removed. Projector pad rollers or "shoes," which hold film against sprocket drives, are calibrated to allow for two thicknesses of film to pass. Heavily built-up splices run the risk of popping open a roller during projection, likely damaging the film.

Splices in 35mm and 70mm prints must also be checked for being in-frame. Since splicers are designed to cut and splice film between perforations, and 35mm and 70mm film have multiple perforations per frame, it is possible to accidentally make splices that leave a frame too short by one or more perforations (e.g., a 35mm frame that is 3 perforations high instead of 4). This is referred to as an "out-of-frame" splice because of its effect upon projection. When an incomplete frame is advanced into the projector aperture, part of the next frame will be projected as well, along with the frame line between them. This throws the image out-of-frame. The image on the screen will remain this way until the projectionist either reframes the image by an adjustment of the projector, or by stopping the show and manually resetting the film in relation to the aperture. Out-of-frame splices are unacceptable, and require immediate correction during the inspection stage. When checking splices in 35mm film, make sure that frames adjacent to a splice, or encompassing a splice, are complete (4 perforations in height). Since 16mm films have one perforation per frame, out-of-frame splices are unlikely.

If a splice occurs in an area of the film that is too dark to see frame lines, it will not be possible to see if the splice was made in-frame (that is, in a proper fashion). This problem can be solved, however, with the use of a film counter. Place the film in the film counter (making sure that it is in-frame with the counter), somewhere to the left or right of the splice, where an image and frame lines are visible. Then, wind the film through the counter, past the splice, to an area on the other side of the splice where you can see the image. If, at this point, the image is still in-frame with the film counter, then you have evidence that the splice was made properly, that is, in-frame.

DAMAGE

Aside from scratches, dirt, and oil appearing on projection prints, any film damage found during inspection should be repaired. Most projection print damage occurs along the edges and perforations, generally appearing as edge nicks, cracked or torn perforations, and minor tears. Occasionally, tears can extend across the film. Creases may also be encountered. The projectionist should have the tools, knowledge, and skills to repair film prints satisfactorily in order to prevent further damage upon projection.

SHRINKAGE

It is common for acetate and nitrate prints to shrink over time. During the inspection process, it is very important to keep this in mind. Film may shrink, but the sprocket drives of a projector do not. Projecting shrunken films can damage the film. All projection prints should therefore be measured for shrinkage. *[Figure 5.10]* A shrinkage rate of 1% is a reasonable threshold for determining whether or not a print can be safely projected without further damaging the object or running the risk of an interruption of the show. The actual amount of shrinkage that film projectors can safely handle, however, really depends on the size and type of drive sprockets (there are several types) and of the intermittent sprocket. Projectors equipped with CinemaScope sprocket drives can more safely project shrunken film because the sprocket teeth are sized smaller, designed for original CinemaScope release prints.

Polyester film is chemically designed to be more dimensionally stable than acetate or nitrate film stocks. If no shrinkage gauge is available, an alternate method of assessing shrinkage is to measure your acetate or nitrate film against a

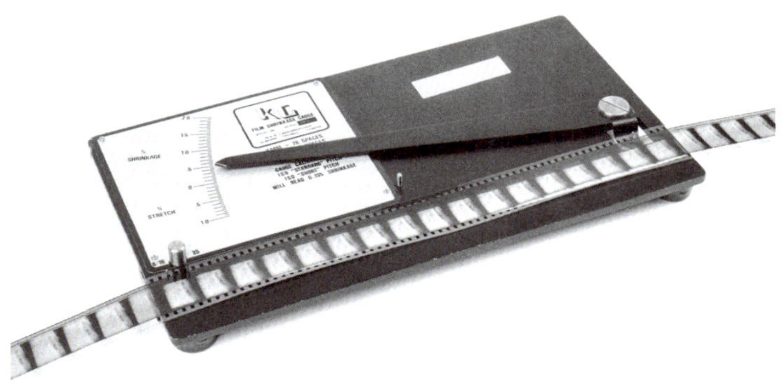

5.10 – **Film shrinkage gauge (KL [Klaus Linnenbruegger], Canada) for 8mm, 16mm, and 35mm film.**

strip of polyester film. If the sprocket holes do not align, the acetate or nitrate print is shrunken. If the acetate or nitrate film is off by one perforation after counting 100 perforations, then it is clearly shrunken by 1%.

CHANGEOVER CUES

In order to achieve a seamless film presentation using two projectors with manual changeovers, the projectionist needs some type of cues to know when to start the other projector and when to change over the picture and sound to that projector. In the silent film era, projectionists often utilized printed cue sheets containing a description of the visuals at the end of each reel, to present an uninterrupted program. Otherwise, seeing title cards such "End of Part One," "Part Two," and so forth, was the norm at each reel change.

CUE MARKS

The practice of printing cue marks on the film to indicate reel changes was introduced by Metro-Goldwyn-Mayer in 1930. The accompanying notice read,

> *In the future, and until further notice, all changeover signals will be visual. These signals appear at the end of the reel in the form of a round black spot appearing steady in the upper right corner of the screen during four consecutive frames.... [T]he signal is fashioned so that it is clearly visible if watched for, but not particularly noticeable to an audience. Two sets of these signals appear at the end of each reel. The first set is the signal to start the motor of the incoming machine, and the second set is the signal to cut over picture and sound.*

The Society of Motion Picture and Television Engineers has standardized the locations of these cues (in its publication *SMPTE Standard 301-1999, Theater Projection Leader, Trailer, and Cue Marks*). From the tail of a reel of film, there should be 18 frames of image, then 4 frames of cues (changeover), then 172 frames of image, then 4 frames of cues (motor start). The cues should appear in the upper right corner

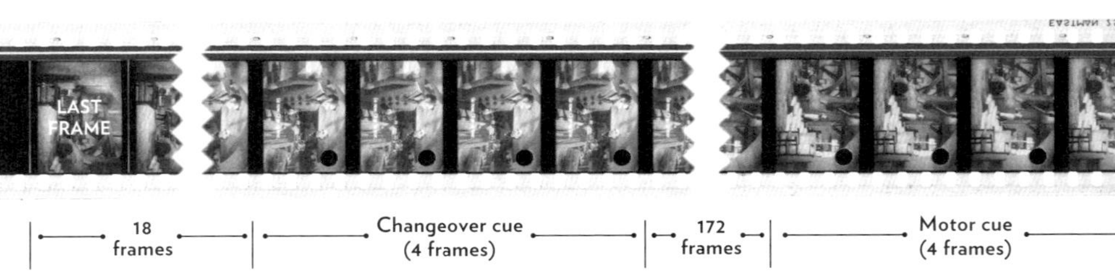

5.11 – **Spacing of motor start and changeover cues for film projection, according to *SMPTE Standard 301-1999*. (*Abismos de pasión [Wuthering Heights]*, Luis Buñuel, Mexico 1954)**

of the frame, as projected on the screen. *[Figure 5.11]* At the sound speed of 24 frames per second, the cues appear 7 seconds apart.

Cues are utilized by projectionists in the following manner: when the first set of cues (motor start) appears on the screen, the projectionist should start the motor on the incoming projector. The lamphouse douser should be opened seconds later, once the film is transporting correctly. When the second set of cues appears (changeover), the projectionist switches the picture and sound to the incoming projector. With the projectors threaded to the proper location on the countdown leader, and the cues placed properly, the projectionist can perform a flawless presentation, without the audience realizing that the film is being projected from several individual reels on two separate projectors. This is the art of film projection at its finest.

SMPTE specifications call for black circles or clear circles for cues, and these are the most common cues printed by film laboratories. Technicolor prints normally feature instead a multi-colored starburst. Projection prints lacking laboratory-printed cues often feature other kinds of markings that have been added by projectionists. These cues are typically circles or diagonal slashes, etched into the emulsion by a cue-marking device or by hand. A less destructive, non-permanent option for adding cues is with grease pencil (also known as a wax pencil or china marker). Drawn by hand, usually as diagonal slashes, these cues should be made on the base side of the film for clean removal after the show. Grease pencil cues added to the emulsion side tend to leave some unwanted residue. When adding temporary grease pencil cues to the base side of the film, place them in the upper-left corner of the image, so that they appear in the upper-right corner on the screen. *[Figures 5.12 through 5.15, see following pages]*

Unfortunately, not every set of cues is placed in compliance with SMPTE specifications, and some projection prints feature

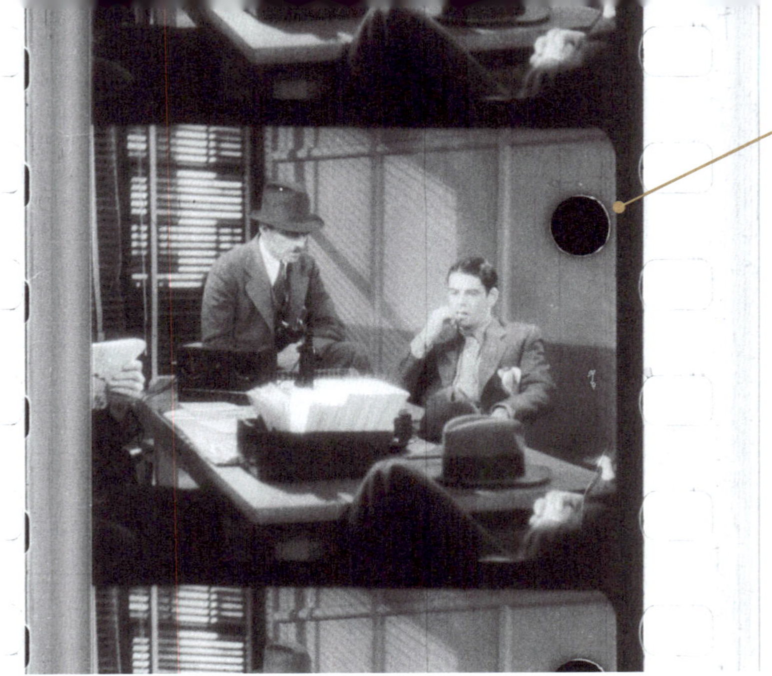

5.12 – 5.15 – **Four examples of common cue marks on 35mm film: black dots, Technicolor "starbursts," scribed circles, and grease pencil slashes.**

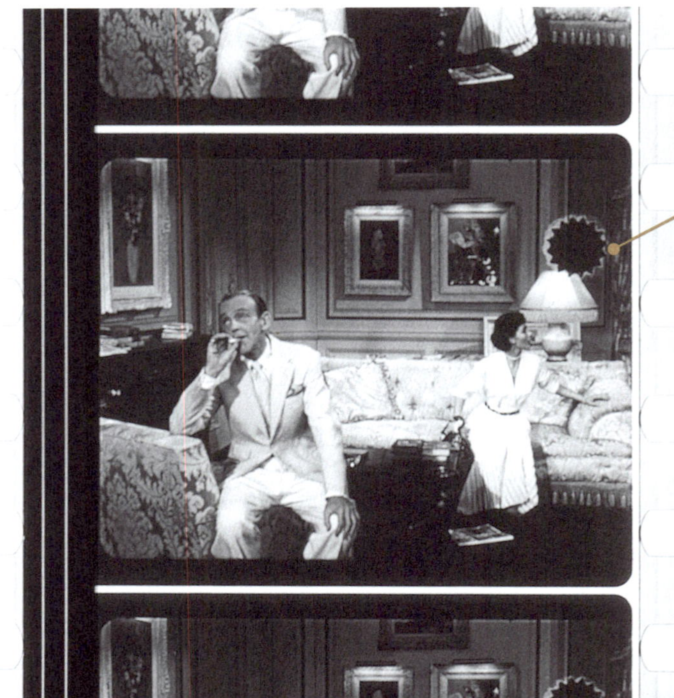

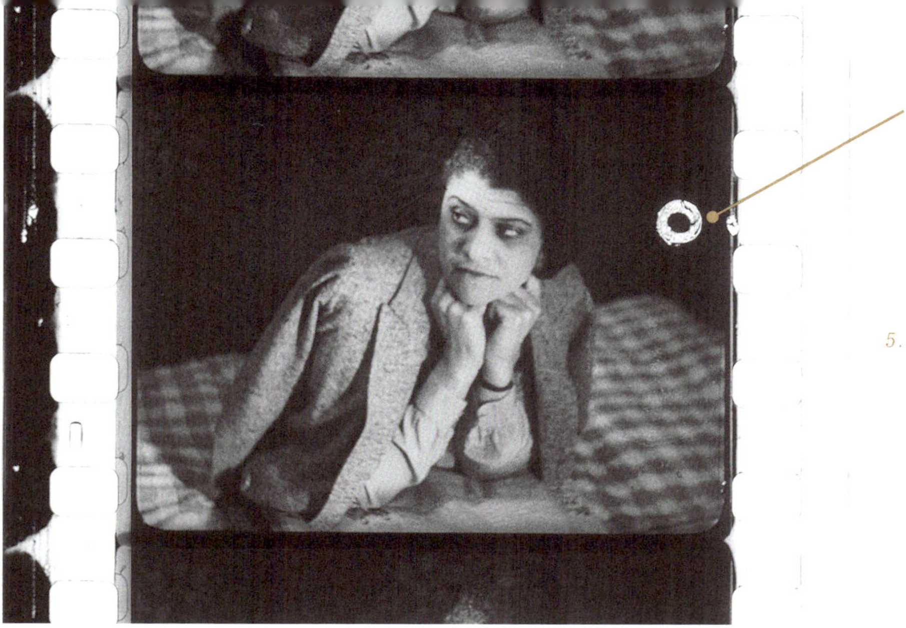

5.14

5.12 – *Scarface* (Howard Hawks, US 1932);

5.13 – *The Band Wagon* (Vincente Minnelli, US 1953);

5.14 – *Borderline* (Kenneth Macpherson, Switzerland 1930);

5.15 – *Men of Honor* (George Tillman Jr., US 2000).

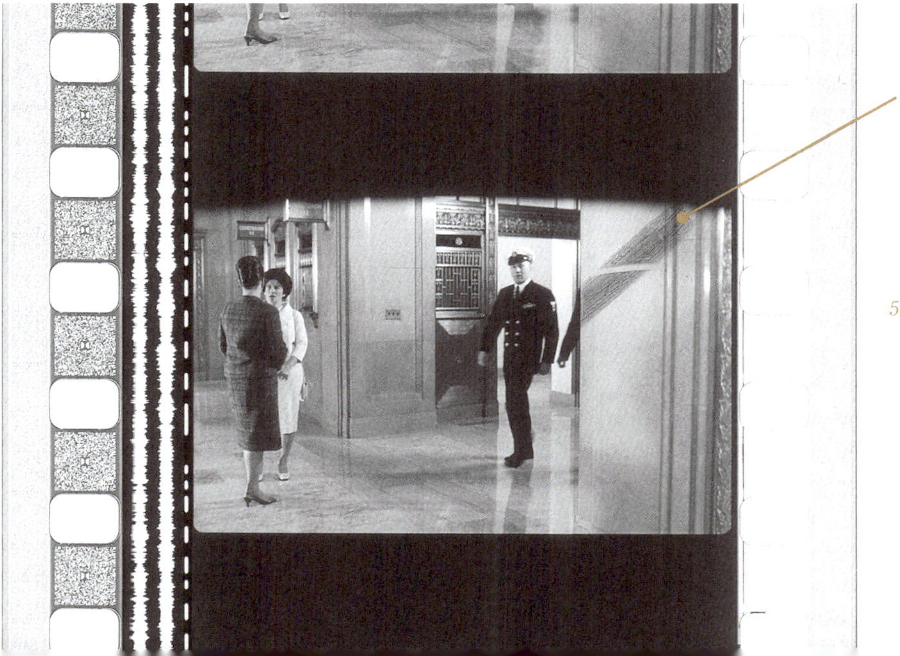

5.15

many sets of cues. Multiple sets of cues may result from prints which have been plattered multiple times, with frames successively being removed from the tail. As film frames are cut from the tail, the existing cues are no longer located where they should be in reference to the tail, so new sets are added. This can result in several sets of cues with different spacing and appearance, posing a real challenge for proper projection.

One solution to this problem is concise documentation. If one set of motor start and changeover cues within the multiple sets is usable and unique in appearance, their spacing and appearance can be noted on the inspection report, indicating to the projectionist the appropriate set of cues to use.

Another solution to overcome multiple sets of cues on a reel is to add a set of temporary grease pencil cues (on the base side) per SMPTE specifications. Adding these temporary cues is a non-destructive way to assure properly spaced, easily identifiable cues, without further damaging the print. The projectionist can then ignore all other cues, except for the newly added grease pencil cues. After the screening(s), the grease pencil cues can be removed, with no harm done to the print. Film cleaning fluid and cotton swabs are effective tools for removing grease pencil (as well as unwanted dirt and adhesive) from film prints.

If existing cues are slightly out of SMPTE specification, judgment should be used in determining whether or not to add additional cues. A few frames will not likely make a difference. An insufficient number of frames after the changeover cue, however, could result in the tail of a reel showing for a brief moment on screen before the projectionist executes the changeover. If the tail leader is black, this is far less jarring to the audience than if the tail leader is clear. If the spacing between the motor start and changeover cues is a bit shorter than 172 frames, the projectionist can compensate for this by threading the following reel that many frames closer to the start of the picture. This eliminates the need to add an additional set of cues, but also necessitates frame-accurate cue documentation on the film inspection report.

When it becomes necessary to add cues to a print, there are several factors to be taken into consideration:

- Spacing – SMPTE specification calls for 172 frames of image between the motor start and changeover cues (4 frames of each cue), and 18 frames of image after the changeover cue, before the end of the reel. On 35mm film, 172 frames equals 10 feet and 12 frames. On 16mm film, 172 frames equals 4 feet and 12 frames. A film counter should be used to assure frame accuracy. Measuring from the tail, the simple math to remember is 18 + 4 + 172 + 4 frames. For reels that end with a fade-out, it's not a bad idea to shift the two sets of cues closer to the tail, so that the fade-out completes before the changeover occurs. The pacing of a film is interrupted when a fade-out at the end of a reel or fade-up at the beginning of a reel is cut short. This is where timing, in the form of cues, countdown leader, and projection performance, is critical to the success of a film screening.

- Visibility – Both the aspect ratio and darkness/lightness of a scene may affect the placement of changeover cues within the frame. Granted, the cues should appear in the upper-right corner on the screen. When adding grease pencil cues to frames that are dark in that corner, however, you may wish to extend the diagonal slash further into the frame, toward a lighter area, to increase visibility for the projectionist. (Remember, the projectionist is the person furthest from the screen image.) You may also wish to choose grease pencil colors that are most noticeable in a given scene (please note that white grease pencil cues appear gray or black on the screen). Projector aperture plates for 1.85:1 aspect ratio can mask changeover cues placed in the upper-right corner. Cues for this aspect ratio should be placed one perforation lower within the frame.

- Placement – Placing cues so that they appear in the upper-right corner of the screen is the responsibility of the film inspector. Most **35mm** projection prints are **A-wind**, meaning that they read correctly when looking at the emulsion side of the film. When adding scribed circle or hand-etched cues (which scratch the emulsion to leave their mark), the cues should be placed in the upper-right corner of the frame on the emulsion side of the film. If adding grease pencil cues to the base side of the film, place the print on the inspection bench with the base side up, and mark the cues in the upper-left corner of the frame. When the film is flipped over, emulsion side up, the grease pencil cues will appear correctly in the upper-right corner. Most **16mm** projection prints are **B-wind**, meaning that they read correctly when looking at the base side of the film. When adding scribed circle or hand-etched cues (which scratch the emulsion), the cues must be placed in the upper-left corner of the frame on the emulsion side of the film. When the film is flipped over, base side up, the grease pencil cues will appear correctly in the upper-right corner. If adding grease pencil cues to the base side of the film, place the film on the inspection bench with the base side up, and mark the cues in the upper-right corner of the frame.
- Necessity – It is usually unnecessary to cue the last reel of a film.

The advent of automation technologies for film projection introduced the need for another type of cue to be added to film prints: the automation cue. **Automation cues** are self-adhesive foil strips that are placed along the inboard or outboard edges of a film print, or on the base or emulsion side of the film, depending on the automation system and the function of the cue. Electronic sensors are installed in the film path of the projector to read these foil cues, which are used to trigger changes in auditorium lighting, screen masking, projector start-up and lamp striking, picture and sound changeover, and the end of the show. Unfortunately, many projectionists leave the foil cues on the films when they break them down after their run.

Foil cues are commonly located just before the beginning of the closing credits of a film (to turn the house lights up halfway) and at the end of the film (for projector shut-down and house lights up full). Automated theaters which employ two projectors per auditorium and build-up film onto 6,000-foot reels generally added foil cues near the end of every third 2,000-foot reel (to implement start-up and changeover to the other projector). It is not uncommon to receive a film print with several sets of foil cues from a variety of venues. Nor is it uncommon to receive prints with adhesive remaining in locations where foil cues have been removed. In either case, it is recommended that all foil cues and adhesive are removed. Use film cleaner, and peel the residue with maximum care to prevent any further damage to the emulsion.

TAIL LEADER

When utilizing a two-projector system with manual changeovers, it is advisable to have black tail-leader for several feet after the last frame of image on every reel. The purpose for this is to minimize any disturbance to the public in the event of a missed changeover. It is far less disturbing to the audience for the screen to go black between reels than for it to flash brilliant white, or display information printed on the film laboratory leader. Tail leader also protects the film from accumulating dirt, debris, and scratches (as does head leader). A generous supply of black leader in the booth will accommodate this need. Fortunately, most reels have black leader printed at the tail when they leave the film laboratory.

DO'S AND DON'TS

ALWAYS

- Thoroughly inspect the print before the show.

- Have a complete and clean set of inspection tools, ready for use.

- Use house reels in excellent condition for feed and take-up in the projector.

- Make sure that the countdown leaders are complete.

- Check the shrinkage rate of acetate and nitrate prints before the screening.

NEVER

- Be in a hurry while inspecting a film print.

- Leave broken perforations and loose splices unrepaired.

- Apply a tape splice only on one side of the film.

- Scratch a changeover cue on the film's emulsion, unless previously agreed with the appropriate parties.

NOTES

NOTES

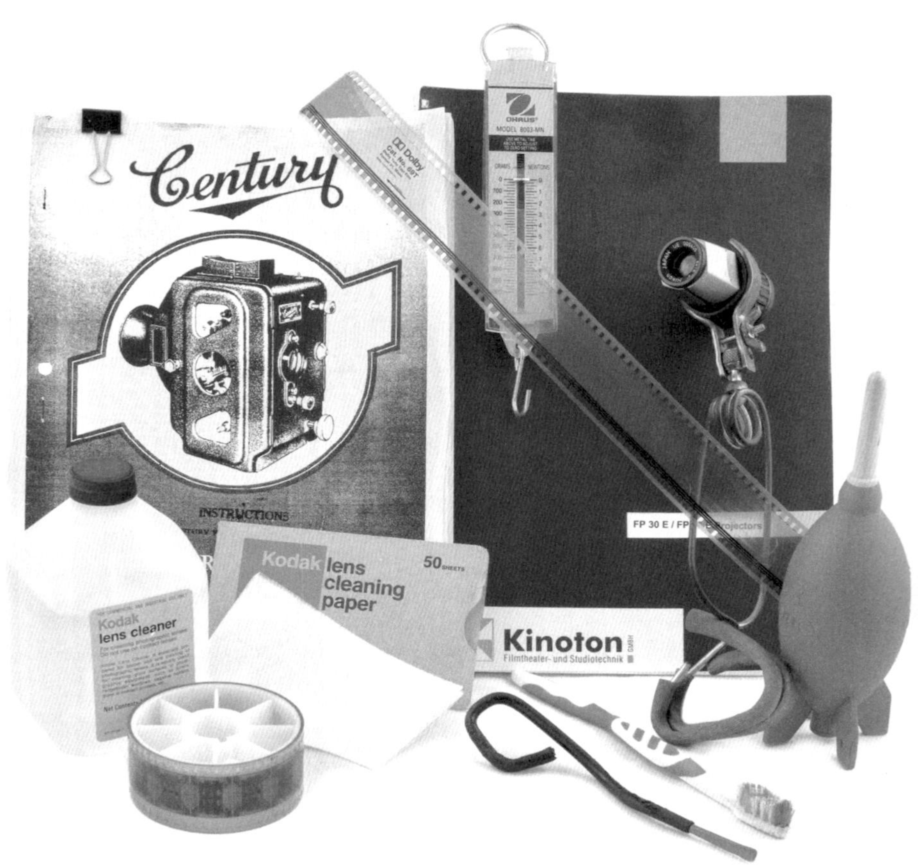
Century
INSTRUCTIONS
Dolby
Cat. No. 69T
OHAUS
MODEL 8003-MN
USE METAL TAB
ABOVE TO ADJUST
TO ZERO SETTING
GRAMS   NEWTONS
0
100
200
300
FP 30 E / FP   Projectors
Kodak
lens cleaner
Kodak lens
cleaning
paper
50 SHEETS
Kinoton GMBH
Filmtheater- und Studiotechnik

6

PREPARING FOR THE SHOW

PREPARATION IS AN integral part of running a smooth and professional show, giving the projectionist the opportunity to test the equipment and address any aspects that could not be determined during print inspection. The preparation stage requires not only technical aptitude on the part of the projectionist, but also a degree of aesthetic sensibility.

No two projection booths are exactly alike. Each installation is designed to meet the needs of the individual theater and to fit the building's architecture. Given the mechanical stability of traditional projection equipment, it is not uncommon for a booth to house technologies that span several decades of film history. For instance, a booth can be outfitted with a projector from the 1940s that has a xenon arc lamphouse from the 1980s and a digital sound reader from the 1990s.

Obviously, these installations require specific instructions regarding operation. Whenever possible, consult the operations manual of a given piece of equipment for proper operating

Fig. 6.1 – **A film projection booth must be stocked with tools and documentation for calibrating, servicing, and operating a variety of equipment.**

procedures. Many film equipment manuals can be found online. At the time of publication, the Equipment Manual Warehouse section of the Film-Tech Cinema Systems website (www.film-tech.com/warehouse/index.php?category=2) is a robust resource for equipment manuals.

Projection equipment models vary, yet their operation does follow a general workflow. Regardless of brand, wiring configuration, and layout of projection equipment, the basics of preparation for projection remain the same: all equipment is checked, powered-up, and set in a logical order.

An important aspect of maintaining proper operation and care of projection equipment is the security of the projection booth. Housing a collection of expensive, precision technology, the projection booth should be secured at all times, with access limited to trained and qualified personnel. Additionally, whenever film prints are located in the projection booth, this area should be treated like a film vault, remaining locked at all times.

This and the next chapter will provide a general overview of how to prepare for the successful projection of a film. While there are many unforeseen variables that may affect the performance (equipment failure, a film break, and so on), a thorough advance preparation helps to prevent problems before they occur. All of the steps described here and in the next chapter should be performed before the screening auditorium is opened to the public.

CHECKING THE EQUIPMENT

Inspect all lenses and the port glass for cleanliness. Dirt, dust, and oil deposits on the lens elements or the port glass can deflect light, distort the image, and result in a loss of luminance. If necessary, clean the lens with lens cleaning tissue and liquid. *Avoid using any materials that contain hard fibers, as they can scratch the lens surface.* If interior lens elements are dirty, always consult lens repair specialists, as they have the proper tools to disassemble, clean, reassemble, and realign the lens. If the port glass is not optically coated, it may be cleaned with non-streaking glass cleaner and a soft, lint-free cloth. If the port glass is optically coated, clean with lens cleaning fluid and lens cleaning tissues.

Check the projector film path for deposits of dirt, dust, particles of film emulsion, and lubricants. Clean the drive sprockets, pad rollers or shoes, intermittent sprocket, gate and trap rails, tension rollers, sound drum, and fire rollers (if any, to prevent the spreading of fire in case of the ignition of a nitrate print) as required. A toothbrush may be used to clean some of these areas, *but never with the projector running*. Manually advance the projector motor in order to access all portions of the drive and intermittent sprockets.

Avoid using any cleaning materials that can leave fibers in the film path. A clean cloth may be used for cleaning the sound drum, tension rollers, and fire rollers, and for wiping down the body of the projector. Sound readers should only be cleaned — very carefully — when necessary, as they are calibrated with factory settings which can easily be altered by careless cleaning procedures. Additional information on this topic can be found in Chapter 9.

Tools used for cleaning projection equipment (such as toothbrushes and cloths) should be replaced when they become dirty or worn. Common tools for cleaning projection equipment include:
- Toothbrush
- Cleaning cloths
- Compressed air
- Lens cleaning tissue and liquid
- Soft camel-hair brush (to remove dust from optics)

Lubrication is essential for projectors with gear-based drive mechanisms. Before lubricating the machine, consult the owner's manual for specific instructions regarding proper lubricants and procedures. Be sure to clean up any excess oil or grease to avoid unwanted contact with the film, the equipment, and the operator.

Projectors with mechanical intermittent movements have some method for gauging the **oil level** in the intermittent mechanism, usually a small glass window. Using the proper oil and keeping it at its required level, as specified in the maintenance manual, is a must. The intermittent mechanism's oil level should be assessed with the projector at rest (not running). Newer projector models may feature an electronic stepper motor for the intermittent movement, which does not require lubrication.

THE APERTURE PLATE AND THE LENS

To maintain a common screen height (or width) while accommodating different aspect ratios, a properly equipped theater must have different focal-length lenses and aperture plates for each aspect ratio. As a rule, lenses and aperture plates are paired and labeled (by aspect ratio) to avoid confusion. Aperture plates can be filed to correct for the keystone effect resulting from projectors located off-axis from the screen (that is, when the light beam of the projector is not perpendicular to the surface of the projection area). In these installations, it is critical to install the aperture plates into the projectors which they were designed for.

The aspect ratio of a given film should be determined in the inspection stage. To set the projectors for the specified aspect ratio, install the appropriate aperture plate and lens on each projector. Insert the proper aperture plate into the aperture slot in the film trap of each projector's picture head. *[Figures 6.2 and 6.3]*

6.2 & 6.3 – **Aperture plates installed in a Century projector (top) and Kinoton projector (bottom).**

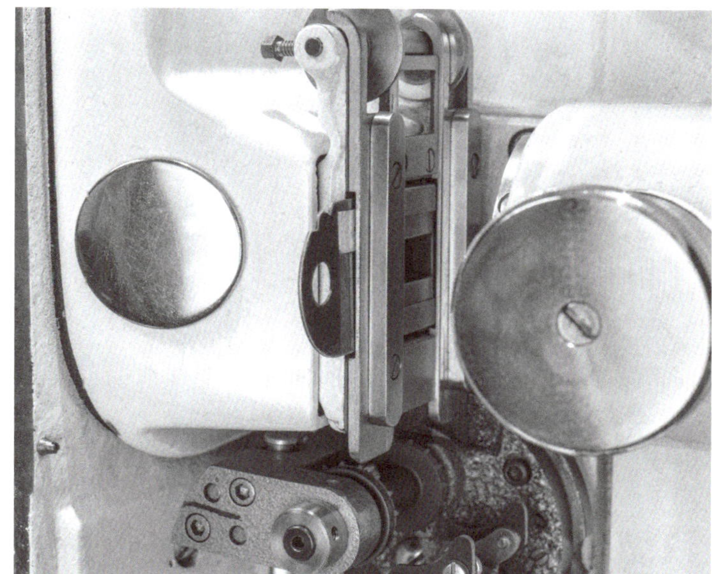

6.2

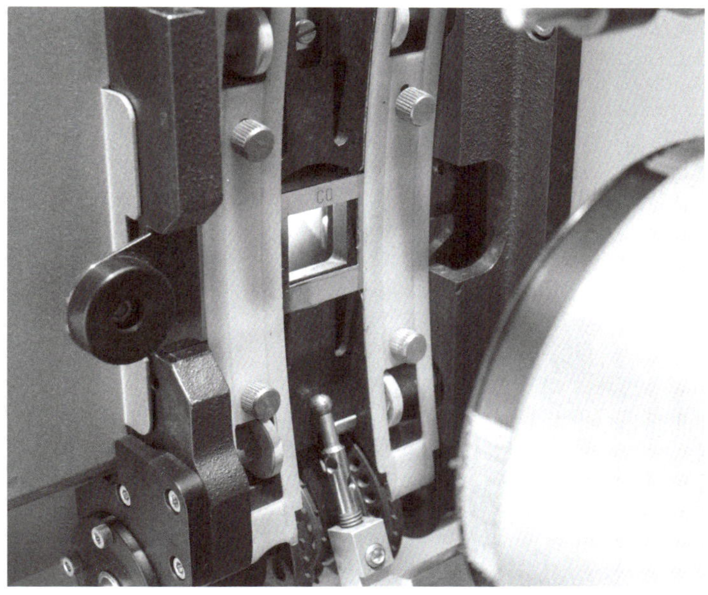

6.3

6.4

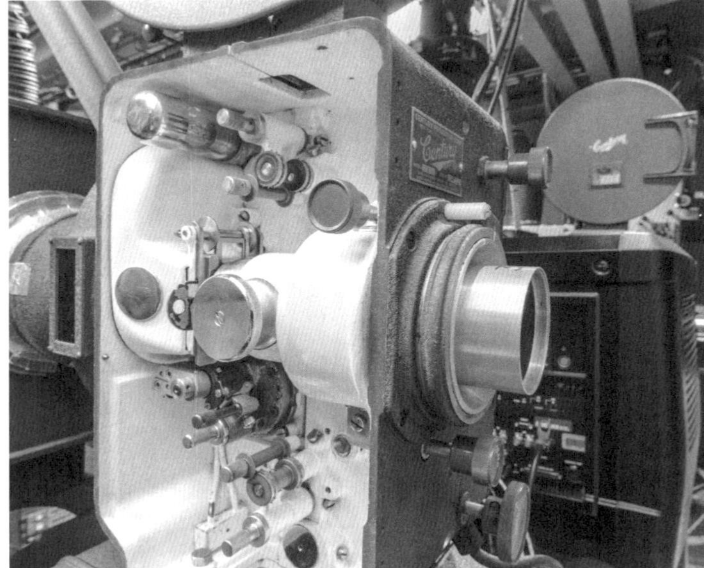

6.5

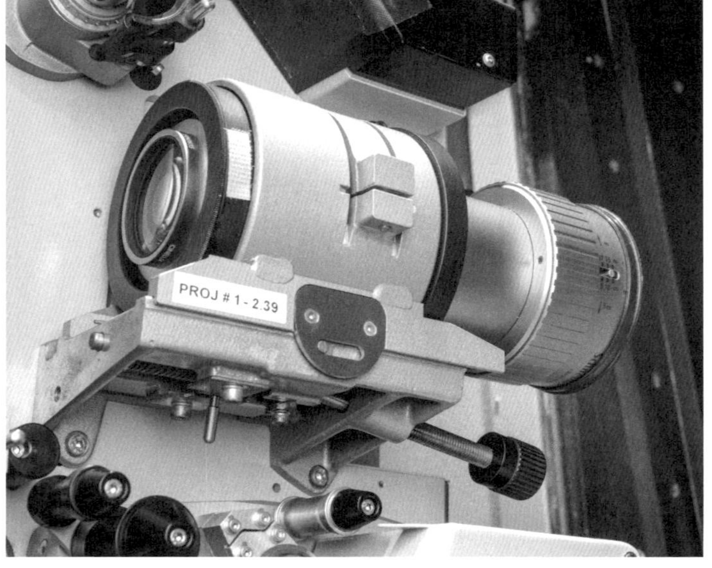

Install the corresponding lenses in the picture heads as well. A mismatch between aperture plate and lens will result in images that are too large, too small, or off-center in relation to the screen.

Most projection lenses are fastened to or within projector lens mounts when they are initially purchased for a theater. To install the lens in the projector, insert the lens mount (containing the lens) into the picture head of the projector, with the front element of the lens facing the screen. While projector picture heads have different configurations, most lens mounts are fastened with an adjustable bolt, clip, or clamp system. *[Figures 6.4 and 6.5]* When installing anamorphic lenses, make sure the alignment is correct (more information on this point is found in the section "Vertical Alignment," in Chapter 7).

If there are any ambiguities encountered when setting the focus (for instance, if the framing looks tight, there is too much head space, or the subtitles are cut off), test the film with other aperture plates. If the aspect ratio looks correct with a different aperture plate, be sure to install the corresponding lens.

POWERING THE EQUIPMENT

Though power distribution varies, depending on the theater's electrical configuration, most equipment is powered by breakers in an electrical breaker box, which is normally located within the projection booth.

6.4 & 6.5 – **A clamp secures the lens mount in a Century projector (top), while a spring mechanism secures the lens mount in a Kinoton projector (bottom).**

While booth configurations differ, the process of powering-up the equipment follows a workflow procedure which can be applied to most projection booths:

- Turn on the exhaust ventilation for the lamphouses.
- Turn on the rectifiers and any other power supplies.
- Strike the projectors' lamps (be sure the lamphouse dousers are closed).
- Turn on the exciter lamps for optical sound (white-light sound heads with separate DC power).
- Power-up the audio rack and all the necessary sound equipment. This includes sound processors, power amplifiers, equalizers, and mixers. Note: In some installations it is preferable to turn on the amplifiers last (and power them down first, before turning off other audio components, after the show has run).
- Turn on the booth audio monitors.

THREADING THE PROJECTOR

The picture head and sound head of the projector is where film threading takes place. The design components of picture and sound heads differ depending on the make and model of the machine. The film path may be relatively straightforward or intricately complex. The incorporation of special sound readers (often referred to as "penthouse" readers) and modifications adds another level of specificity to the threading process. All variations aside, the basic components of a film path remain universal.

The intermittent advancement of film in the gate assembly (of the picture head) necessitates the creation of an upper loop of film — formed between the first drive sprocket and the gate — and a lower loop of film, formed upon exiting the intermittent movement. Analog optical sound readers are located later in the film path because continuous movement is required for sound reproduction. Pad rollers (also called "pad shoes") hold the film against the sprocket drives, and tension rollers provide surface tension for the film around the sound drum. With these characteristics in mind, it is possible to approach any picture and sound head with a general understanding of how it should be threaded along the following path in the projector:

- Upper loop between the drive sprocket and the gate;
- Intermittent or pull-down movement;
- Lower loop following the intermittent or pull-down mechanism;
- Optical sound head (sound drum and photocell);
- Pad rollers or shoes, and tension rollers.

[Figures 6.6 and 6.7, see following pages]

MOUNTING THE REELS

Before threading the projector, the print should be wound onto house reels in good condition. Ideally, this has already occurred during the inspection process.

For 35mm film projection, reels should be wound heads-out, emulsion facing outward, with film coming off the reel in a *counterclockwise* direction. Place the reel on the feed-spindle of the projector so that the film comes off the reel counterclockwise, with the soundtrack facing "outboard" (toward the projectionist). Lock the reel onto the spindle. *[Figure 6.8, see page 192]*

For 16mm film projection, the reel should be wound heads-out, with film coming off the reel in a *clockwise* direction. For single-perforation film prints, the perforations should face "outboard" (toward the projectionist), with the soundtrack facing "inboard" (toward the projector). Lock the reel onto the spindle. *[Figure 6.9, see page 193]*

See Chapter 5 for more information on orienting silent 16mm prints on reels for projection.

6.6

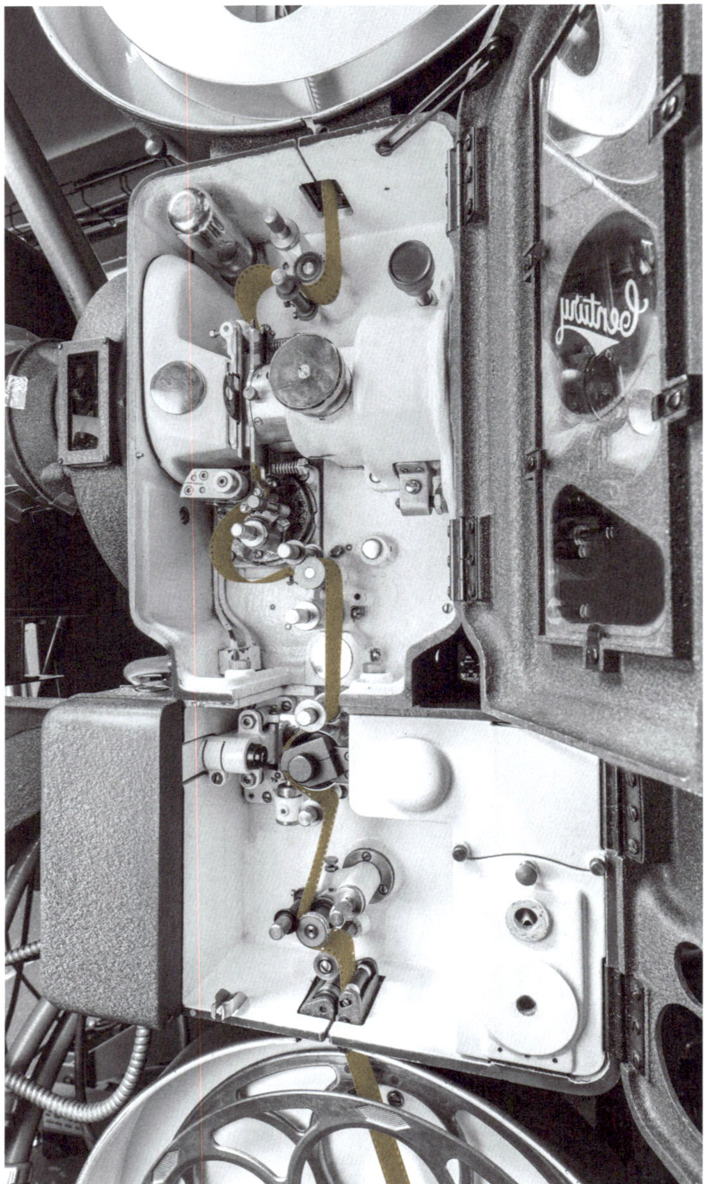

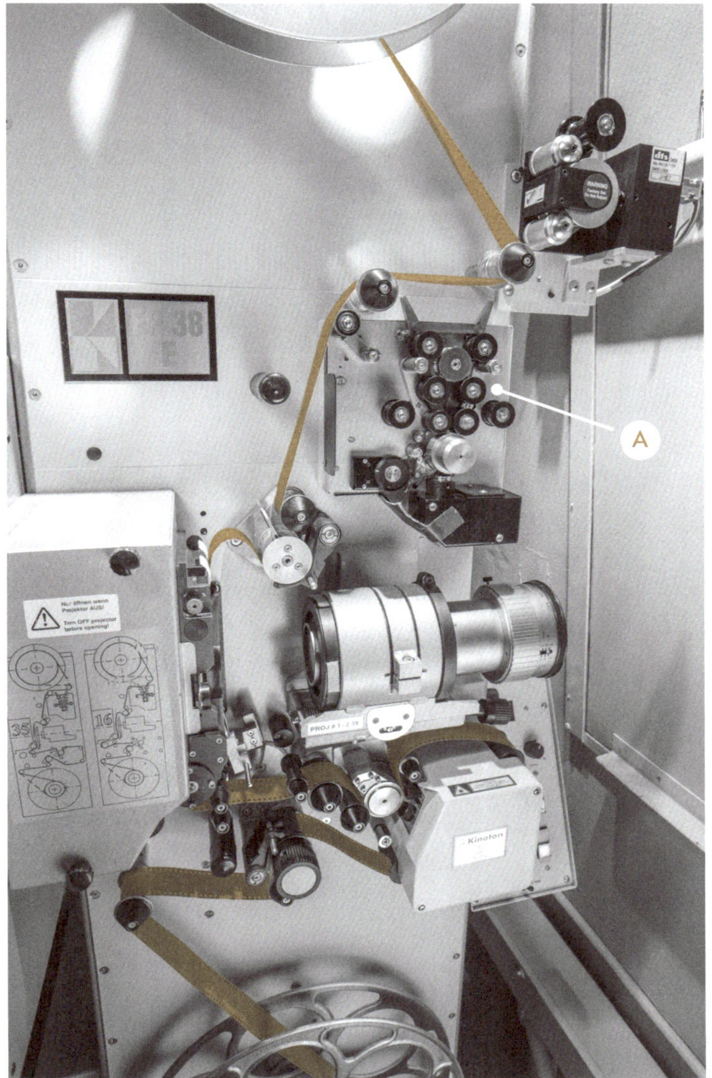

6.7

6.6 & 6.7 — **35mm film threading paths in a Century projector (left) and Kinoton projector (right). Kinoton's 16mm sound head (A) is bypassed for 35mm projection.**

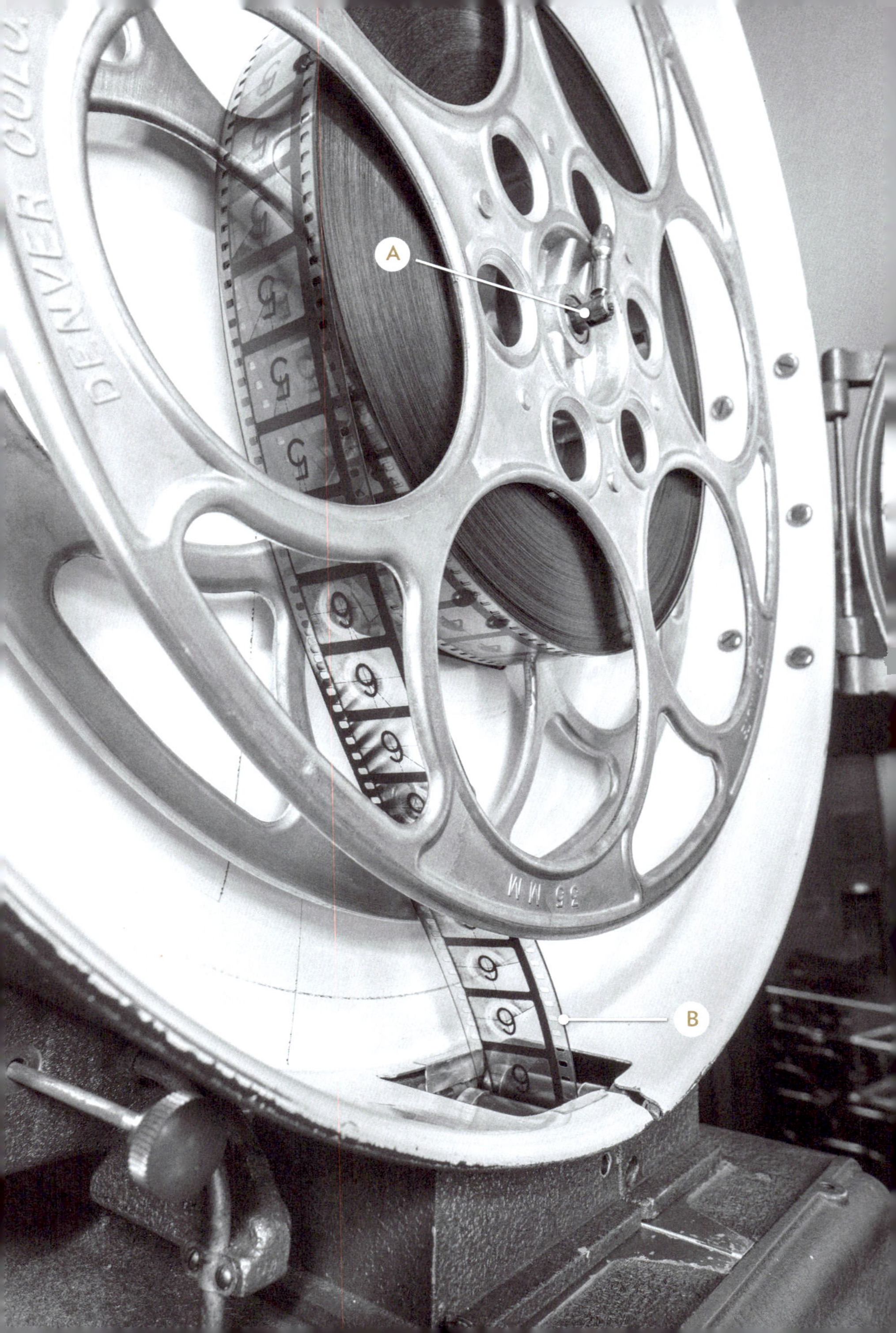

DENVER COLO
35 MM
A
B

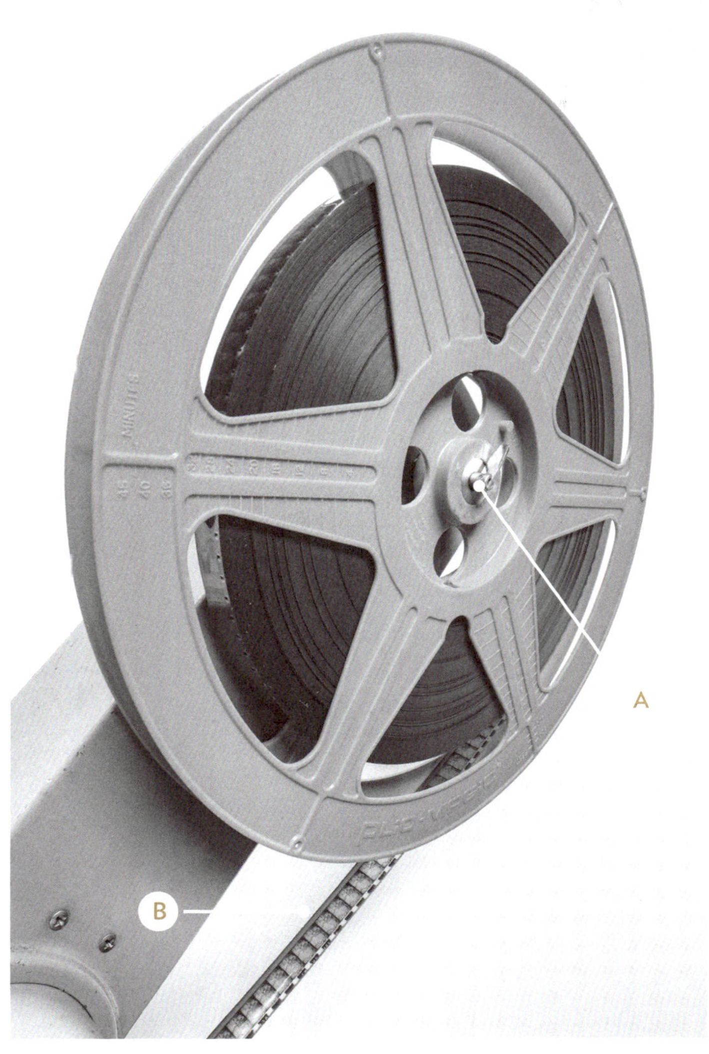

6.8 & 6.9 – **Feed reels properly oriented and mounted on a Century 35mm projector (left) and a Kodak 16mm film projector (right):**

A. LOCKED SPINDLE   B. SOUNDTRACK SIDE OF FILM

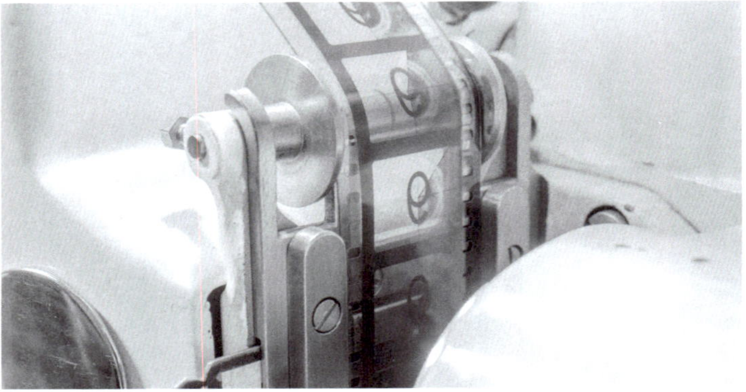

6.10

SETTING THE INTERMITTENT

For projectors with mechanical intermittent movements (Geneva movement or pull-down claw), the movement needs to be set before threading the projector.

Setting the intermittent on a Geneva movement involves manually advancing the projector motor by hand until the intermittent sprocket is at rest (in the "dwell" position, when the sprocket is at rest and not mid-cycle). This assures that the image frame, when the film is properly threaded, will be in alignment with the aperture during operation. The mechanical intermittent movement is also used, on many projectors, as the framing device for the image. By means of a framing knob, the entire intermittent movement is either rotated (in Simplex projectors, among others) or raised and lowered (in Century projectors, among others) to adjust the vertical framing of the image. As part of setting the intermittent, prior to threading the projector the projectionist should always check and adjust the position of the framing knob so that it is in the center of its range of motion, in order to accommodate reframing in either direction if necessary.

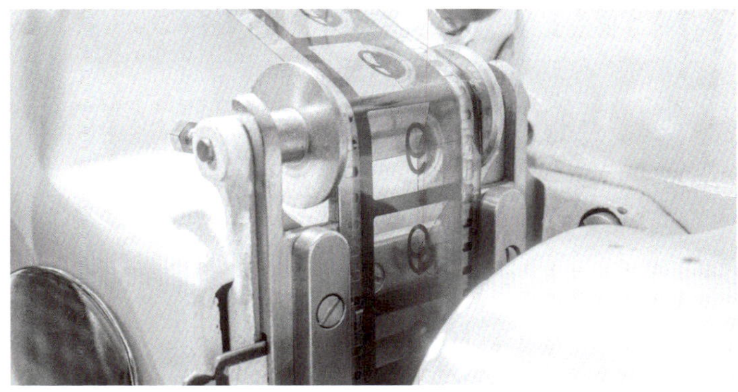

6.10 & 6.11 – **35mm film threaded in-frame (left) and out-of-frame (right) within the threading aperture of a Century 35mm film projector.**

Setting the pull-down claw on a projector is achieved by advancing the projector motor by hand until the claw has retracted into the gate. This allows insertion of film into the gate without damaging the claw mechanism. Once the projector has been fully threaded and the gate closed, advance the projector motor by hand until the claw properly engages with the film perforations.

Projectors with electronically driven intermittent sprockets should be advanced for a few seconds prior to threading.

FRAMING AND THE INTERMITTENT SPROCKET

In order to minimize reframing of the image during projection, the film should be carefully threaded in-frame within the projector aperture in the first place. This is achieved by placing the film in the trap so that a frame of countdown leader lines up within the projector aperture. *[Figures 6.10 and 6.11]* The perforations should also align with the sprocket teeth on the intermittent sprocket, located just below the gate.

For 16mm projection, since one perforation corresponds to each frame, as long as the perforations register with the pull-down claw or intermittent sprocket, the image should be in-frame, requiring only minor adjustment via the framing knob. On mechanical projectors, the framing knob should be set to its center, to allow for plenty of movement in both directions when vertically framing the image.

THREADING THE COUNTDOWN LEADER IN THE PROJECTOR

Whether a film print contains Academy countdown (measuring feet) or SMPTE countdown (measuring time, in seconds), 35mm projectors are typically threaded, at the aperture, to a point that is 8 or 9 feet before the first frame of image. This position relates to the spacing of Motor Start and Changeover cues. As outlined in Chapter 5, the SMPTE specified distance between the Motor Start and Changeover cue is 172 frames, regardless of film gauge. At a projection speed of 24 frames per second, this equals just over 7 seconds (7.16 seconds, to be exact). To enable a well-timed changeover, the countdown leader must be threaded at a length which takes into account human reaction time, projector motor acceleration time, and placement of the cues. Ongoing experience in projecting film with a particular equipment will allow a committed projectionist to fine-tune the threading distance.

When threading a complete Academy countdown, the frames marked "9" and "8" refer to 9 feet and 8 feet from the head of the film.

When threading a complete SMPTE countdown, 9 feet corresponds to the first frame of "6" (adjacent to "7"), and 8 feet corresponds to the 16th frame of "6" (or, 8 frames before the first "5"). *[Figure 6.12]*

6.12 – **35mm Academy (left) and SMPTE (right) countdown leaders with corresponding 9-foot locations.**

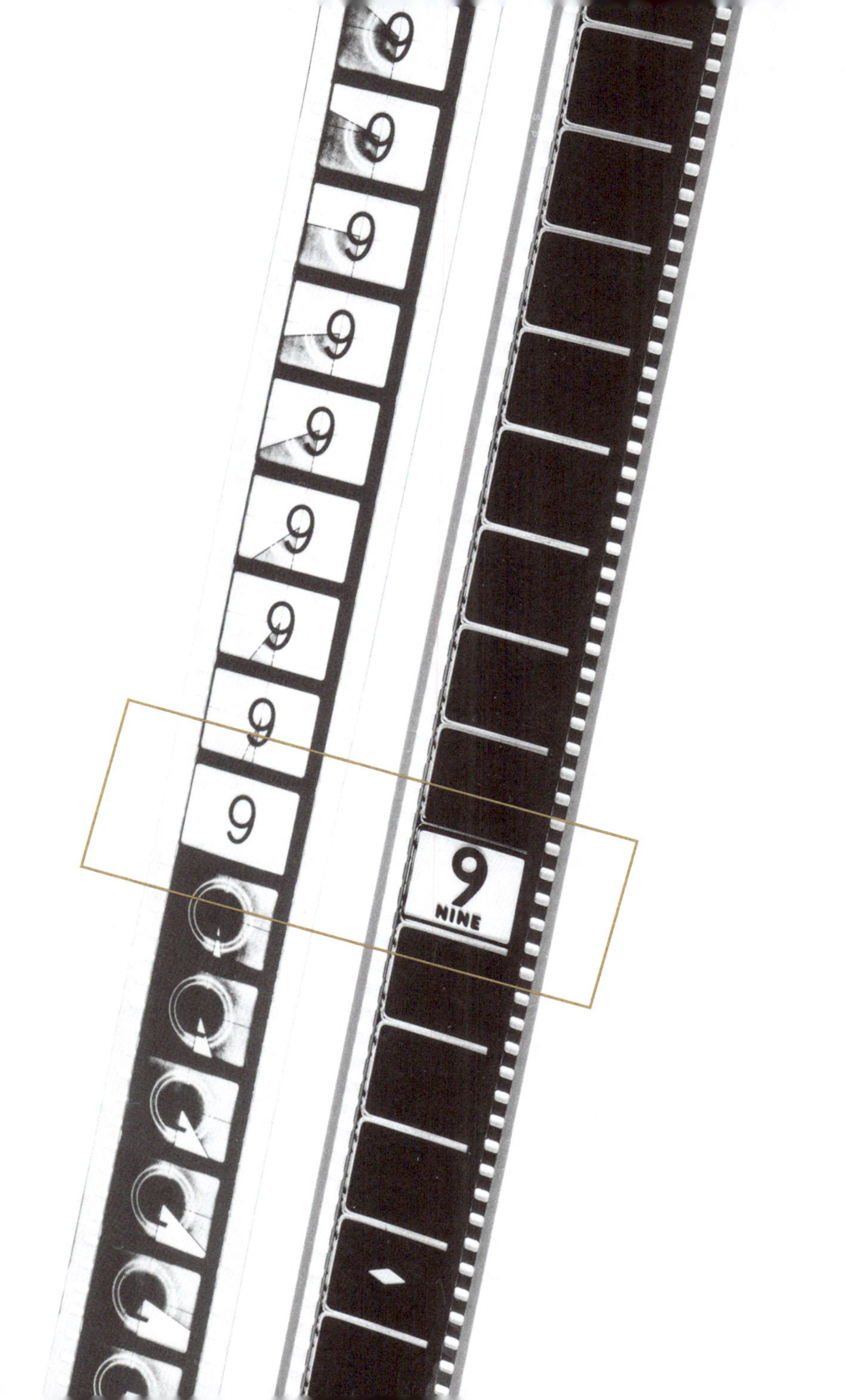
9
NINE

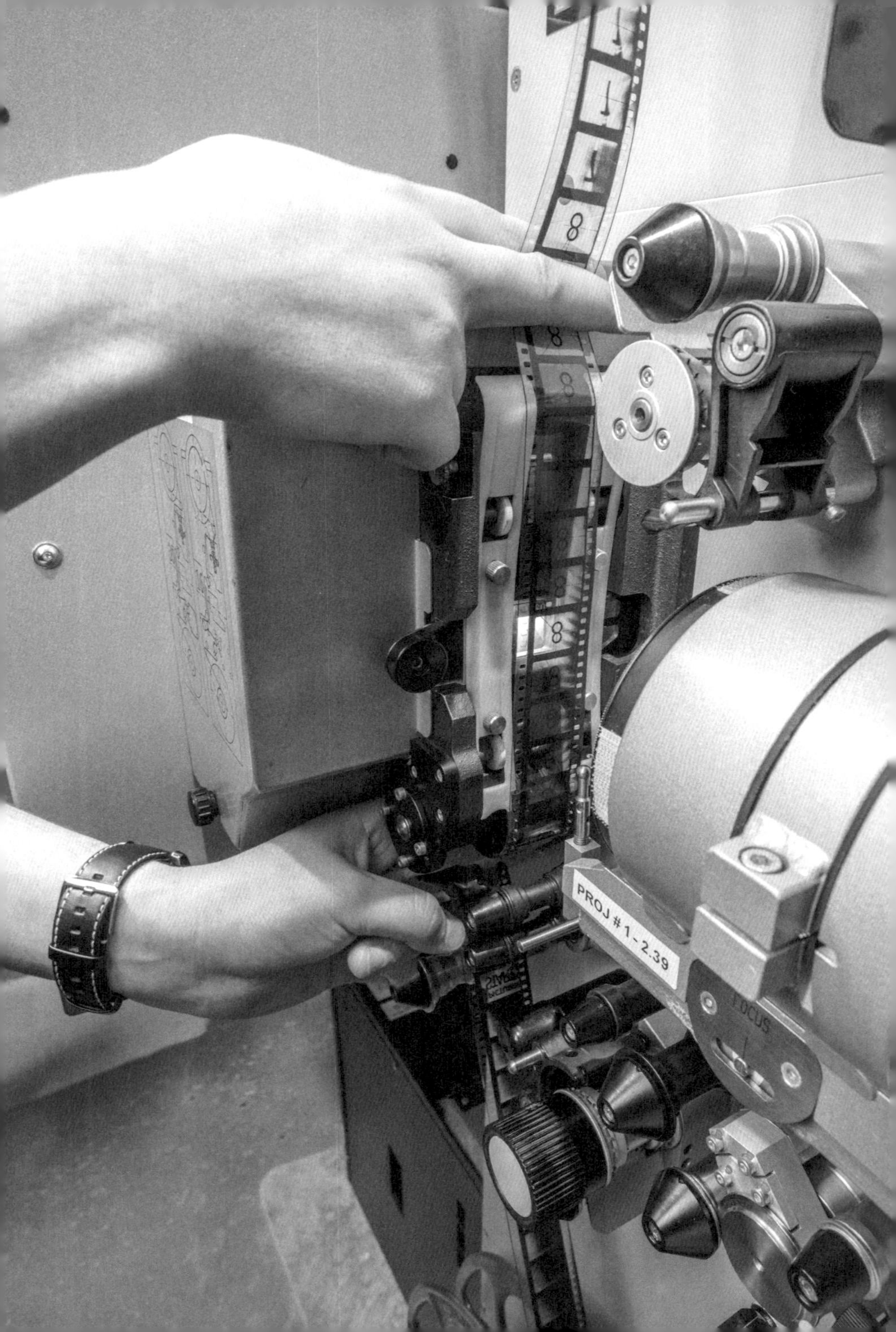

PROJ # 1 - 2.39
FOCUS

For 16mm projection, the same threading positions apply, as both Academy and SMPTE countdowns account for the different measurements pertaining to 16mm stock.

Before threading the countdown leader in a projector, retract the gate and open all pad rollers or "shoes" to allow for access. After setting the intermittent, it is best to secure the film in the gate first, in-frame, before threading the remainder of the projector. To do this, engage the film on the intermittent sprocket so that a complete film frame is in-frame within the aperture, and the film is lying flat in the trap. *[Figure 6.13]* Carefully close the gate to secure the film in the trap.

It is advisable to initially thread the countdown ahead of where you want to "park" the projector, allowing room to hand-advance the motor after threading, in order to check for proper film alignment and sprocket engagement along the film path. We shall return to this in Chapter 8 when discussing the changeover process.

UPPER LOOP

The upper loop is formed in the picture head between the first drive sprocket and the gate assembly. The loop creates slack to ensure safe travel of the film between the continuous motion of the drive sprocket and the intermittent motion through the gate assembly.

If the loop is too small, it can cause excess tension, resulting in gate clatter, unsteadiness, and possible film damage. If the loop is too big, the film can come into contact with surfaces within the picture head, resulting in scratches on the print.

6.13 – **35mm film engaged with intermittent sprocket, threaded in-frame with the aperture on a Kinoton projector.**

6.14

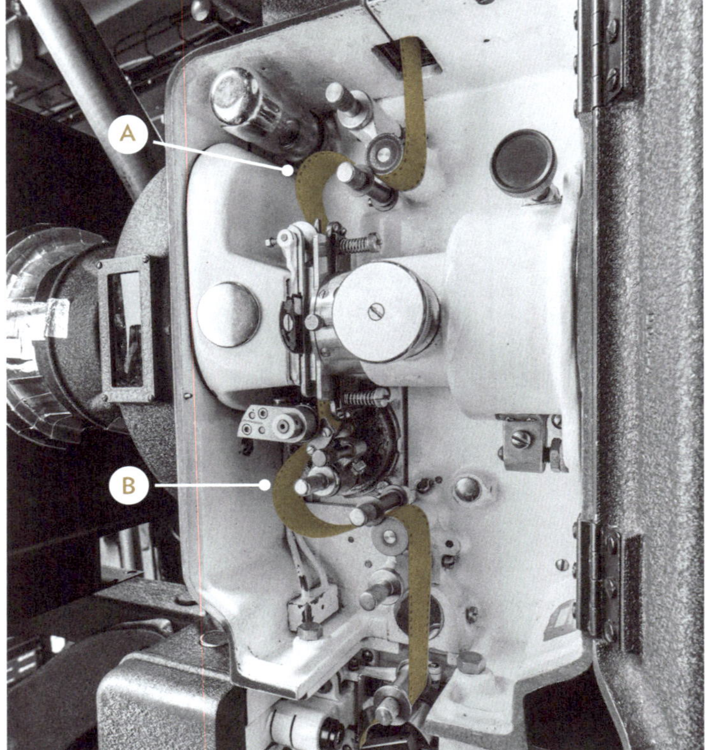

6.14 & 6.15 – **Upper and lower 35mm film loops in the picture head of a Century projector (left) and a Kinoton projector (right).**

A. **UPPER LOOP**   B. **LOWER LOOP**

With the countdown leader secured in the gate assembly, form the upper loop and thread the film onto the first drive sprocket, locking it in place with the pad roller or "shoe." The loop size is adjusted by opening the pad roller or "shoe," disengaging the perforations from the sprockets, and moving the film to make the loop bigger or smaller. Once the loop is formed, close the pad roller or "shoe" to secure the film against the drive sprocket. *[Figures 6.14 and 6.15]*

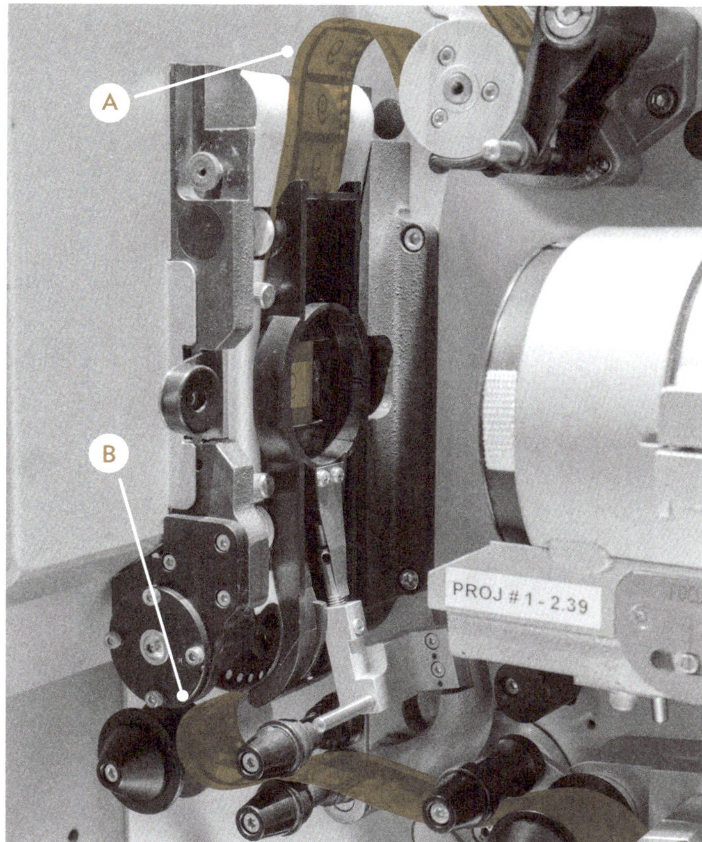

6.15

LOWER LOOP

The lower loop is formed between the intermittent sprocket and the next drive sprocket. Depending on the make and model of the projector, the next drive sprocket could be in the picture head, or located after the sound reader, in the sound head. As with the upper loop, the same rules for loop formation and loop size apply. On some projectors, too large a loop can cause uneven travel along the sound drum, producing pitch fluctuations during playback.

According to the specifications of the Society of Motion Picture and Television Engineers (SMPTE), the audio information in 35mm optical film soundtracks is printed 21 frames (+/- ½ frame) in advance of its corresponding image, and 26 frames (+/- ½ frame) in advance for 16mm film with an optical soundtrack. Adjusting the size of the lower loop affects the audio/image sync, as this loop determines the number of perforations between the image in the gate and the optical soundtrack in the sound reader.

SOUND HEAD

There are a number of different sound heads and sound reading technologies a projection operator may encounter. Among them are forward-scan and reverse-scan white-light analog sound readers, containing an exciter lamp and a slit lens, which combine to project the fluctuations of the optical soundtrack onto a solar cell. There are also reverse-scan infrared (IR) LED and red LED analog sound readers which employ light-emitting diode (LED) light sources, and there are signal pick-up assemblies to achieve the same effect. Red-light readers were introduced to read cyan-dye optical soundtracks, developed in the late 1990s. Cyan-dye optical tracks read poorly with white-light readers. *[Figures 6.16 – 6.18]*

Magnetic readers are installed in many kinds of projectors for 16mm, 35mm, and 70mm prints with magnetic soundtracks. The reader assemblies for these magnetic tracks may be located within or above the picture head. Threading patterns vary

6.16 – 6.18 – **Analog optical sound readers on 35mm projectors: forward scan white-light reader on a Simplex projector (top); reverse-scan infrared LED reader on a Century projector (middle); reverse-scan dual red LED reader (analog and Dolby Digital) on a Kinoton projector (bottom).**

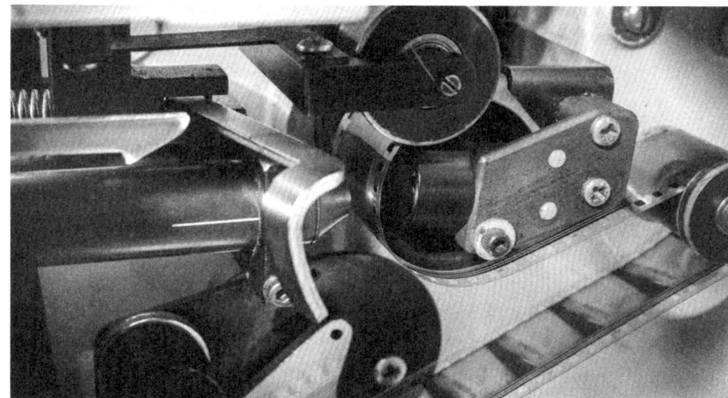

6.16

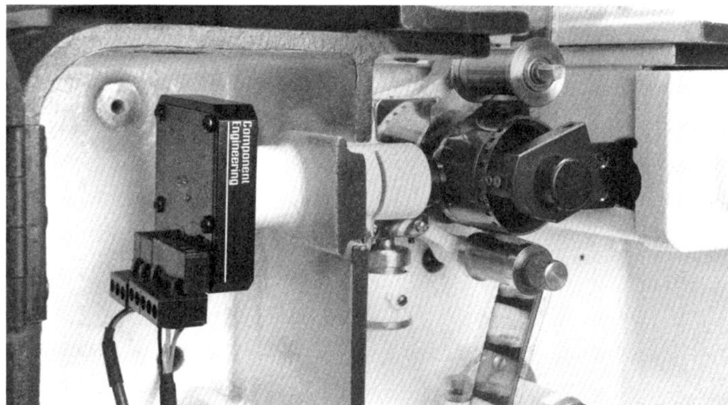

6.17

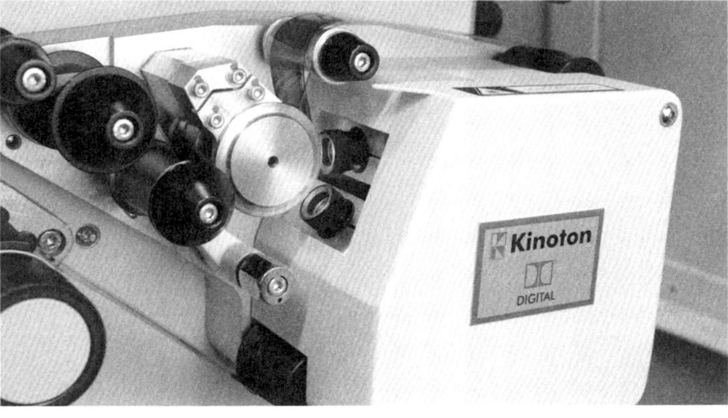

6.18

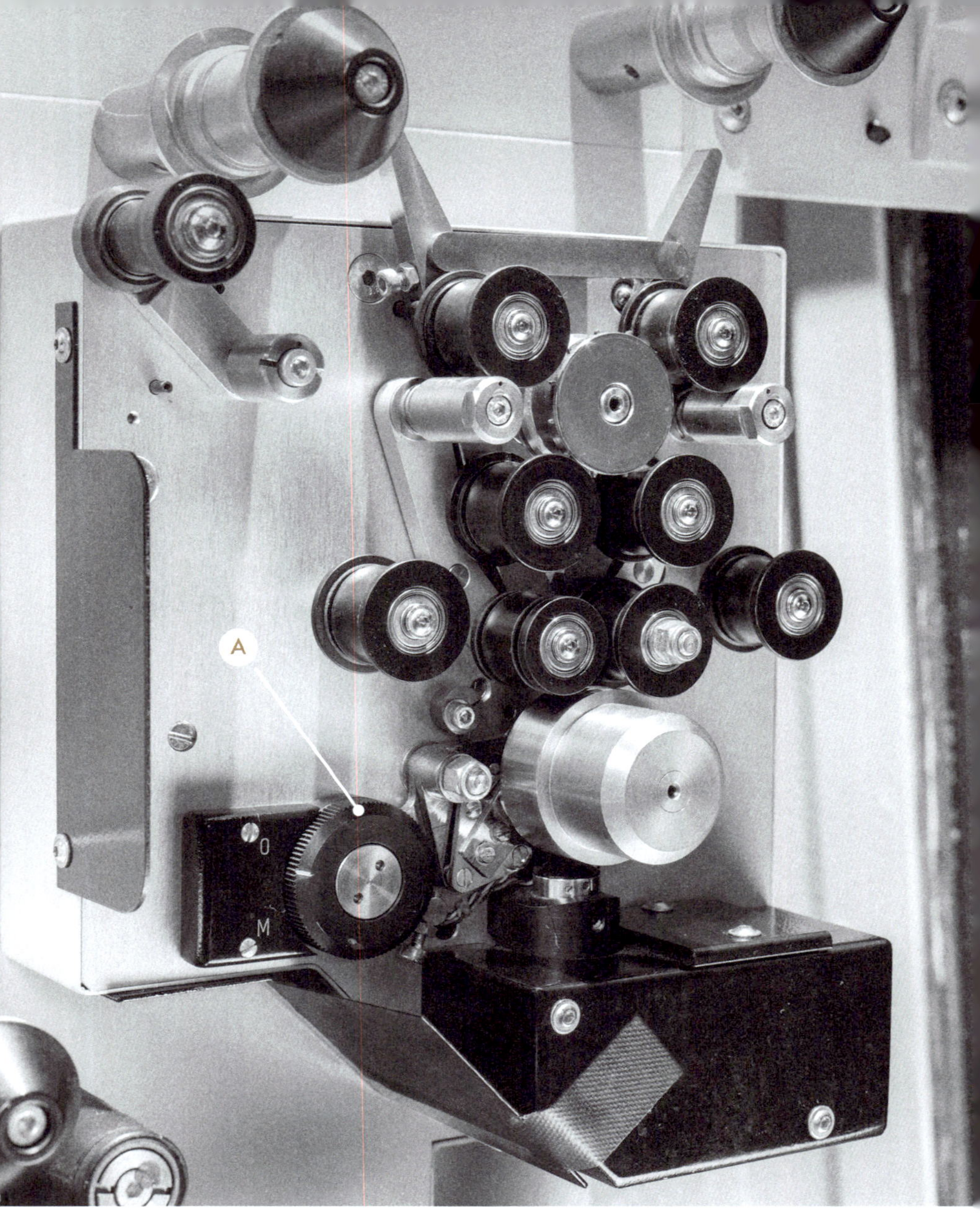

6.19 – **16mm magnetic/optical sound reader on a Kinoton projector:**

A. MAGNETIC / OPTICAL SOUND TOGGLE KNOB

according to the manufacturer. Be mindful of any switches which may have to be activated when reading magnetic audio tracks. *[Figures 6.19 and 6.20]*

One may also encounter a variety of digital film sound readers: Dolby Digital, DTS (Digital Theater Systems, later marketed as Datasat Digital Entertainment), and SDDS (Sony Dynamic Digital Stereo). Unlike optical analog sound readers, which are positioned below the gate, digital sound readers are positioned either above or below the gate, as the decoding software is

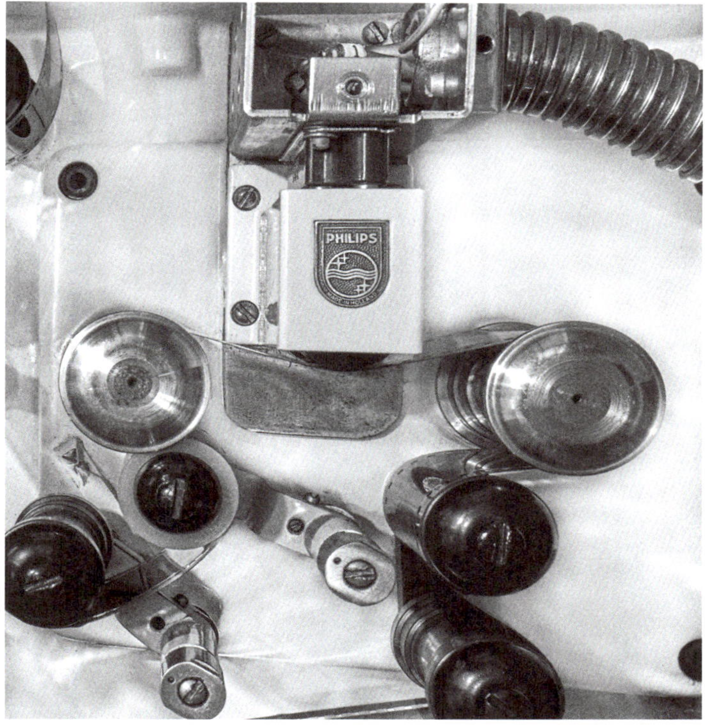

6.20 – Magnetic reader assembly within the picture head of a Norelco DP70 35/70mm film projector (The Netherlands, ca. 1959) at Kodak Center Theater, Rochester, NY.

capable of producing a digital delay that properly synchronizes the sound with the image. The optically printed digital soundtrack area is illuminated by a red LED, and is read by a charge-coupled device (often called CCD) for the movement of the electrical charge. *[Figures 2.17 – 2.19. see pages 65–66]*

Most sound readers, analog or digital, for motion picture film follow the same basic principle. The film is threaded around a freely rotating drum (usually connected to a flywheel) with enough tension for the film to turn the drum, which works to provide smooth continuous movement of the optical soundtrack across the sound reader.

The sound drum is the only component of the projector film path that comes into contact with the image area. For this reason, it is critical to keep the sound drum absolutely clean and turning freely.

To obtain an even reading of the soundtrack, it is important to thread the film around the sound drum with enough tension (via tension rollers, or tension roller and holdback sprocket, depending on the manufacturer) for the traveling film to rotate the sound drum mechanism. Proper threading and tension around the sound drum is critical to avoid audio distortion and film damage. *[Figures 6.21 and 6.22]*

Depending on the configuration of the projector, there can be additional factors to address when threading the film (fire rollers, for example).

6.21 & 6.22 – **35mm film threaded through the sound head of a Century projector (top) and a Kinoton projector (bottom).**

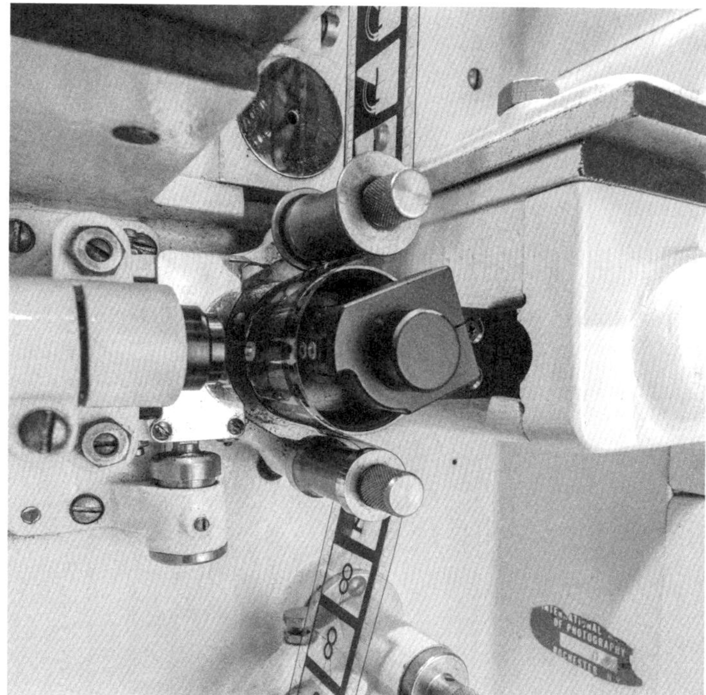

6.21

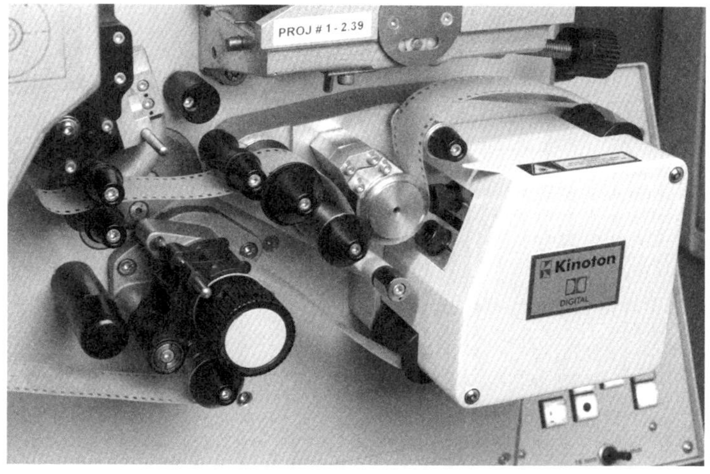

6.22

TAKE-UP

Film should be taken up onto house reels in excellent condition, with the reel locked onto the spindle. Wrap the film tightly around the reel hub in a clockwise fashion, using only tension to hold the film onto the reel. If the head leader preceding the countdown is too short to wrap around the reel hub securely, splice a piece of scrap film onto the beginning of the leader to extend its length. Advance the reel by hand until all slack is taken up.

Avoid taping the head of the film to the reel hub, as this causes excess tension upon rewind, possibly breaking the leader, and leaves tape or adhesive on the leader and reel hub. Using the threading slot in the reel hub is preferable to using tape. Some projector models have a switch to engage and disengage the feed and take-up tension. Before threading, the tension should be disengaged; once threading is complete, the tension should be re-engaged.

After thread-up has been completed, re-examine the film path to double-check for any problems.

Things to watch for include:
- The reels are secured in place on spindles with spindle locks.
- The size of the upper and lower loops is correct.
- The film is threaded in-frame.
- The gate assembly is closed.
- Film perforations are properly engaged with sprocket teeth. (When the projector is in idle mode, run your finger over film that is engaged with sprocket drives, using your sense of touch to make sure that the sprocket teeth are protruding through the perforations.)
- The sprocket pad rollers or shoes are closed. Pad rollers should turn freely.

- The guide rollers and tension rollers are threaded correctly.
- Tension is correct on the sound drum.
- The take-up tension is engaged (on some models of film projectors).

Once the film path has been inspected, the projector should be manually advanced (when possible) through several frames. Look and listen to the film as it travels its path and engages with sprockets to assure that it travels and engages smoothly. This step ensures that the film is threaded properly.

DO'S AND DON'TS

ALWAYS

- Check the proper path for the film thread from the feed reel to the take-up reel. When done, check again.

- Be accurate in threading the countdown leader.

- Thread the film around the sound drum with enough tension for the traveling film to rotate the sound drum mechanism.

NEVER

- Clean projector lenses with materials containing hard fibers.

- Tape the head of the film to the hub of the take-up reel in the projector.

- Neglect to verify the correct sizes of the upper and lower film loops.

NOTES

NOTES

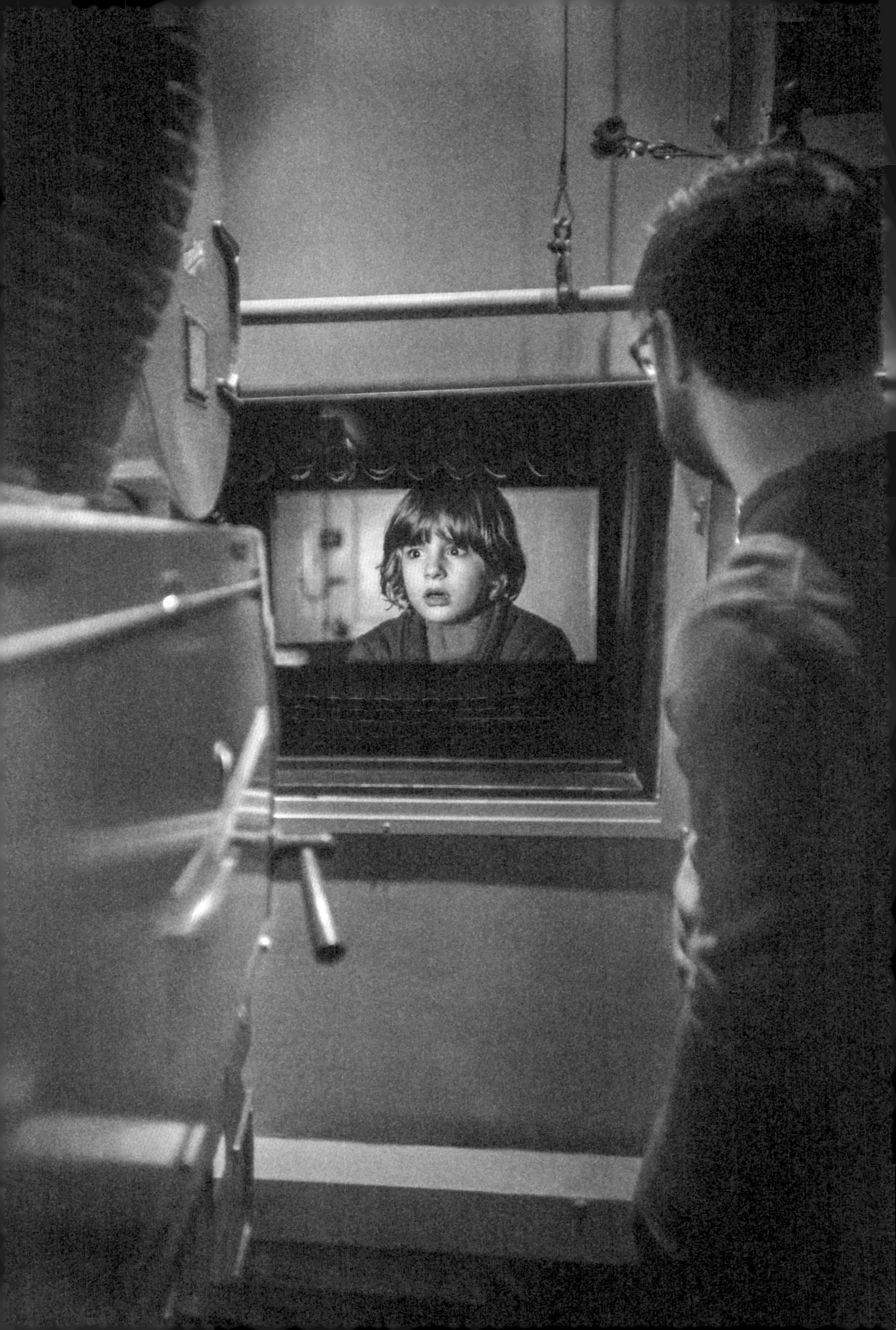

7

THE FINAL TOUCH: PRE-FOCUS

SETTING THE PROPER audio format, gate tension, focus, vertical alignment (for anamorphic prints), sound level, and screen masking are of primary importance in preparing for a screening. While some operators choose to calibrate the focus using a test film or film loop, such as the *SMPTE RP 40 Projector Alignment and Image Quality Test Film*, it is best practice to run the actual print. Not only does this provide an opportunity to optimize the visual and audio components of the presentation, it also affords the opportunity to address any variables which may have surfaced during the inspection of the print. Reels of the film should be threaded on each of the very projectors to be used for the screening.

Fig. 7.1 – **A projectionist pre-focusing a projector with a reel of film (*The Shining*, Stanley Kubrick, UK/US 1980) prior to the entry of an audience.**

The final stages of preparation for a film screening involve an actual **projection test** ahead of the show, consisting of eight fundamental steps:

1. Setting the audio format.
2. Adjusting the gate tension.
3. Setting the focus.
4. Vertical alignment of the anamorphic lens (where applicable).
5. Setting the sound level.
6. Setting the masking.
7. Making any necessary adjustments.
8. Unthreading the projector.

Begin by turning on all relevant equipment in the booth.

AUDIO FORMAT

The cinema sound processor located in the booth will likely have several options available for reproducing the various possible soundtracks on film prints, be they optical (analog or digital) or magnetic. The appropriate audio format for a print should be determined when inspecting the print (see Chapter 4), and should be identified on the film inspection report (see Appendix A). Consult the report to determine the proper option to select on the cinema sound processor. *[Figure 7.2]*

With the projectors threaded and checked, dim the lights in the auditorium. Beginning with the first projector, start the motor. When up to speed, open the lamphouse douser and activate the picture and sound changeover mechanism.

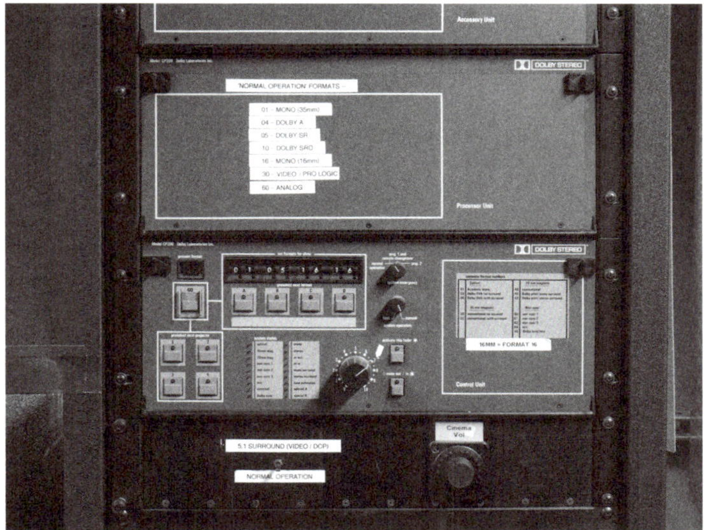

7.2 – **Dolby CP200 sound processor mounted on a sound rack in a film projection booth.**

GATE TENSION

Most 35mm film projector gates are spring-tensioned, with a means for adjusting the amount of tension. Tension in the gate is necessary to keep the image stable, in the vertical plane, avoiding jitter and jumps. The minimum gate tension necessary to hold an image stable is recommended. To achieve this, slowly decrease the gate tension until the image begins to jump, then increase the tension until the image stabilizes. Image stabilization tends to be more of an issue with 16mm film projection. Most 16mm portable projectors do not have adjustable gate tension. *[Figures 7.3 – 7.6. see following pages]*

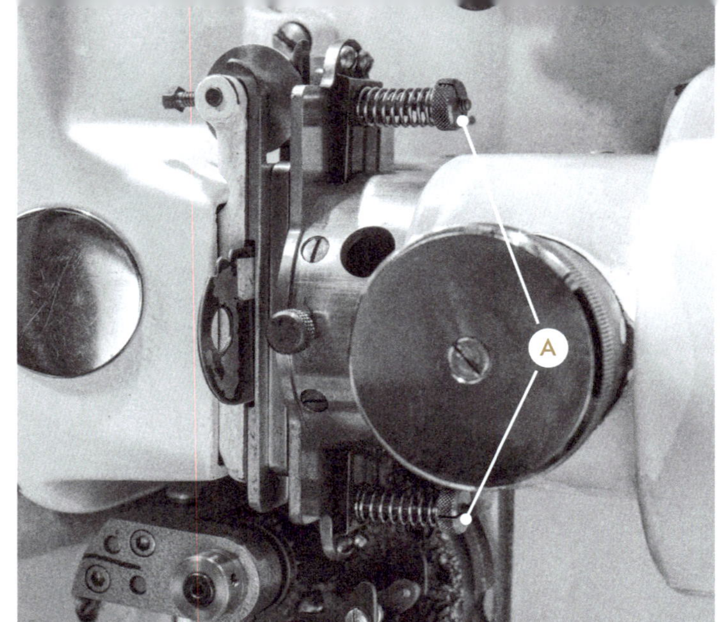

7.3

7.3 – 7.6 – **Gate tension adjustments on:**
(7.3) a Century 35mm projector, (7.4) a Kinoton 16mm/35mm projector,
(7.5) a Simplex 35mm projector, and (7.6) an Eastman Model 25
16mm projector.

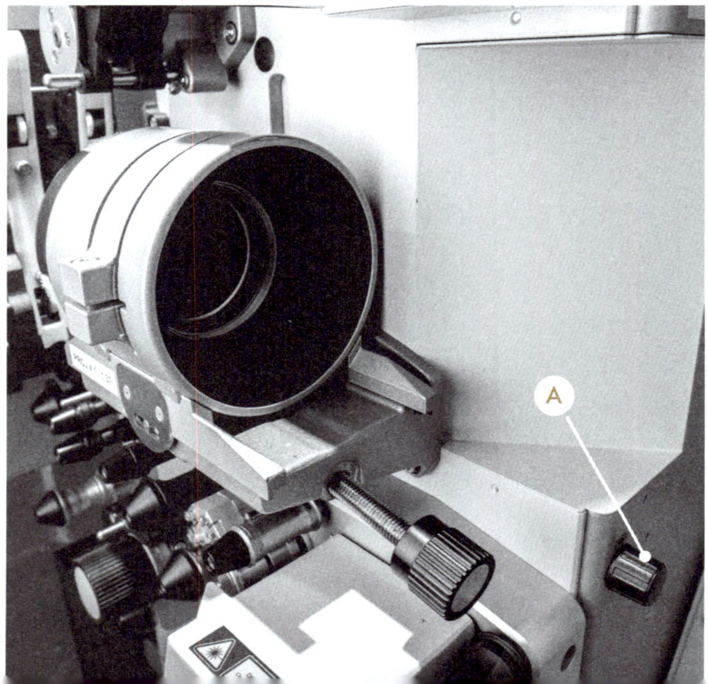

7.4

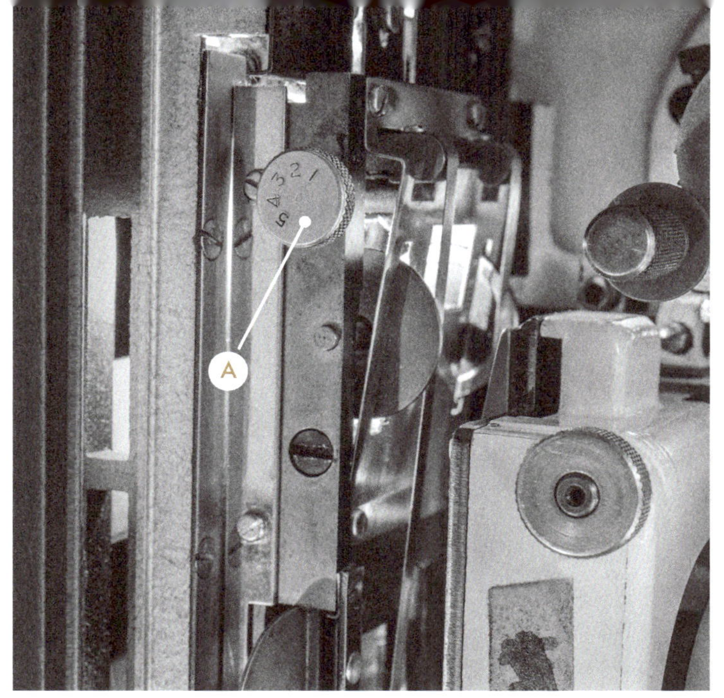

A. GATE TENSION ADJUSTMENT KNOB

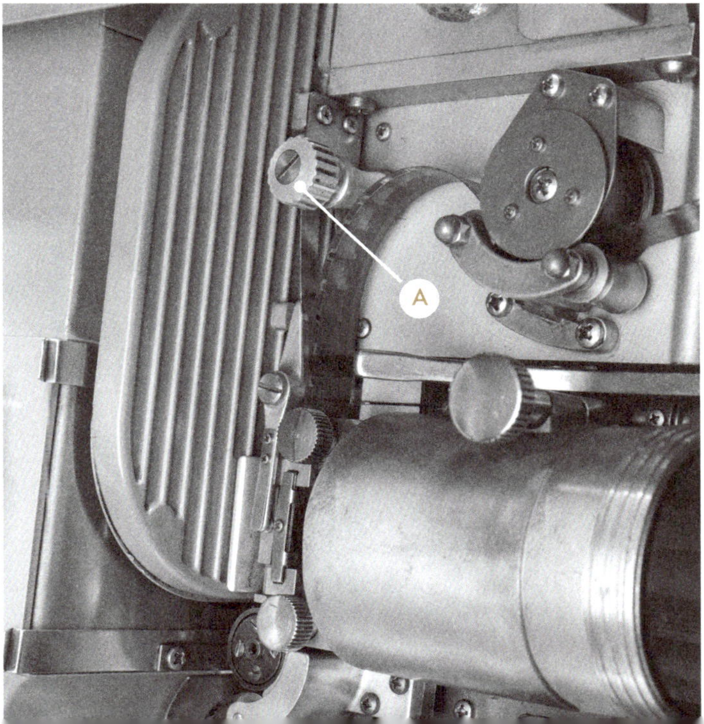

FOCUS AND FRAMING

The desired result is to yield an image that meets the following criteria:

- The sharpness of the image is even at the sides and at the center.
- The visible grain of the film is sharp.
- No frame lines appear on screen.
- Framing is adjusted to present the intended composition.

Focus is set by adjusting the projector's focus knob. To set the focus, turn the focus knob until the image appears sharp at the center and both sides. If the grain of the film appears sharp, the image is in focus. Projecting warped film can result in fluctuations of focus. Projectors with curved gates are believed to improve the stability of focus. Ideally, the focus of the print should not fluctuate once it has been set. There are some instances, such as poor splices, which may alter the focus temporarily. Prints which combine elements from multiple sources may also cause fluctuations in focus, as the thickness of film stock changes. These prints should be closely monitored during projection.

It is ironic that the person responsible for image focus is also the one who is farthest from the screen. To overcome this disadvantage, it is recommended to procure one or two monoculars, or a pair of binoculars, for the booth. Using optical magnification to bring the projectionist "closer" to the image will greatly assist in setting the focus. Focusing on the film grain is a reliable way of obtaining ideal focus. If using optical devices to help you focus, first make sure that the optics of the device are focused for your vision.

Other important aspects to be considered during the pre-focus test:

- Framing, whereby the film frame is moved vertically relative to the projection aperture, is adjusted via a knob or buttons on the projector, depending on whether a mechanical or electronic movement is used. Adjustment of the image framing depends on the intended and printed aspect ratio of the film.

- Films with 1.33:1, 1.18:1, and 2.35:1 or 2.39:1 aspect ratios have very thin frame lines, leaving little room for adjustment. Vertically adjust the framing so that no frame lines appear on screen.

- Films with a 1.37:1 aspect ratio ("Academy" aperture) have very wide frame lines, but the image area should be only slightly larger than the aperture plate. Vertically adjust the framing to center the image on screen.

- Flat widescreen films (1.66:1, 1.75:1, and 1.85:1) printed with hard mattes leave no room for artistic license; the correct aspect ratio of the image is printed onto the film. Vertically adjust the framing to center the image on screen.

- Flat widescreen films printed at the 1.37:1 aspect ratio, which is common, present a challenge to the projectionist as to where to properly center the frame. Frame the image too low, and unwanted artifacts on the floor of the set may appear on screen. Frame the image too high, and microphone booms may appear above the performers' heads. The disposition of the film's opening credits may provide the best target for properly framing the film (this is an equally useful method for other aspect ratios). Keeping an eye toward not cutting off people's heads in shots is another guide to proper frame adjustment. *[Figures 7.7 – 7.10, see following pages]*

To obtain the best focus, framing, and proper sound level, and to fine-tune screen masking, it is recommended to invite a person in the auditorium to provide feedback on these factors.

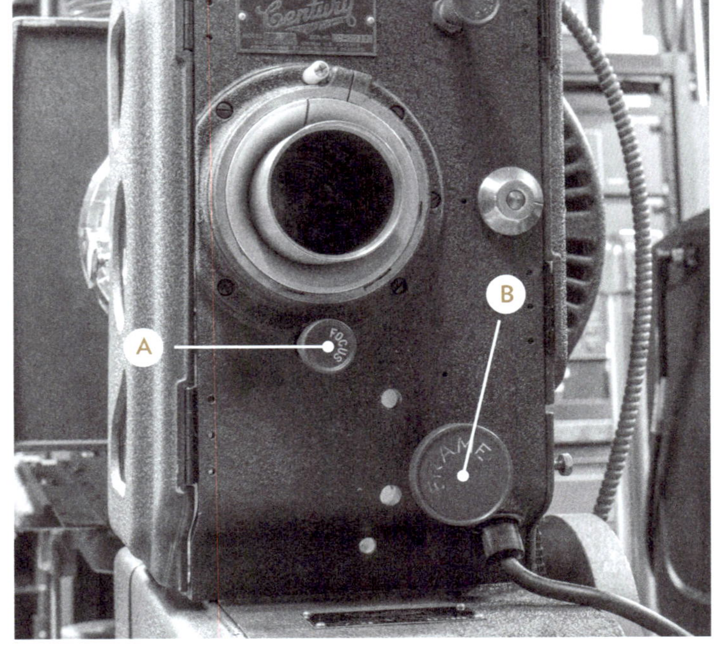

7.7 – 7.10 – Focus and framing adjustments on:
(7.7) a Century 35mm projector, (7.8) a Kinoton 16mm/35mm projector,
(7.9) a Simplex 35mm projector, and (7.10) an Eastman Model 25 16mm projector.

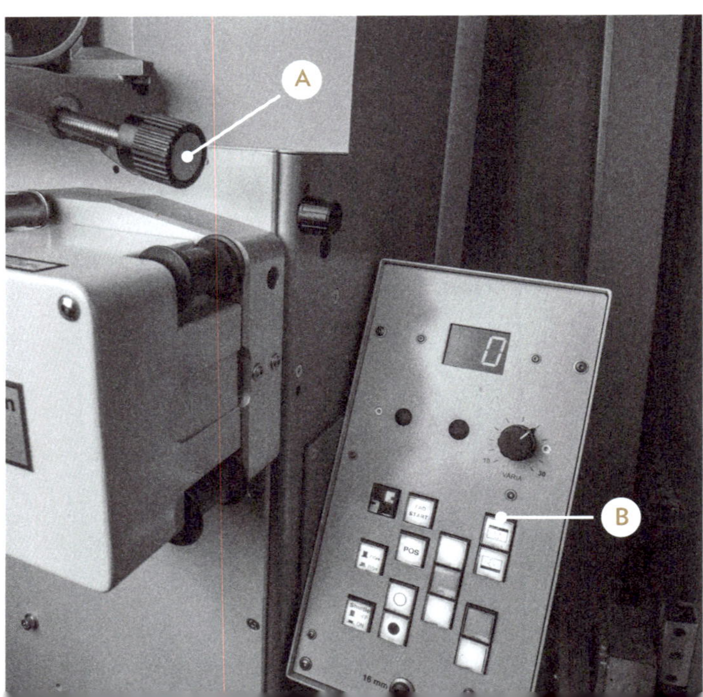

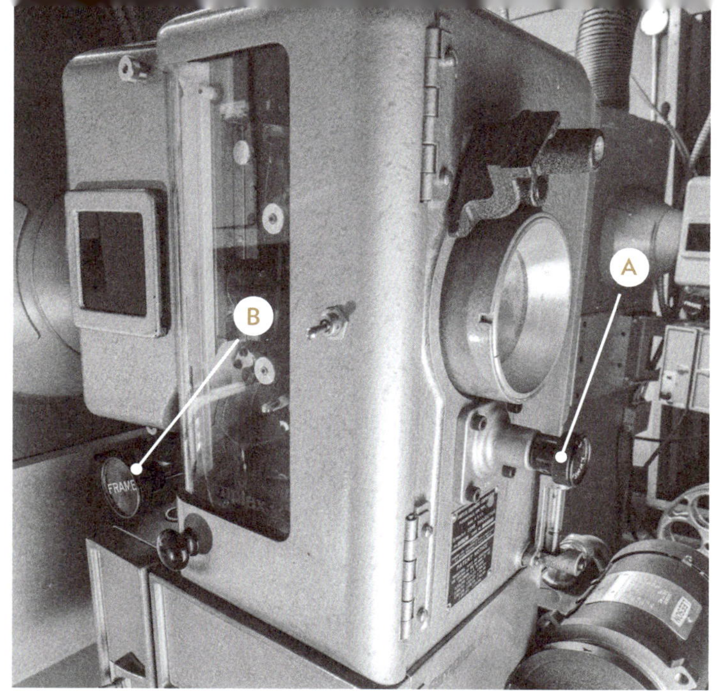

A. FOCUS ADJUSTMENT KNOB   B. FRAMING ADJUSTMENT KNOB

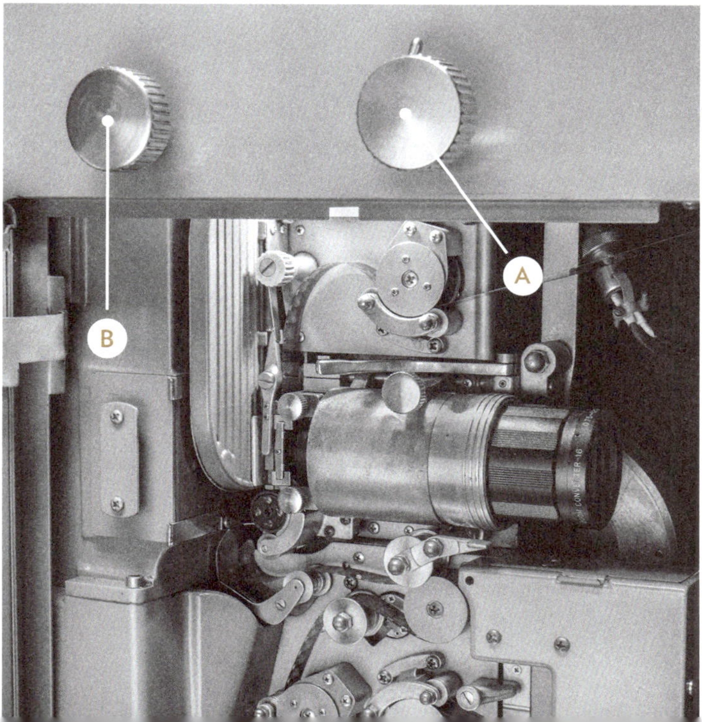

VERTICAL ALIGNMENT

When projecting anamorphic prints, such as CinemaScope films, it is necessary to address the radial orientation of the projected image to achieve proper vertical alignment. When placing an anamorphic lens assembly into the projector, the radial orientation is critical to maintaining proper image orientation on the screen. Depending on the brand of film projector, the vertical alignment of an anamorphic lens may be established when the lens is initially installed within the lens mount, collar, or holder. Some projectors may feature an alignment pin located above the lens area. An adjustable stop ring affixed to the lens collar of an anamorphic lens may be positioned so as to align with the pin on the projector, resulting in proper vertical alignment. If the vertical alignment of the anamorphic lens is not preset, or does not have a vertical alignment mechanism, then the projectionist must manually rotate the lens to achieve vertical alignment during this pre-focus stage.

While the film is running, loosen the lens clamp, and, holding the lens barrel so as not to shift any adjustable settings which may be incorporated into the lens, slowly rotate the lens while watching the image on screen. When the vertical lines within the image are straight up and down on the screen, correct alignment has been achieved, and the lens assembly may be secured in position.

Conversely, one can frame the image up or down to expose a frame line, then rotate the anamorphic attachment until the frame line is parallel to the top or bottom masking. Keep in mind that if the lens is moved forward or backward while rotating it, the image will go out of focus. *[Figures 7.11 and 7.12]*

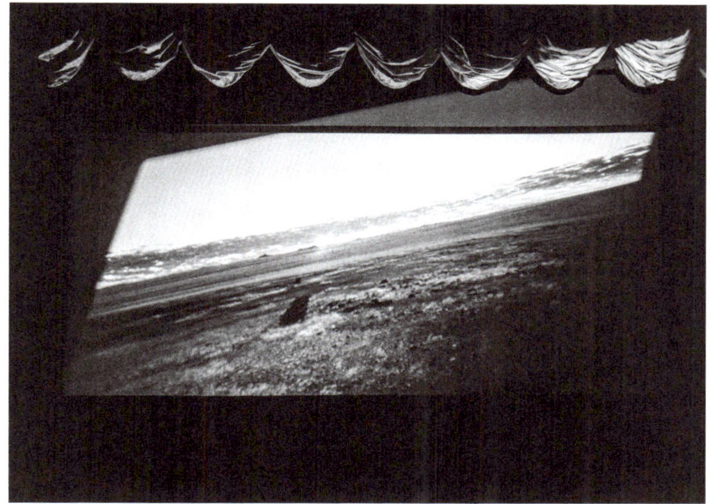

7.11

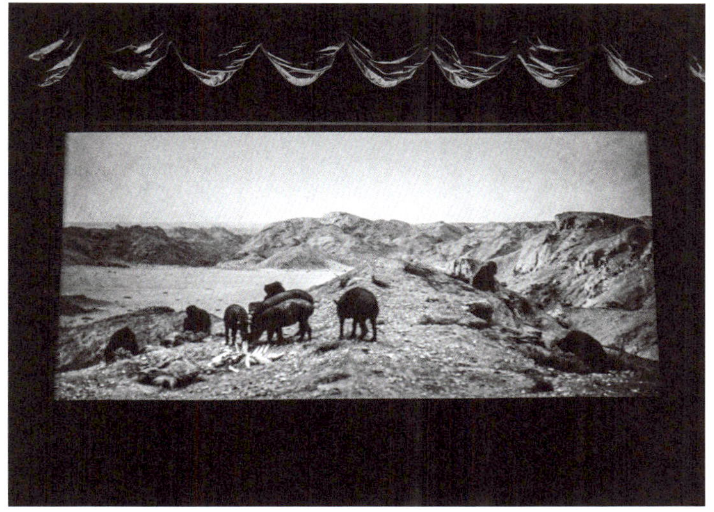

7.12

7.11 & 7.12 – An anamorphic image projected *out* of vertical alignment (above), and *in* vertical alignment (below) (*2001: A Space Odyssey*, Stanley Kubrick, UK/US 1968).

SOUND LEVEL

If there is a default volume level set for the theater, it is best to begin the sound check at this level. To properly monitor and judge the volume and quality of the audio, the projectionist or the theater manager should be in the auditorium for this step.

While checking the sound, the projectionist should listen for both dialogue and music levels. In some cases, music and effects tracks may be mixed louder than dialogue; by adjusting the sound level based solely on dialogue or music, there may be a discrepancy during the show, requiring audio levels to be adjusted. An optimum audio level enables dialogue to be heard clearly, without strain.

The projectionist should also check to ensure that all speakers are functioning properly. For mono optical tracks, the sound should be emanating from the center speaker (behind the screen). For non-Dolby stereo optical tracks, there should be separate audio coming from the left, center, and right speakers. For Dolby stereo optical tracks, there should be separate audio coming from the left, center, right, and surround speakers (one channel), with low frequencies reproduced by a separate subwoofer (if equipped). With DTS and SRD (Dolby Digital) digital audio tracks, there should be separate audio coming from the left, center, right, left-surround, and right-surround speakers, and subwoofer. Wiring configurations in theaters can vary, resulting in different outputs.

Some auditoriums may have left-center and right-center speakers behind the screen for separate audio channels provided by SDDS. SRD and DTS digital audio can also support extended surround channels, providing separate audio for a center-surround channel.

The acoustics of the theater will change as it is fills with people. Depending on the size of the crowd, it may be necessary to boost the audio level once the show has started. Once a satisfactory audio level is found, it is desirable to avoid further adjustment of the volume while the film is running.

SCREEN MASKING

The purpose of screen masking is twofold: to provide a crisp edge to the image, while masking (hiding) the unused portion of the screen. Projecting film onto a screen without masking results in an image with soft edges.

Painted black borders for the screen were in use during the silent film era to ensure that the picture had sharp margins, thereby improving the theatrical presentation. The evolution of film presentation resulted in multiple aspect ratios, which had to be followed on a case-by-case basis. A wide screen, with movable screen-masking fabric, was eventually developed in order to accommodate a variety of aspect ratios. *[Figures 7.13 and 7.14, see following page]*

A screen is properly masked when all edges of the image are sharp, with minimal spillover of image onto the masking material, and no unused (blank) screen space visible. When setting the masking during pre-show, it is best to avoid using dark scenes (e.g., credit sequences), as it is difficult to see the edge of the image or black frame line(s).

Theater auditoriums feature a variety of screen masking systems. Setting the masking varies considerably from one system to another. In some cases, there may not even be any masking to set. Portable screens used for small-gauge projection tend to be manufactured without any masking options.

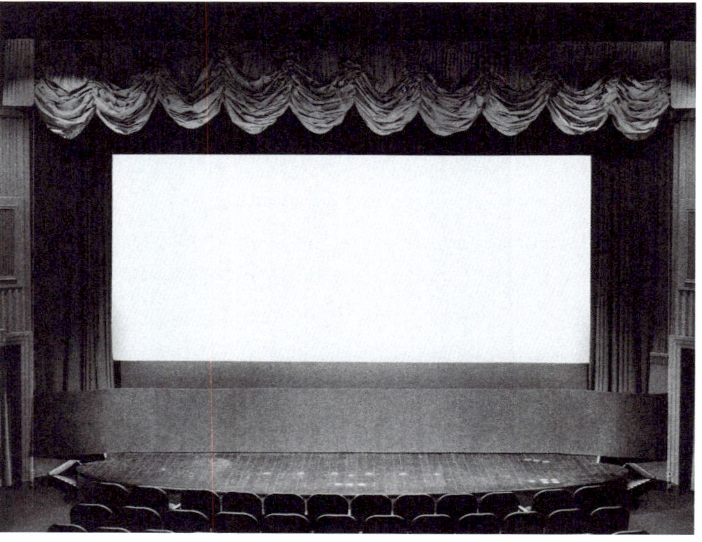

7.13 & 7.14 – Movable screen masking, set for 1.33:1 and
2.39:1 aspect ratios.

What follows is a very **brief summary of the two basic types of screen masking**:

- **Automatic masking** is set from the booth using a touchpad or switch corresponding to a given aspect ratio. With automatic masking, pre-programmed aspect ratios can be switched during a show. One possible disadvantage, however, is that these set-ups may lack the ability for fine adjustments of the masking. Furthermore, these systems are sometimes programmed to accommodate the most common aspect ratios (1.85:1 and 2.39:1).

- **Manual masking** is set at the screen itself, with the possible inclusion of hinged boards or curtain material activated via a traveler system. The masking position may be fine-tuned while setting the focus during the pre-show. There are also implications for switching aspect ratios during a show, as the projectionist may be required to exit the booth and take the time to adjust the masking manually, or ask an assistant to do this under the projectionist's instructions.

TWEAKS AND ADJUSTMENTS

This stage of the pre-focus process provides the projectionist with a final opportunity to assure that the film presentation is optimized, and, for older films, presented in a manner as close as possible to the way they were originally presented (minus the cigarette smoke in the auditorium). In addition to focus and audio level, observing the chosen aspect ratio for correctness, fine-tuning of the framing, screen masking, and adjustment of the projection speed for silent films, are all best accomplished while the film is running. From within the auditorium, the theater manager or an assistant projectionist should look for issues that could negatively affect the audience's experience of the film. It is important to address these matters before the auditorium opens to the public and the screening begins.

UNTHREADING THE PROJECTOR

After all the parameters are set and adjustments made, the projectionist should stop and unthread the projectors, rewind the film, and rethread the proper reels before showtime. In order to unthread the machine, the projectionist must first close the lamphouse douser, then stop the motor. The gate can now be opened, along with all sprocket pad rollers or shoes.

Since the projectionist may be unthreading the print mid-reel, it is extremely important that great care is taken when handling the film. The projectionist should avoid touching the image area of the film, handling the print from the edges only. Wearing clean cotton gloves during this process is recommended. When removing film from the sprockets, one should carefully lift it off the teeth, avoiding any contact with the open roller or shoe. Once the print has been disengaged from the sprockets, the projectionist can proceed to remove the film from the gate and unthread the projector, gently removing the film from the film path. The reels can then be rewound on the rewind bench or projector (if the projector is equipped for this).

DO'S AND DON'TS

ALWAYS

- Listen to both dialogue and music when determining the optimal sound levels for the show.

- Work with a theater manager to check image and sound quality from the auditorium, or do so directly with an assistant projectionist in the booth while the film is running.

- Have a monocular or a pair of binoculars in the booth in order to check that the film is in focus.

NEVER

- Open the auditorium to the public without having completed the pre-focus procedures.

- Take for granted that an automatic masking preset matches the aspect ratio of the print you are about to project.

- Touch the image and soundtrack area of the print with bare fingers when unthreading it after pre-focus.

233

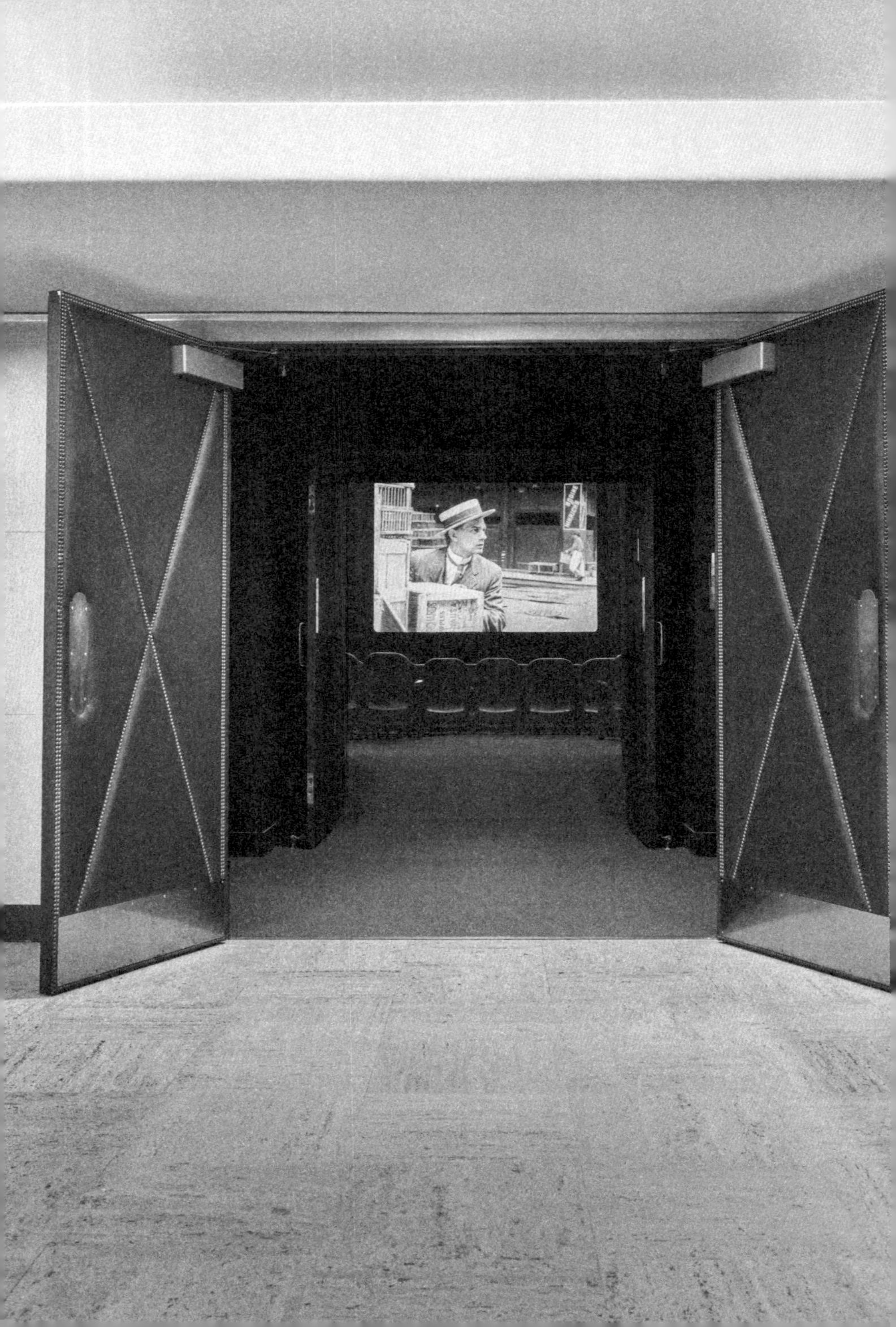

8

THE SHOW

THIS CHAPTER PROVIDES information on recommended film projection practices, along with solutions to some common problems that may occur during projection.

The first section addresses the **basic practices for projectionists**, outlining standard operations necessary for archival film projection.

The second section addresses **troubleshooting** specific issues that may arise during a show.

The information in this chapter is applicable to most locations where film is projected. To ensure the safety of the projectionist, the physical integrity of film prints, and the successful presentation of a screening, it is necessary for the projectionist to become familiar with the equipment, the venue, and any and all circumstances relevant to film exhibition.

Fig. 8.1 – **The time that a projectionist spends preparing and practicing culminates in the ultimate goal of projection: the exhibition of a cinematic work for an audience (*Too Much Johnson*, Orson Welles, US 1938).**

I. Basic Practices for the Projectionist

STARTING THE SHOW

In a film exhibition venue, there are a number of factors (aside from the film itself) that need to be addressed in conjunction with film presentations. These factors may include pre- and post-show music, auditorium lighting, on-screen display (if any) before and after the screening, film introduction, post-screening discussion, and curtain etiquette. It is not uncommon for the projectionist to manage these operations from the booth, so it is important that there is communication with the theater manager to establish the proper protocols for these procedures. Presentations involving guests, multiple media, or nitrate film may require the scheduling of an additional operator. Audio or video recording of guests may also be required.

Before going any further, it is time to draw attention to three things a projectionist should **never** do at any time during the show:

- Leave the projection booth unattended while a projector is running.
- Bring food or liquids into the projection booth. (This also applies to all the other activities held in the booth before and after the show.)
- Allow unauthorized personnel in the booth, under any circumstances. Film exhibition requires a high degree of mental concentration and physical coordination. Therefore, nobody must stand in the way of the projectionist in the course of the performance, unless the operator has explicitly agreed otherwise.

A successful film presentation begins long before showtime. Preparation of the film print and projectors is covered in the previous two chapters. Before the auditorium is opened to the public, however, additional preparations are in order. Through effective communication, the projectionist and the theater manager should be on the same page about the protocol for the screening. A wide array of decisions need to be made in advance of the show.

Most screenings follow a protocol that becomes second-nature to the projectionist. Guests and special events require advanced planning so that the projectionist can accommodate the technical and operational requirements of the presentation. Equipment may need to be procured, and contractors or additional booth personnel may have to be hired for the occasion. To successfully present a show, the projectionist must have all the information and resources available well in advance to perform technical checks and make sure that everything is in working order prior to the presentation.

Before the auditorium opens to the public, everything in the booth should be ready for the presentation: pre-focus complete, pre-show music and on-screen display (if any) playing, auditorium lighting and curtain (if any) set, microphone level(s) preset (and muted to prevent amplifying ambient noise or pranksters), booth equipment powered-up, sound format selected, Reels 1 and 2 properly threaded on the projectors, and booth lighting set for show mode. Many booths have general lighting for routine activities and task lighting for work within the booth during projection. Prior to opening the auditorium to the public, adjust the projection booth lighting to avoid any unwanted spill of light into the auditorium. Once all of this is set, the pre-showtime period allows the projectionist time to communicate with the theater manager, address last-minute details in the booth, or take a bathroom break.

While it is not required to have Reels 1 and 2 threaded on the projectors before the auditorium opens to the public, make sure they are properly threaded before showtime.

Once the show begins, projectionists becomes performers as well, focusing their actions on the requirements of the show. Their undivided attention to the presentation onscreen and to the operation of film equipment in the booth requires that there are no distractions. Securing the entrance(s) to the projection booth during screenings is necessary to minimize any interference from the outside. Keeping the booth locked when not in use, and whenever film prints are within, is also a recommended practice.

Before we begin our film exhibition, let's take a moment to address curtain etiquette. For screening venues which incorporate traveling or rising curtains in front of the screen, setting a protocol for use of the curtain (and auditorium light levels) with film presentations is very important. This protocol should be agreed upon well ahead of the show, and communicated to all projection staff.

The projector lamps should be struck (turned on) several minutes before the screening begins. This allows time for their arcs to stabilize. Before striking the lamps, however, make sure that the projection exhaust system is also turned on, and that the lamphouse dousers are closed.

The first rule that a projectionist should learn is to keep the lamphouse douser closed until the film is running through the gate. If film is sitting still in the gate with the projector lamp on and the douser open, the film will melt, or, if it is nitrate stock, burst into flames.

With a two-projector set-up (a requirement for projecting archival film prints), before the show begins, the picture and sound should be activated on the projector that is *not* going to be running the first reel of film. This way, when the projector with the first reel is started, no audio will be heard as the countdown leader passes across the sound head.

When showtime finally arrives, an agreed procedure should be followed for dimming the auditorium lights and opening the curtain. Once the lights are down, the projectionist should begin projecting the first reel as quickly as possible, to avoid leaving the audience waiting in the dark for too long. Start the motor on the projector carrying the first reel. As soon as it's running at full speed (a couple of seconds), open the lamphouse douser. Watch the film as it passes through the picture head. After the countdown leader passes through the gate, and before the first image or sound appear, activate the picture and sound changeover for that machine. This will allow the image and sound to project into the auditorium without cutting off the beginning of the film.

CHANGEOVERS

The two-projector system for motion picture projection — requiring manual changeovers between the projectors from one reel of film to the next — was the standard in film exhibition for most of the 20th century. The advent of xenon lamps and platter projection technology eliminated the need for two-projector systems in commercial theaters. The dual projection system, however, remains the standard for film museums, archives, and repertory screening venues wishing to exhibit prints of preserved films, which are not allowed to be cut or spliced under any circumstances.

To properly exhibit multiple-reel film prints with a two-projector set-up, it is necessary to perform a picture and sound changeover at the end of each reel in order to properly transition the picture and audio from one projector to the other. This process is known as the **changeover**. Performing precisely timed projector changeovers ensures a film's smooth, uninterrupted exhibition.

Changeovers are governed by **two sets of visual cues**, appearing within the image **at the tail end of each reel**. These cues, located in the **upper-right corner** of the image, can take many shapes and forms, but their function is always the same: to indicate to the projectionist when to start the motor of the projector, and when to change over the picture and sound to that projector.

The first set of cues appearing on screen is the **Motor Start cue (MS)**. The second set is the **Changeover cue (CO)**. The MS cue signals the moment when a projectionist should start the motor of the incoming projector; the CO cue indicates when to change-over the picture and sound to the incoming projector. This topic has been thoroughly discussed in Chapter 5.

Used in conjunction with the Motor Start and Changeover cues, located at the end of each reel, are the **countdown leaders**, which are located at the head of each subsequent reel. The count-down leader allows the projectionist to thread the film in the projector to a point that is in advance of the beginning of the reel, typically 8 or 9 feet. During projection, as one reel of film nears the end, the other projector is activated. As the film on the outgoing projector approaches the end of the reel, the film on the incoming projector is nearing the beginning of the reel. Achiev-ing a perfect transition between reels is dependent upon proper timing of the changeover between the outgoing and incoming reels. This is where the art and craft of manual changeover pro-jection comes in. A combined knowledge of the process, of the projection equipment, and of the film print itself is crucial in the achievement of a flawless cinematic performance.

THREADING THE COUNTDOWN LEADER FOR CHANGEOVERS

The basics of threading the countdown leader in the projector have already been explained in Chapter 6. It is now time to apply this knowledge to changeover projection: the goal is to ensure that no image or sound are truncated at the time of transition to the next reel. The type of countdown used (SMPTE vs. Academy) is not important, but its completeness is. An incomplete countdown can mislead the projectionist when threading a projector, resulting in the beginning of the reel passing through the gate before the changeover process is conducted.

Keep in mind that SMPTE countdown is calibrated in seconds with 24 frames per number, and that Academy countdown is calibrated in feet, with 16 frames per number. Upon inspecting the film, it is important to check and assure that each countdown is complete. A few frames short may not make a great difference at the time of projection; but missing more than a few frames can affect the presentation by cutting off the beginning of a reel.

Threading film in the projector to the proper point is an important part of the changeover process. Changeover projection is all about timing. The projectionist is responsible for performing the transitions from one reel to the next so that the audience is unaware of any interruption in the presentation. Coordinating the threading of each projector with the spacing of cues on each reel allows the projectionist to perform successful, virtually invisible changeovers. Improperly timed changeovers can result in the end of a reel being cut off, the beginning of a reel being cut off, or a gap of time appearing between two reels. These occurrences can and must be avoided.

Much of what we are about to explain has been outlined in Chapter 5, but is worth repeating here. According to SMPTE specification, Motor Start and Changeover cues are placed 172 frames apart. With the film running at 24 frames per second (sound speed), this equals a time of 7.16 seconds between cues. In order to properly time the transition from one reel to the next, it is necessary to thread each projector to a specific distance before the beginning of the reel. Since SMPTE specification cues are spaced 10 feet plus 12 frames on 35mm film, one might assume that threading a 35mm film projector to a point of 10 feet plus 12 frames before the reel begins would be appropriate. This would not take into account, however, the reaction time of the projectionist (to see the cues and start the incoming projector), or the brief time it takes for the incoming projector to get up to full speed. These factors may seem minor, but they are important when addressing the split-second timing of changeovers. Therefore, to perform successfully timed changeovers, it is necessary to thread the projectors to a point that is shorter than the distance between Motor Start and Changeover cues. On 35mm motion picture projectors the threading distance is normally 8 or 9 feet. The precise distance should be determined based on the ramp-up speed of projectors and the reaction time of the projectionist.

Changeover timing can be further complicated when cue marks are not located per SMPTE specification. Astute projectionists can address this issue by adjusting the threading distance of any reel based on the cue spacing of the previous reel.

In this context, it is good to memorize the following tips:
- To compensate for cues which are placed **less** than 172 frames apart, measure the distance between the cues (in frames) and subtract this number *from* 172. With the resulting number of frames, thread the following reel on the projector that many frames **closer** to the beginning of the reel than you normally would.

- To compensate for cues which are placed **more** than 172 frames apart, measure the distance between the cues (in frames) and subtract 172 from the measured number. With the resulting number of frames, thread the following reel on the projector that many frames **farther** from the beginning of the reel than you normally would.

A dedicated projectionist can receive great satisfaction from performing impeccable changeovers at all times, regardless of the material condition of film prints. Another example of the art and craft of cinema projection!

CHANGEOVER MECHANISMS

There are **four mechanisms involved in performing manual changeover projection**:

1. The first mechanism is the **projector motor**, typically activated by a flip or push-button switch. Located on the projector itself or nearby, the switch activates and deactivates the projector motor, turning the projector on and off.
2. The second mechanism is the **lamphouse douser**, located on the front of the lamphouse. The douser is manually opened after the projector is turned on, with film running through the gate.
3. The third mechanism is the **picture changeover device**, usually electro-mechanical in design. Located atop or within the picture head of each projector, this mechanism contains a metal shutter which either blocks or unblocks the light from the lamphouse entering the picture aperture of the projector. This device is activated by a switch, which may be a button, lever, foot pedal, or flip-switch located on or near the projector. Manual activation of the mechanism may also be possible. On two-projector systems, the picture changeover

mechanisms are generally wired to each other, so that when activated the mechanism on one projector opens while the mechanism on the other projector closes. This prevents images from both projectors from being on-screen at the same time. *[Figure 2.13. see page 57]*

4. The fourth mechanism is the **sound changeover**, which is primarily an electronic function. When activated by a switch located on or near the projector, the sound changeover mechanism cuts electrical power to the sound head of one projector while supplying electrical power to the sound head of the other projector. The component affected may be the light source, the reader (optical or magnetic), or both.

Depending on the equipment installation in the booth, the picture and sound changeover mechanisms may be activated by one switch (accomplishing both), or by separate switches. Greater coordination is required for changeovers involving separate switches for picture and sound, as they need to be activated simultaneously. *[Figures 8.2 and 8.3]*

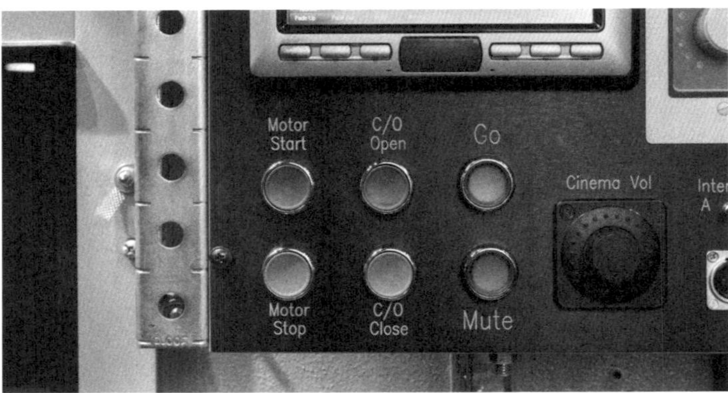

8.2 – **Control panel with switches for motor start and changeover (integrated picture and sound).**

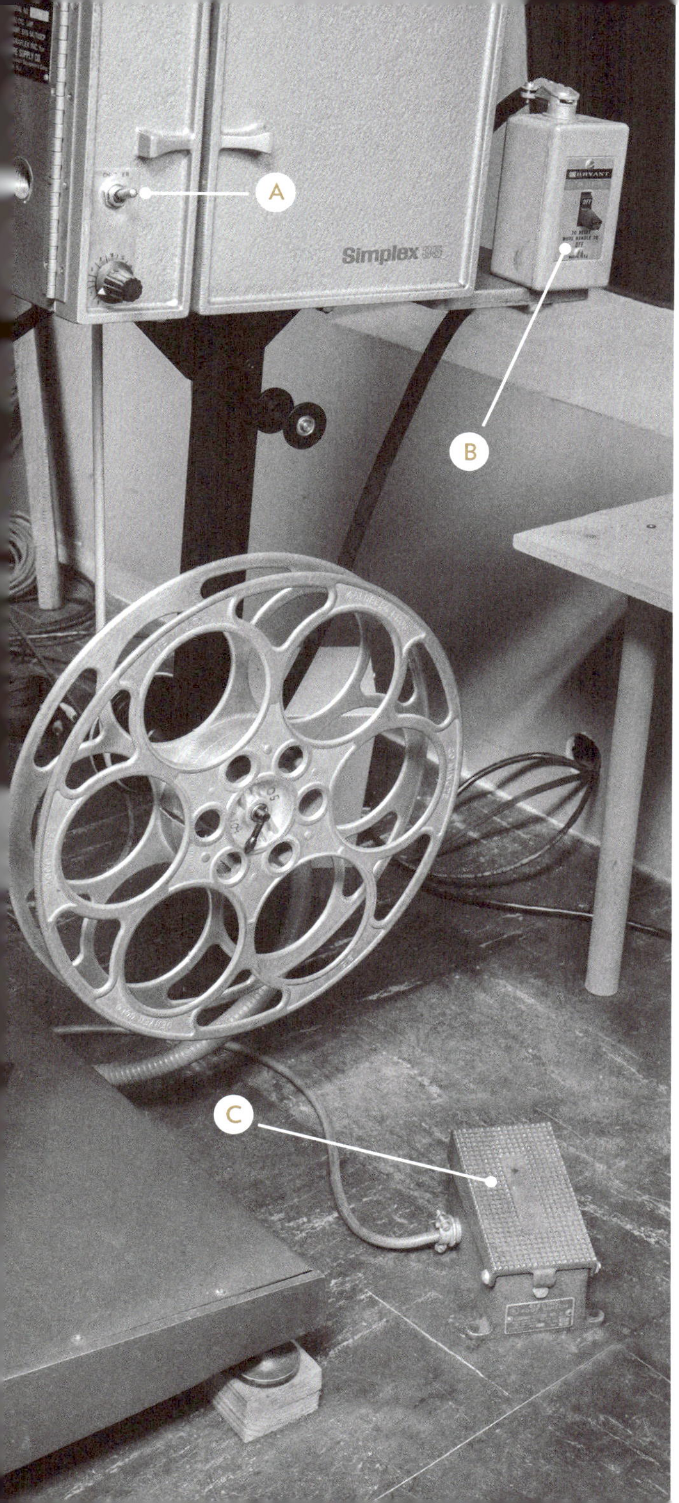

8.3 –

Separate switches
for activating
motor start, picture
changeover, and
sound changeover.

A. SOUND
   CHANGEOVER
   SWITCH

B. MOTOR
   START SWITCH

C. PICTURE
   CHANGEOVER
   PEDAL

PERFORMING A CHANGEOVER

Making a seamless changeover requires keen observation, coordination, and ongoing practice. The actual process is straightforward and easy to understand. The following steps demonstrate the process, describing the first changeover from Reel 1 to Reel 2. Projector 1, the outgoing projector, contains Reel 1, and Projector 2, the incoming projector, contains Reel 2. These steps should be applied to every changeover throughout the film presentation. Both lamphouses are on at this point.

Step 1: As Reel 1 nears the end, position yourself near the Motor Start and Changeover controls of Projector 2, with the ability to clearly see the screen.

Step 2: Watch closely for the **Motor Start cue** in the upper-right corner of the screen. When it appears, activate the motor of Projector 2.

Step 3: Observe and listen to Projector 2 as it starts up. Ensure the film is running smoothly and feeding/taking-up correctly.

Step 4: If the film is running properly, open the lamphouse douser of Projector 2.

Step 5: Watch the screen closely for the designated **Changeover cue** in the upper-right corner of the screen. When it appears, activate the picture and sound changeover switch(es) for Projector 2. This will block the picture and sound from Projector 1, and allow the picture and sound from Projector 2 to reach the screen.

Step 6: Observe and listen to ensure that Projector 2 is operating correctly. Watch the screen for any framing or focusing problems, and listen for any variations in the soundtrack. Make the appropriate adjustments if necessary.

Step 7: Turn off the motor and close the lamphouse douser on Projector 1. Remove Reel 1 from the take-up spindle, clean the film path in the projector, and thread the next reel for projection.

Repeat Steps 1 – 7 until the final reel.

Performing changeovers requires much from a projectionist in a very short period of time — the time between MS and CO cues is less than 8 seconds for film running at 24 fps. It is important for the projectionist to be prepared and focused to perform this task. Technical familiarity with projection equipment and practice with changeovers will build confidence and allow the operator to develop the split-second timing skills to perform smooth change-overs. Ironically, the best compliment projectionists can receive is that no one has noticed their work. The focus of an audience should remain on the film itself, not on its presentation.

BETWEEN REELS

When projecting film, it is best practice to **clean the film path between each reel**. This promotes the longevity and integrity of the film print and equipment. It is important to remove any dirt or build-up from the film path that may scratch a print or adversely affect any mechanical part of the projector over time. Areas to focus on include the gate/trap, sprocket drives, pad rollers or shoes, and the intermittent. A thorough brushing with a dry, soft toothbrush can be accompanied by a wipe-down with a cleaning cloth. Compressed air can be used to address the least accessible areas, if and when necessary.

Between changeovers, the projectionist is responsible for handling the reels which have just been projected and preparing the projectors for the following reels. This involves rewinding the previous reel and threading the next reel.

Even though venues may have different set-ups and equipment, the following tips and guidelines are useful in ensuring that the show runs efficiently and that the film is handled properly:

- Use only metal house reels in good condition (preferably new) for feed- and take-up reels, regardless of what the film print is shipped on.
- Ensure that each reel of film involved in a given show has been inspected, is heads-out, properly wound and labeled, and easily accessible.
- Threading a projector during a show is different from threading a projector before the show. Threading which occurs before a show is often accomplished in an environment with ample light, relatively low noise levels, and without urgent time constraints. During a show, the projectionist is normally working in a darkened booth with loud, operating machinery, the film soundtrack playing through booth monitors, and the necessity of getting the next reel threaded in time for the changeover. Have threading diagrams for all projectors in easily visible places (they may be placarded onto the projector itself), and, if necessary, carry a small flashlight or headlamp for spot-checking the threading pattern and reading the diagram.
- If the projectors have a mechanical intermittent, remember to manually advance the projector motor by hand until the intermittent comes to rest (its stopped position) before threading the projector.
- Once a reel has been threaded in the projector, check and double-check that:
    a. Feed and take-up reels are secured on their spindles, and that the film is oriented properly.
    b. The film has been correctly positioned within the aperture (in-frame) and threaded to its proper location in the countdown.
    c. The film has a sufficient upper loop and lower loop, and is in registration with the intermittent and all drive sprockets.

    d. The film path matches the threading diagram and there
    is no unnecessary contact between the film and the
    equipment.

- Have a system in place for rewinding and storing film reels
  after they have been shown. Once a reel runs through the
  projector, it will be necessary to remove the film and replace the
  take-up reel. Have plenty of empty reels in good condition on
  hand during the show, kept in an easily accessible location.
  Decide where to temporarily store film once it screens and
  when to rewind the film off the take-up reels. Some venues
  allow rewinding of film during a screening, while others require
  the projectionist to wait until the end of a show.

- Prevent film damage during rewind by handling the film
  with the utmost care. Winding film back onto cores or reels
  requires attention and diligence. If left unattended, high-
  speed rewinding can damage lots of film very quickly! When
  rewinding film onto a reel or core, *always start the rewind
  slowly*, and monitor the wind to make sure the film pack is
  smooth, without any film edges sticking out (protruding
  edges are asking to be damaged!). When possible, acquire a
  collection of plastic reels in good condition (as giveaways),
  in order to replace reels that arrive damaged. Secure the end
  of the reel (6 inches of a low-tack adhesive tape, often
  referred to as "artist tape," is recommended) to prevent the
  film from unwinding during shipment. *[Figures 8.4 and 8.5.
  see following page]*

Threading, rewinding, and properly storing film once it has been
projected are important parts of running a show and preserving
the physical integrity of the film print. Your meticulousness and
care are critical for a film's health and well-being, and its ability
to be presented in the future.

8.4

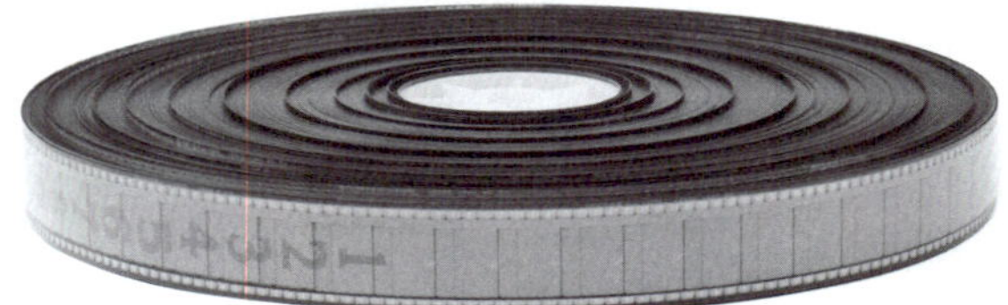

8.5

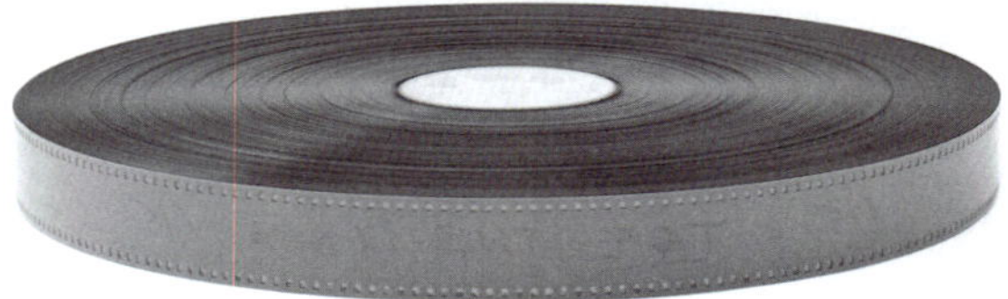

8.4 & 8.5 – Uneven film winds (top) expose film edges to potential damage. Smooth film winds (bottom) are critical to prevent edge damage to film prints during handling and transit.

FOCUSING AND FRAMING THE IMAGE

Setting the focus and framing for a show should occur before the show begins (see the section "Focus and Framing" in Chapter 7). However, it may also be necessary to adjust the focus and framing while the film is running. It is the projectionist's responsibility to accomplish any adjustments in a timely fashion, without distracting the audience.

The following guidelines can be useful in minimizing disruption to the viewing experience:

- Be mindful of focusing and framing immediately following the changeovers, as this is when shifts in sharpness and image orientation are most likely to occur.
- If the film print is warped, image sharpness may be adversely affected. When projecting warped film, the projectionist should pay close attention to focus, as image focus is more likely to change unexpectedly. Increasing gate tension may help with focus stability of warped prints.
- Out-of-frame splices are bound to alter the framing of the image when they pass through the projector gate. *Always thoroughly inspect film before projection and repair any suspect splices.*
- If framing needs adjustment mid-reel, making the adjustment during a shot in which the camera is moving will be less noticeable to the audience. Framing adjustments are far more noticeable during shots with a static camera.

SOUND ADJUSTMENTS

When projecting sound film in a theater, it may be necessary to raise or lower the volume level during a show. Although sound levels are usually set before the show, the perceived volume can change with the amount of people in the auditorium (see the section "Sound Level" in Chapter 7).

The following suggestions are intended to achieve an enjoyable audio experience for the audience:

- The theater manager should be in the theater at all times, but especially during the first reel, and should *listen to both the music and dialogue* of a given soundtrack to assess whether or not the sound levels need adjustment.
- If the sound levels *do* need adjustment, make changes slowly to avoid abrupt changes in volume and minimize disruption of the viewing experience.
- Keep open lines of communication with the theater manager, who should report any problems or complaints regarding the sound.

ENDING THE SHOW

It is important to have established procedures in place to end the screening gracefully, to allow the audience to exit safely, or to set the stage for guests for a post-screening discussion. Auditorium lighting, curtain operation, exit music, and microphone(s) are components which the projectionist will need to address in consultation with the theater manager. If guests are to be recorded (audio or video), the projectionist may be involved in these activities.

Once the show is over, the projectionist still has a number of duties to perform regarding equipment maintenance and storage of the film print.

1. **Ending the Last Reel**
   - The Film Inspection Report (see Appendix A) should indicate how a film ends by providing a description of the last image that the audience should see, and how it ends (e.g., "The End" title fades to black). This informs the projectionist when to shut off the image and sound of the film to end the show. This is important because you do not want to ruin the end of the presentation by bombarding the audience with disruptive audio or imagery (such as laboratory leader at the tail of a reel) not intended for the audience to see and hear! If, during inspection, it is discovered that a print ends with a long sequence of image without audio activity, muting the audio during this sequence will prevent the audience from hearing any dirt or damage on the audio track. Likewise, if a film ends with exit music and no image, closing the lamphouse douser during this section will prevent the audience from seeing scratches in the film, if they are present.
   - The most efficient way to end the show is to perform a changeover to the "dead projector" (the other projector no longer in use).
   - Once the image and sound have been cut, bring up the house lights and lower the curtain following established procedures. Play exit music, if appropriate.
   - If a post-screening discussion is scheduled, change the applicable settings on the audio equipment to allow for microphone amplification within the auditorium. Monitor the session for proper audio levels. Be prepared to audio-record the discussion, if equipped and requested.
2. **Storing the Print**
   - Carefully rewind the reels onto large cores or shipping reels. Monitor for a smooth wind, and be sure to secure the

loose ends with at least 6 inches of low-tack artist tape. Place the wound cores or reels securely in their cans and/or shipping containers.

- Complete any necessary reports (for the screening venue or film distributor) and inform the print provider of any film damage incurred, or about problems with the print.
- Return the print to a secure storage location or properly prepare and package it for shipment.

3. **Cleaning the Projectors**

- Use a toothbrush, cleaning cloth, and compressed air to clean the entire film path. With more time for cleaning than in-between changing reels during projection, now is the time to perform a thorough job of cleaning. Pipe cleaners are handy for cleaning in hard-to-reach areas of the projectors. In addition to the film path, the projectionist may choose to clean the projector surfaces, lenses, port glass, and floor.
- Remove the projector gates for cleaning and store them nearby for the next screening.
- Release the tension on any spring-tension parts (most commonly the trap and pad rollers or shoes).

4. **Turning Off the Equipment**

- Given the variety of equipment and electrical configurations in any projection booth, it is impractical to suggest a specified sequence for powering-down equipment. However, a generic **shut-down sequence** may follow this order:
  a. Turn off the projection lamps first, in order to conserve lamp hours and allow lamps to cool;
  b. Exciter lamps (optical sound);
  c. Amplifiers;
  d. Booth monitors;
  e. Audio racks;

 f. Rectifiers / lamphouse power supplies;

 g. Exhaust system.

Note: Do not turn off the rectifiers or exhaust system until the lamphouses are cool to the touch.

The recommended practices outlined in this chapter are fundamentals of good projection, and contribute to both the quality of the presentation and the care of the film print and equipment.

The next section will offer recommendations for addressing some general problems which may occur during a screening.

II. Troubleshooting

Once a show is underway, the projectionist should be vigilant and prepared to address any issues that could disrupt a screening, damage the film, or harm the equipment. Equipment failure, film breaks, poor image or sound quality, or other issues, are always a possibility. A thorough knowledge of projection booth equipment and functions, along with a **calm demeanor**, are the best tools for diagnosing a problem and implementing a solution.

Communication with the theater manager is important when addressing issues that affect the presentation. If an issue arises that requires stopping the show for more than a few seconds, it is important to raise the lights in the auditorium. Never leave an audience sitting in the dark. This creates anxiety, and is a safety hazard. Raising the auditorium lights will also indicate to the theater manager that you are aware of and addressing a problem.

Any damage to a print should be reported to the print provider. Some organizations prefer to make their own repairs should damage occur; in this case, the screening venue must inform the print provider that the repair has taken place.

Any mechanical malfunctions should be noted, preferably in logs maintained for each projector. (See Appendix B.) This information is very useful for tracking problems and addressing repair work. Any repair work should also be noted in the projector logs.

UNSTEADY PICTURE

The mechanics of film projection necessitate a constant state of movement of the film while passing through the projector. Despite this fact, the image on screen should appear stable, without any movement induced by the projector. **Jump**, **weave**, and **focus fluctuation** are types of instability which can be evident on the screen.

Jump is vertical movement of the image. Jump can be caused by multiple factors, such as an upper loop that is too large, improper gate tension, or a worn or faulty intermittent mechanism. Regulating the loop size when threading film and adjusting the gate tension when projecting film allow for control of these factors. If you suspect a projector's intermittent to be worn or faulty, inspect the device when not projecting or contact a qualified technician.

Weave is horizontal or lateral movement of the image. It is usually caused by malfunctioning lateral guide-rollers in the picture head. It is not practical to address these rollers while the film is running. If you notice weave on a particular projector, inspect and service these rollers between screenings or after a show. If you are unfamiliar with servicing rollers, consult the projector's manual or contact a qualified technician.

The *SMPTE RP 40 Projector Alignment and Image Quality Test Film* is a valuable diagnostic tool to determine the amount of jump and weave that a projector may have, using particular target areas printed on the film. Other target areas allow you to measure lens resolution, verify focus, identify aspect ratios, and observe "ghosting." Using the *SMPTE RP 40* test film enables you to assess the performance and optics of your projectors. *[Figure 8.6]*

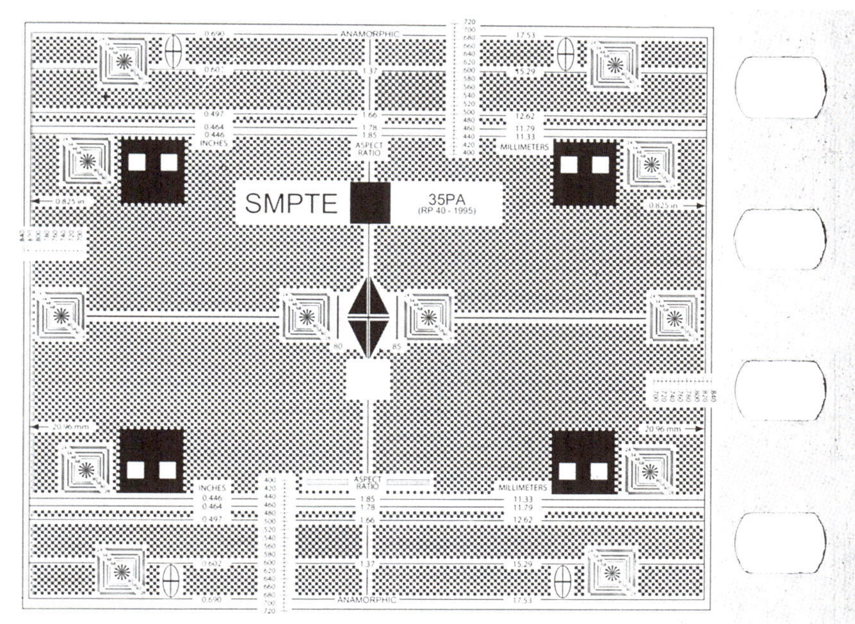

8.6 — *SMPTE RP 40* test film. Frame enlargement from a 35mm acetate print. © SMPTE

Focus fluctuation — the inability to maintain sharp focus within a film presentation — may be caused by a number of factors: warped film prints, poor optics (for instance, old lenses, or fast lenses with poor depth of focus), and focus "flutter."

- **Warped film prints** present a challenge, as there is nothing you can do to improve the flatness of the film print. Projecting the film in a curved-gate projector may yield slightly more stable focus. Increasing gate tension may also be of some help. Employing lenses with a greater depth of focus should result in a lesser focus fluctuation on the screen.

- Projecting with **old lenses** can have adverse effects on every screening. The lens elements within older lenses are generally cemented in place. As the cement ages and dries, elements within the lens may shift, affecting the ability to focus the image. The capability of attaining focus across the width of the screen may be lost. Moisture condensation within a lens, scratched lens surfaces, and damaged lens coatings also negatively affect the image quality on the screen.

- **Fast lenses**, designed with a larger aperture diameter to allow for greater transmission of light, provide less depth of focus (comparable to depth of field in photography). Warped prints and accentuated projection angles make it more difficult to attain focus across the entire width or height of the screen with fast lenses. Slower lenses increase the ability to maintain focus across the image plane. The speed of lenses is usually indicated by f-stop or t-stop numbers. The lower the number, the faster the lens.

- **Focus "flutter"** is an effect that occurs within the gate of the projector when each film frame is momentarily exposed to the light and heat intensity of the projector lamp. The sudden exposure to the heat component of the light source causes the film frame to buckle temporarily when first exposed. The minute movement of the film plane can have an adverse influence on focus. Projectors with two-blade shutters expose each frame of film twice before advancing to the next frame. High-speed capture studies about focus "flutter" show that the frame flexes less on its second exposure to light or heat.

There are at least two ways **to minimize focus "flutter"**:

a. Incorporating heat filters within the lamphouse to minimize transmission of heat to the picture head.

b. Employing slower lenses on the projectors to increase depth of focus of the image upon the screen, thereby minimizing focus instability caused by the movement of each frame.

FILM BREAKS

Film breaks are a fact of life when it comes to film projection. Inspecting film prints prior to screening, a mandatory practice, is the most effective way to avoid film breaks. As each reel is inspected, any film damage should be documented and repaired.

Polyester film stock is stronger and more durable than either acetate or nitrate film stock. As nitrate, diacetate, or triacetate film stock ages, it tends to shrink and become brittle, especially when stored in environments that are not climate-controlled for long-term film storage. Handling a film during inspection will provide a good indication of the flexibility remaining in a print.

Acetate film stock was widely used for 35mm and 16mm projection prints prior to the introduction of polyester film stocks in the mid-1990s. Nitrate film stock was widely used for 35mm projection prints before it was discontinued (in the United States) in 1952. Therefore, the handling and projection of acetate and nitrate film requires greater care to avoid film breaks during projection.

Handling a film break during a show should follow a set of procedures which minimize damage to the film and allow the projectionist to resume the show as quickly as possible. Staying in close proximity to the operating projector during a show is the surest way to minimize damage and interruption in the event of a film break.

A recommended set of procedures follows:

a. As soon as a film break occurs, immediately close the lamp-house douser, mute the audio, and turn off the projector motor. It is important to do so in exactly this order, to prevent the film from burning or melting in the projector aperture and feeding or unraveling within the projector. **This is critically important when projecting flammable nitrate film, in order to prevent a fire from starting! Once a nitrate film catches fire, it cannot be extinguished.**

b. Turn on the lights in the auditorium so that patrons are not sitting in the dark.

c. Wind the "tail end" of the broken film onto the take-up reel and remove the take-up reel from the projector, setting it aside for later repairs. **Do not attempt a quick repair.** Save this procedure for later, when you have time to perform a quality repair.

d. Remove any film remaining in the film path and manually advance the projector, looking and listening for mechanical malfunction.

e. If no mechanical failure is evident, place an empty take-up reel on the projector and rethread the projector with the remaining film.

f. Lower the auditorium lights and restart the show, using standard start-up procedures.

DEBRIS IN THE GATE

Another common problem when projecting film is the possibility of dirt, hair, or other small debris becoming trapped in the projector gate. Any small object caught in the light path will cast a distracting shadow on the screen, especially with smaller-gauge projection. Furthermore, any object trapped in the gate has the potential to scratch or damage the film.

Three approaches are recommended:

a. Cleaning dirty film prints. Hair, dirt, and fibers on film prints are the most common cause of visible debris in the gate. Ultrasonically cleaning a dirty film print is the surest way of presenting a show without accumulations in the gate.

b. Preventative maintenance will help minimize accumulations in the picture head. Regularly clean all components related to the light path, with particular emphasis on the gate, trap, aperture plate, lenses, and port glass.

c. While the film is running in the projector, use compressed air to remove any objects which become lodged in the trap or aperture plate. If using canned compressed air, hold the can upright, and use short bursts to remove the unwanted object(s). It is best to position yourself perpendicular to the light path and to use the plastic extension nozzle that often comes with the can. Follow any safety instructions printed on the compressed-air container.

LOSING A LOOP

Properly sized upper and lower film loops in the picture head allow film to travel safely between the constant-feed sprockets and the intermittent sprocket. Occasionally, a loop may shrink, or be lost entirely, due to a loss of engagement between the perforations and the sprocket teeth. Losing one of the loops can subject the film to damage, make the image jump on screen, and cause the film to rattle loudly in the gate.

Losing a loop tends to occur more commonly with 16mm projectors, which employ a claw mechanism for film advancement.

Thick splices, blocked perforations, poor perforation repairs, and torn perforations are the most common causes affecting loops. Diligent film inspection and repair can prevent this problem. When a loop is lost, it is important to respond quickly in order to prevent damage to the film and to the projection equipment.

If a loop is lost **(35mm)**:

a. Immediately close the lamphouse douser, mute the audio, and turn off the projector motor. This will help prevent further damage to the film.

b. Turn on the lights in the auditorium so that patrons are not sitting in the dark.

c. Examine the film for damage. It may be necessary to examine it further and repair it after the screening.

d. Remake the loop(s) to the proper size, check the film threading path, and manually advance the projector, looking and listening for mechanical malfunction.

e. If no mechanical failure is evident, lower the auditorium lights and resume the show, using standard start-up procedures.

f. If a mechanical malfunction is evident, immediately inform the theater manager, and avoid using that projector until proper repair can be made. Consider finishing the show using the other projector, with brief interruptions between the reels (the theater manager should inform the audience accordingly).

If a Loop is lost **(16mm)**:

a. If the projector has a loop-former, activate this function
   immediately to try resetting the loop. This may fix the
   problem right away.

b. If Step 1 doesn't fix the problem, stop the projector and
   follow the same steps (a) – (f) described for 35mm projection.

DO'S AND DON'TS

ALWAYS

- Use only metal reels in excellent condition for the feed- and take-up reels.

- Keep the lamphouse douser closed until the film is running through the projector gate.

- At the beginning of the show, activate picture and sound on the projector that is *not* going to be running the first reel of film.

- Clean the film path of the projector at the end of each reel and after each show.

- Keep a clear and accurate maintenance log for each projector.

- Promptly report any print damage to the film provider.

NEVER

- Leave the projector unattended during the show.

- Leave the audience sitting in the dark when the film is not running.

- Bring food and liquids into the projection booth.

- Allow unauthorized personnel and visitors to be in the booth during the show.

- Leave a high-speed rewind machine unattended while it's in operation.

- Attempt a quick repair of broken film at the time of the show.

- Turn off the rectifiers or exhaust system until the lamphouses are cool to the touch.

265

NOTES

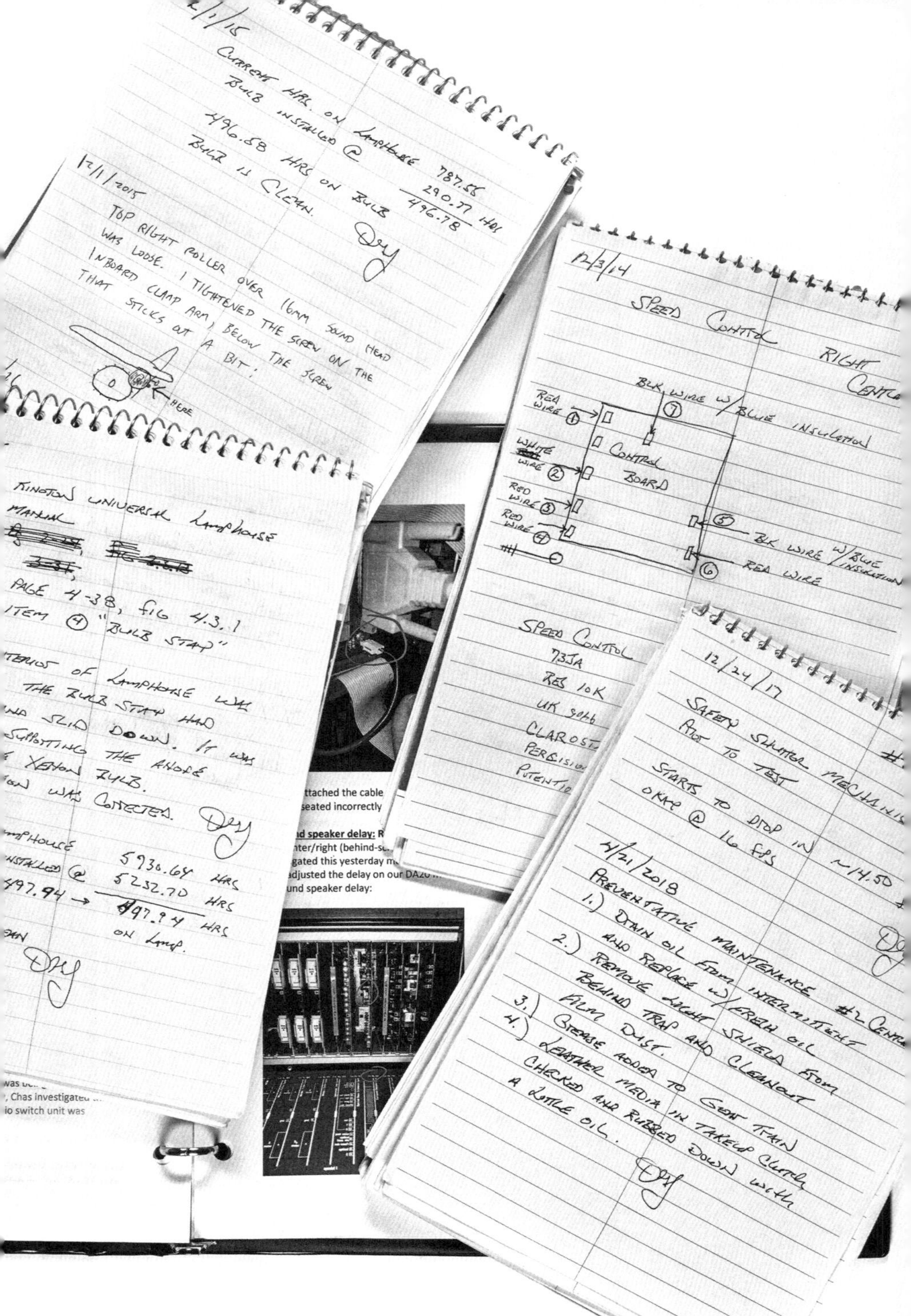

1/1/15
CURRENT HRS. ON LAMPHOUSE   787.56
BULB INSTALLED @   290.77 Hrs
496.58 HRS ON BULB   496.78
BULB IS CLEAN.

12/11/2015
TOP RIGHT ROLLER OVER 16MM SOUND HEAD
WAS LOOSE. I TIGHTENED THE SCREW ON THE
INBOARD CLAMP ARM, BELOW THE SCREW
THAT STICKS OUT A BIT.
HERE

KINOTON UNIVERSAL LAMPHOUSE
MANUAL
PAGE 4-38, fig 4.3.1
ITEM (4) "BULB STOP"
BEARINGS OF LAMPHOUSE WH
THE BULB STOP HAD
SLID DOWN. IT WAS
SUPPORTING THE ANODE
XENON BULB.
WAS CORRECTED.
LAMPHOUSE
INSTALLED @   5930.64 HRS
497.94 →   5232.70 HRS
497.94 HRS
ON LAMP.

12/3/14
SPEED CONTROL   RIGHT   CENTE
BLK WIRE W/BLUE INSULATION
RED WIRE (1)→
WHITE WIRE (2)
RED WIRE (3)
RED WIRE (4)
(7)
CONTROL BOARD
(5) BLK WIRE W/BLUE INSULATION
(6) RED WIRE

SPEED CONTROL
73JA
RES 10K
UK 5046
CLAROST
PERCISIO
PUTENTIO

ttached the cable
seated incorrectly
nd speaker delay: R
center/right (behind-s
gated this yesterday m
adjusted the delay on our DA2
und speaker delay:

was be
, Chas investigated
io switch unit was

12/24/17
SAFETY SHUTTER MECHANIS
NOT TO TEST
STARTS TO DROP IN ~14.50
OKAY @ 16 FPS

4/21/2018
PREVENTATIVE MAINTENANCE #2 CENTE
1.) DRAIN OIL FROM INTERMITTENT
AND REPLACE W/FRESH OIL
2.) REMOVE LIGHT SHIELD FROM
BEHIND TRAP AND CLEANOUT
FILM DUST.
3.) GREASE ADDED TO GEAR TRAIN
4.) LEATHER MEDIA IN TAKEUP CLUTCH
CHECKED AND RUBBED DOWN WITH
A LITTLE OIL.

9

CLEANING AND MAINTENANCE

CLEANING AND MAINTENANCE of projection equipment and of the projection booth are essential to properly care for and exhibit motion picture film prints. Preventing projection damage to film prints is one of the most important duties of a projectionist. Operating projection equipment in poor repair or filthy condition can cause irreparable harm to the print being projected. Daily maintenance and cleaning activities are necessary to keep equipment operating in optimum condition, thereby promoting successful screenings, minimizing the risk of damage to film prints, and maximizing the life of projection equipment (a huge financial investment). Cleaning routines and maintenance schedules should be established and followed by all projection staff. Maintenance logs are recommended for each film projector in order to document malfunctions and failures, as well as repair work or parts replacement.

Fig. 9.1 – **The practice of keeping detailed records of service and malfunctions is necessary in order to understand and maximize a machine's performance.**

A description of all the spare parts for projection equipment that should be held in storage at a cinema exhibition venue (either within the projection booth or in an adjacent area) is well beyond the scope of this book. Suffice it to say that a good projectionist knows which parts are more subject to wear and tear, or require replacement on a regular basis: xenon lamps (or other light sources), lenses, and lamphouse mirrors are only a few in a potentially very long list of items, some of which are very difficult to obtain. Maintaining an accurate inventory of the available spare parts, understanding which ones must be kept handy in the projection booth, and researching the best available sources for precision parts engineering should be matters of priority for all film projection managers. Documentation and training sessions held on a periodic basis are also vital for sharing knowledge with the projection staff, and for providing them all with the most appropriate, uniform, and up-to-date set of skills. Last but not least, remember that — contrary to common belief — film projectors are not inert objects. They need to be kept in operation in order to function at their best. A film projector that is left inactive and untuned for a prolonged period of time is eventually bound to "die" without a film running through its sprockets, not unlike a concert piano without a performer.

CLEANING THE BOOTH

Cleaning projection equipment and the booth is an ongoing exercise. Motion picture film projectors should be cleaned daily. Good exhibition practice promotes cleaning the film path of projectors between reels, during each screening. Lamphouse mirrors require periodic cleaning. Film-handling equipment, including the inspection bench, should be cleaned daily as well. Use alcohol to wipe down the inspection bench, as this removes oil and adhesives that may accumulate during the film inspection process. Throw out any unwanted papers or tape. The floor should be regularly vacuumed and equipment racks cleaned on a periodic basis. Venting on all electronic equipment should be kept free of dust accumulation. Projection ports should be inspected and cleaned as necessary. The port glass may be coated: use lens-cleaning fluid and tissues, as the coating could be damaged by harsher cleaning fluids. Establishing a cleaning schedule for daily, weekly, and monthly activity will prevent equipment from being overlooked.

Performing daily cleaning procedures during and after a day's screenings will leave the booth and equipment ready to go for the next day. Be sure to put away all equipment and supplies (restock as necessary) that have been used in the course of the screening. This will enable other projectionists to find everything they need to run the show. Leaving the booth as clean and orderly as possible is not only professional and courteous, it is also necessary for the safety of projection staff and the successful presentation of films.

CLEANING THE PROJECTOR

A methodical approach is recommended for cleaning motion picture projectors. If available, refer to equipment manuals for cleaning instructions, as they may alert you to areas requiring special care. Projectionists should take their time to perform a thorough cleaning, and the booth and projector should be well-lit to accommodate this. Common sense suggests that it is best to clean from the top to the bottom, as dirt will fall downward. Projectors featuring enclosed film paths (usually older projectors designed to run nitrate film) require more cleaning than newer projectors with open film paths, as the enclosures provide many nooks and crannies for dirt to accumulate.

Items needed to clean the projector include a clean cloth, alcohol, a toothbrush, cotton swabs, pipe cleaners, compressed air (to be used sparingly), and a small vacuum. Use the alcohol, if needed, to clean rollers and surfaces. Cotton swabs, pipe cleaners, or the small vacuum may be used for hard-to-get areas. While compressed air may appear handy for cleaning, it simply blows the dirt around, while a vacuum will remove dirt. If using compressed air in a can (which is actually not air), never shake, tilt, or invert the can. Hold the can upright when spraying to prevent compressed liquid from spraying out. Always read the safety precautions on the can. The toothbrush is used for cleaning sprocket drives, but *never* when the projector is running.

Begin by opening the film magazines (if equipped) and any enclosures along the film path. Open all pad rollers away from their sprocket drives, and open the gate in the picture head. If the projector is equipped with enclosed magazines for feed and take-up reels, clean the upper magazine first, wiping its interior with the clean cloth. Use the cloth (and toothbrush, if necessary) to clean the rollers located at the exit from the feed magazine. Slip the cloth into the film path between the rollers, and work the cloth up and down. If the rollers between the feed magazine and picture head are actual fire rollers, they can be a significant source of film scratching if not turning freely. It may be necessary to apply a drop of oil on the pin-type shafts to keep them turning. A small syringe-type oiler (which can be found at a model-railroad shop) is ideal for this purpose. Oil for intermittent mechanisms or a very light oil may be used for lubrication. Many projectors feature rollers between the magazine and picture head; they are not fire rollers, but are mounted in the same-style casting. These are less likely to cause scratching, but they should be cleaned and lubricated as needed to insure smooth rotation. *[Figure 9.2]*

9.2 — **Fire rollers in the feed magazine of a Century 35mm film projector.**

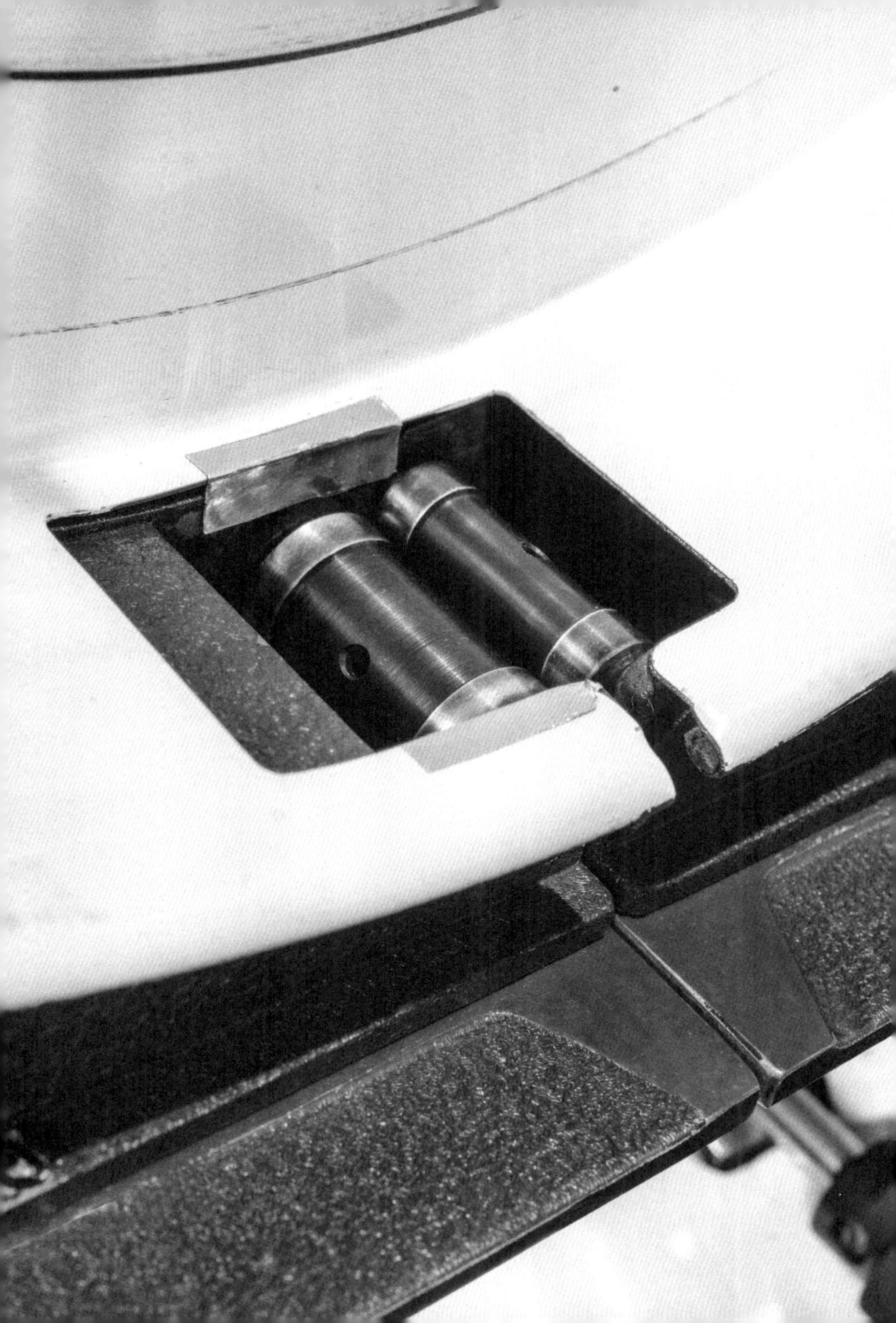

Continue cleaning by slowly working your way downward along the film path, through digital and magnetic sound readers (if any), picture head, sound head, and finally, the lower magazine. Optical readers for digital and analog optical tracks, and magnetic readers for magnetic soundtracks, should be cleaned with care, and only when necessary, per manufacturer instructions (if available).

The film path of a projector contains several **sprocket drives** which advance the film through the projector. Pad rollers (also known as "pad shoes") hold the film against the sprocket drives. All pad rollers or shoes in the picture and sound heads should be wiped down, with attention given to the inside corners of the flanges. The toothbrush works well in these corners for stubborn deposits. Sprocket drives (including the intermittent sprocket) should be brushed with the toothbrush. Advance the projector mechanism *by hand* to rotate the sprocket drives for cleaning the entire circumference. *Never* clean sprocket drives with the motor running. Equipment damage and personal injury can easily result by doing this. Also, be mindful of your hands when cleaning around sprockets, as the sprocket teeth can easily bite! Some projectors employ a pad "shoe" to hold the film against the intermittent sprocket. Make sure to clean the pad roller or shoe with a toothbrush and cloth.

If the trap in the picture head is removable, remove it for cleaning. The gate on most projectors is removable. Both of these components require cleaning. **Gates and traps** come in a variety of configurations. Some are curved; others are straight. Some traps feature rigid surfaces for the film to ride on, while others contain flexible steel bands to hold the film in place.

Regardless of the type of trap and gate, they are the toughest component which film has to move through, and more likely to harbor the build-up of dirt than any other part of the projector.

Because the film is literally dragged through the trap and gate, it can easily be scratched if these components are not kept clean and free from build-up. Dolby Digital and SDDS soundtracks can be ruined by a poorly maintained gate and trap. Build-up of debris can also give rise to focus issues. Use the toothbrush to thoroughly clean these areas, followed by the cloth.

The sound-reading area of the projector features the optical sound-reading components — solar cell and light source — as well as a series of guide rollers and sound drum in the film path.

Wipe the **guide rollers** with a cloth, using alcohol if necessary. The **sound drum** requires careful cleaning, as it is the only surface in the film path which comes into contact with the image area of the film. Wipe it with a lint-free cloth, and alcohol if necessary. Keep the sound drum clean, while lubricated enough so that it can turn freely, thus preventing it from scratching the film and causing audio fluctuations.

To remove dust from **sound-reader optics**, a clean camel-hair brush is sufficient. Avoid the urge to touch the bristles of the brush, as you may leave oil from your fingers on the brush. Alternatively, quick, gentle sprays of compressed air, directed at a 90-degree angle across the optics, will suffice. Never spray compressed air directly toward the sound-reader optics. If the optics of the sound reader are oily or dirty, clean them with lens tissue wrapped around the end of a cotton swab, moistened with a drop of lens cleaner. Then immediately wipe them with a dry lens tissue wrapped around a cotton swab. The optics should be cool before cleaning (turn the light source off for several minutes before you set to work cleaning). If the solar cell is not protected behind a lens, consult a sound engineer for cleaning recommendations, as misalignment and damage could result.

Magnetic sound heads, generally located above the film gate or picture head, require periodic "degaussing" in order to remove the magnetic build-up on playback heads and rollers. The recorded signal on magnetic prints may be damaged or erased by stray magnetic fields. Avoid using magnetized tools (like screwdrivers) near film projectors. If you are involved with projecting film with magnetic soundtracks, ensure that you are completely trained in the safe handling of these materials. Improper use of magnetic tracks can quickly ruin them. Consult a sound engineer if you have questions.

If the projector is equipped with an **enclosed take-up magazine**, first clean the rollers located at the entrance to the magazine, then wipe the magazine interior with a clean cloth. Slip the cloth into the film path between the rollers and work the cloth up and down. (See earlier comments relative to the upper magazine rollers.)

If your projection booth is equipped with **film threading bins** on the floor for the projectors, clean these last to displace any dirt that may have accumulated over time, or fallen into them during the cleaning process. Keeping the bins clean helps keep the film clean.

Projection lenses should be checked before each screening and cleaned, very gently, only if necessary. Gentle brushing with a clean camel-hair brush, or gently blowing compressed air across the front and rear lens elements, will remove any dust accumulation (again, never spray compressed air directly toward optics). Lens-cleaning tissue and lens-cleaning fluid should be used to remove any fingerprints, oil, or dirt on the lens, as most lenses have coatings which could be damaged by harsher cleaners. Clean the lens by placing a few drops of cleaning fluid onto a folded tissue and gently wipe the lens glass, starting at the center, in an outward circular motion. Use the corner of the tissue to pick up any debris which may accumulate between the glass and its metal housing. Immediately wipe with dry lens-cleaning tissue.

As mentioned earlier, good exhibition practice entails **cleaning the film path of projectors between each reel during a**

screening. This will help maintain the quality of the print and of the screening itself. After stopping the projector and removing the reel of film from the take-up spindle, clean the gate, the trap, all sprockets, pad rollers or shoes, and rollers. Brush and wipe any dust and dirt out of the projector. Be careful not to knock the aperture plate out of alignment.

Since film can easily become statically charged, do not clean the film path with film mounted on the projector, as any dust stirred up would likely attach itself to the film. Once the film path has been cleaned, the next reel can be mounted and threaded.

As mentioned earlier in this book, the projectionist should be mindful to regard every film print as an irreplaceable artifact, to be treated with the utmost care. Cleaning projectors between reels is necessary to preserve the longevity of the print and of the equipment.

Once a projector has been cleaned at the end of the day, it is recommended that all pad rollers or shoes and the gate are placed in such positions as to minimize their spring tensions. This will promote the longevity of the spring's capacity.

If the projector employs a mechanical shutter, the shutter blades will need periodic vacuum cleaning. Once-a-year cleaning should be sufficient with projectors using xenon lamps. When operating with carbon-arc illumination, quarterly cleaning of shutters is recommended.

The **projector lamphouse** also requires periodic cleaning. Electrical power to the lamphouse should be shut off at the circuit breaker prior to performing any cleaning or work on the lamphouse. On xenon lamphouses, the exterior screen or grille covering the internal cooling fan should be vacuumed periodically to keep it dust-free.

The **cooling fan** itself necessitates periodic cleaning and lubrication. These fans are typically of the "squirrel cage" design (so-called because it looks like that of a hamster wheel). Remove the grille covering the fan, and clean each blade of the "squirrel cage" with a toothbrush. Then, vacuum the fan and the interior of the lamphouse before restarting the fan. Follow the manufacturer's instructions regarding lubrication. Cleaning the fan blades once a year should suffice.

It is recommended to access the lamphouse only when the lamp has cooled, preferably on an afternoon or day when it isn't in use. Temporarily enclosing the xenon lamp in its protective enclosure (a plastic housing or fiberglass "blanket") and removing it in careful fashion, per manufacturer's directions (wearing a protective face shield, clothing, and gloves, and using a protective enclosure for the xenon lamp), will allow you to vacuum the lamphouse and clean the mirror(s) and heat filter, if equipped.

Do not handle the xenon lamp with bare hands, as the oil from fingerprints can weaken the glass envelope at high operating temperatures. If a heat filter is removed for cleaning (use lens-cleaning tissues and fluid for this), make sure you return it in the same orientation, with the reflective coating facing the lamp.

Cotton wipes moistened with alcohol work fine for cleaning mirrors. Follow this by wiping the mirror(s) with cotton wipes moistened with distilled water, to remove any streaking remaining from the alcohol. Dry thoroughly with cotton wipes. Wear cotton gloves while cleaning these items to avoid leaving fingerprints on the optical components. Be sure to read the manufacturer's instructions before cleaning, as the procedure may vary from one model to another. When cleaning interior components of the lamphouse, check the electrical connections, especially the DC leads to the xenon lamp. Clean, tight connections will prevent arcing and damage.

Lamphouses utilizing carbon-arc illumination require daily cleaning, due to the smoke and soot generated from the burning carbon rods. Drippings from copper-coated negative carbons also need to be removed.

If the power supply (rectifier) for the lamphouse is not built into the projector console, it is generally located on the floor, adjacent to the lamphouse. Since this electrical component generates heat, it is very important to keep any venting areas free of dust and dirt to promote air circulation.

EQUIPMENT MAINTENANCE

Aside from keeping projection and booth equipment clean, most maintenance work focuses on lubrication and calibration. Preventive maintenance is key to maintaining high projection standards.

While some **calibration** work is best left to technicians with proper test films and monitoring equipment, most ongoing maintenance should be performed by trained projection staff. Unless a staff member has the requisite knowledge, 35mm calibration films, and tools to perform critical alignment and calibration of audio and optical components, a service contract with an individual or organization specializing in film projection installation and maintenance is a must. Typically, contracts include annual or semi-annual preventive maintenance visits, as well as specific rates for travel and time for unscheduled visits.

Lubrication of projection and booth equipment should be carried out on a regular basis; the frequency depends on the equipment. Drafting a maintenance schedule that includes lubrication will prevent items from being overlooked. (See sample Projection Booth Maintenance Log in Appendix B.) Check equipment manuals for maintenance suggestions and lubricant specifications. Most parts of the projection equipment require oil for lubrication, but there are different oils for different applications, and some parts may require grease, damping oil, graphite, or other lubricants. It is important to apply the lubricant of the appropriate kind, and in the correct amount.

While the specifications of film projectors and their components vary according to their manufacturer, they have many features in common.

Areas to assess for lubrication are the following:
- Feed and take-up reel shafts.
- Slip clutch on the take-up reel shaft.
- Sprocket drives and their pad rollers.
- Spring-loaded lateral guide roller (located above the aperture).
- Intermittent mechanism.
- Sound-drum shaft (Do not lubricate if the shaft turns in sealed ball bearings. This applies to any shaft which turns in sealed ball bearings. Consult the projector's manual for details.)
- Tension roller(s) for the sound drum.
- Fire rollers.
- Drive gears.
- Changeover mechanisms (Lubrication is generally not required. Refer to the projector's manual for details.)
- Chain drive.
- Motor (Few modern motors require lubrication. If a vintage motor has oil or grease cups, then lubrication is required. Consult an electric motor technician for details.)
- Lamphouse fan.

Be aware that **certain lubricants can damage parts made of plastic**. If a plastic part will not perform correctly without lubrication, ensure that only oils and greases which are compatible with plastics are used for lubrication. Model-train shops are excellent sources for plastic-compatible lubricants.

LUBRICATION: SOME PRECAUTIONS

Any moving part on a film projector likely requires lubrication, though some parts may be sealed without need for further lubrication. Rollers should move freely, and be free of dents or cracks. Prior to lubricating them, clean the shaft and inside bore of the roller. Oil levels should be checked when the equipment is at rest, preferably after several hours.

Do not add oil to the projector while in operation, and don't bother checking oil levels right after the projector has been run. Any assessment of oil levels made while the projector is running, or immediately afterwards, would be inaccurate.

If equipped with a mechanical intermittent, the projector's intermittent oil level should be checked before each screening. It is also recommended that the oil is changed at regular intervals (say, every 500 hours). (Changing the oil once a year should suffice.) Make sure to replace with oil of the same viscosity.

Electronic intermittent movements require no lubrication at all. Some projectors incorporate a damping pot for stabilizing tension rollers at the sound drum. This pot requires special oil and disassembly to check its level.

When adding oil, grease, or other lubricants to any part of a projector or other equipment, be careful not to overdo it. Excess oil, if not wiped up immediately, can work its way onto film prints, inadvertently lubricate pulleys which require tension to drive belts, or find its way to the floor, causing a safety hazard.

It is important to restate here that the operation and maintenance manual of the specific equipment being maintained should be consulted first, if available.

Aside from projectors, other equipment in the projection booth is likely to require lubrication on a regular basis:

- Film inspection bench shafts and motor.
- Rewind bench shafts and motor.
- Exhaust fan motor(s), which may be located outside the projection booth.

MECHANICAL PARTS

Variable-speed DC motors, installed in some projectors and rewind/inspection benches, need to have their motor brushes replaced from time to time. Monitoring their wear, purchasing spares, and replacing the motor brushes when worn to manufacturer's recommended lengths will help prevent unwanted surprises.

For projectors with mechanical shutters or electronically driven shutters, **shutter timing** is important. Correct shutter timing prevents "ghosting" of the image (most noticeable during credit sequences with white lettering on a black background). Projectors may have a shutter-adjustment knob on the picture head to fine-tune the shutter timing. When replacing or manually retiming a two-blade or three-blade shutter, remember to set the shutter adjustment knob to its mechanical center.

Drive sprockets and the intermittent sprocket should be checked periodically for worn or damaged sprocket teeth. A magnifying glass will do. Undercutting of the sprocket teeth, most common on the intermittent sprocket drive, is a sure sign of wear. When wear is detected, the sprocket may be pulled from its shaft, turned over, and reinstalled, allowing the unworn portion of the teeth to engage the film, until a replacement sprocket has been procured.

Projector heads may be driven by **gears, chains, or drive belts,** or a combination of these. Gears may require grease lubrication or reside in an oil bath, necessitating periodic oil changes. Drive belts should be replaced at regular intervals, per manufacturer recommendations.

Both chain and belt drives should be adjusted to proper tension. Belt and pulley cleanliness and tension should also be monitored whenever belts are used to drive take-up reels on projectors.

LAMPS AND ILLUMINATION

It is important to monitor **screen luminance (brightness)** on a periodic basis. Screen brightness changes as lamps age, the screen becomes dirty, and whenever lamps are rotated or replaced. Screen luminance is measured in **footlamberts (fL)**. SMPTE specifications for indoor theater screens allow for a range of 12 to 22 fL in the center of the screen, with 16 fL being ideal. The light should be uniform across the screen, without any "hot spots" or dark areas. The corners of the screen should be within 75% of the center reading, and never less than 10 fL.

A **reflectance light meter,** which reads light reflected from a surface, should be used for measuring screen luminance. *[Figure 9.3]* The most useful meter is a screen brightness meter,

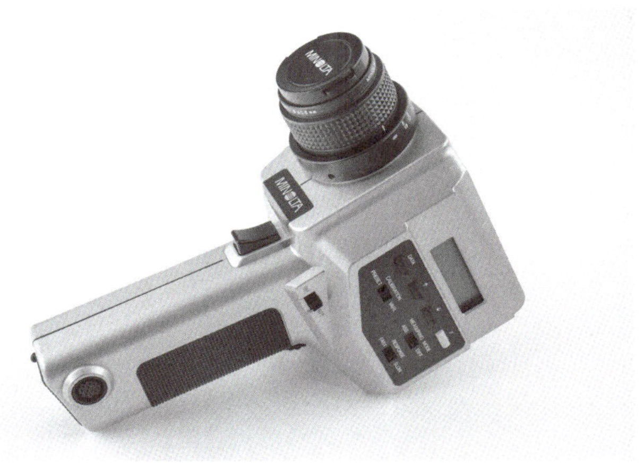

9.3 – **The Minolta Chroma Meter CS-100 measures luminance and chromatic values of light sources or reflective surfaces.**

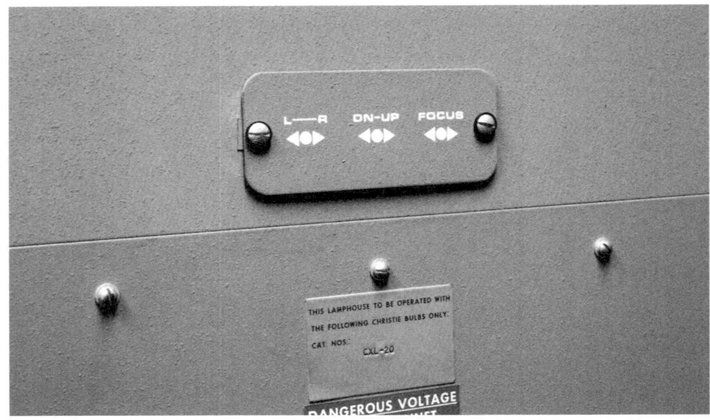

specifically designed for this kind of work, which allows the reading of small areas of the screen. (A photographer's or cinematographer's spot photometer is *not* designed for this application.)

Readings of bare screen light should be made from the auditorium's center, with the lamp warmed up, the projector running, and with no film in the aperture. Measuring screen brightness with the CinemaScope aperture (2.39:1) has been recommended, along with focusing the lens (with film) before taking readings.

The lamphouse douser should be closed between readings, to prevent lens damage from the heat of the lamp. Open the douser for no more than 20 to 30 seconds at a time. Readings should be made for each projector in the booth. (For further information, see the publication *SMPTE Standard 196M-1995, Indoor Theater and Review Room Projection – Screen Luminance and Viewing Conditions.*)

Operating xenon lamps at their specified current range will help maintain proper screen luminance. As lamps age, the output from the rectifier may need adjustment to keep the specified current level (amperage). Xenon lamphouses feature adjustments to position and focus the lamp. *[Figure 9.4]* Lamps should be focused

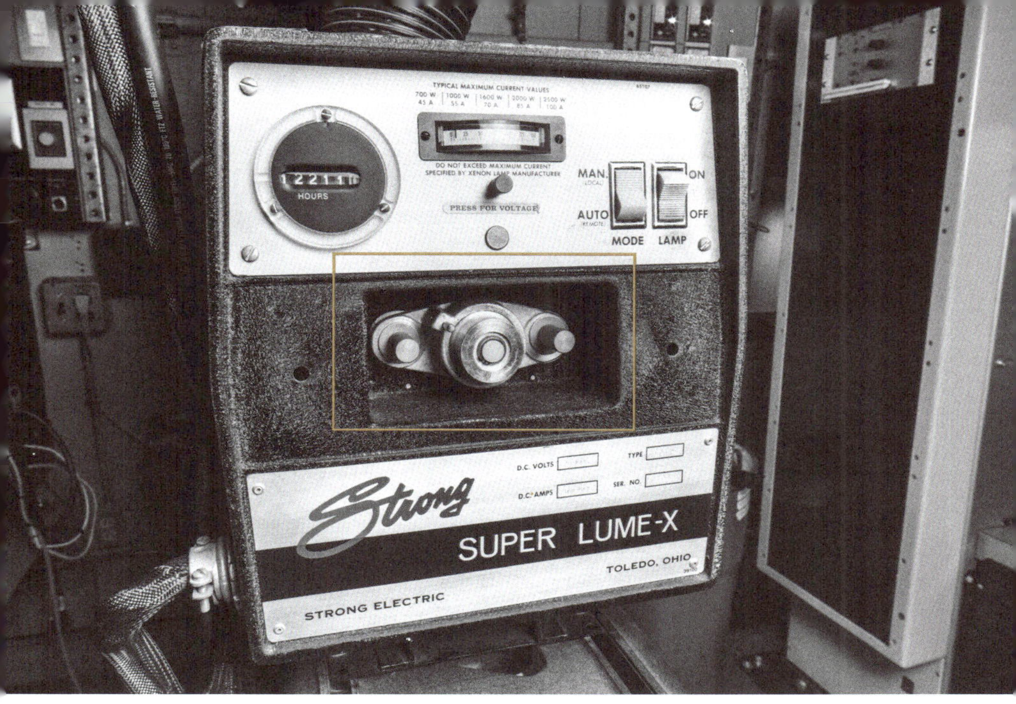

9.4 — **The positioning adjustments of a xenon lamp on a Christie lamphouse (left), with protective panel in place, and on a Strong lamphouse (right), with panel removed.**

(BOX) ADJUSTMENT AREA

to provide as bright and even a light as possible, without an apparent "hot spot" in the center.

Xenon lamps have a **manufacturer-recommended lifespan**, measured in hours. The lamps should be operated at specified currents, checked at regular intervals, and retired before they reach the threshold of their life expectancy. Operation beyond the manufacturer's recommended lifetime increases the risk of explosion, which would likely damage or destroy the mirror(s), heat filter, and other components.

Xenon lamps should be inspected every six months to ensure that the quartz glass is free from any visible defects. It is generally not necessary to remove the bulb for this inspection.

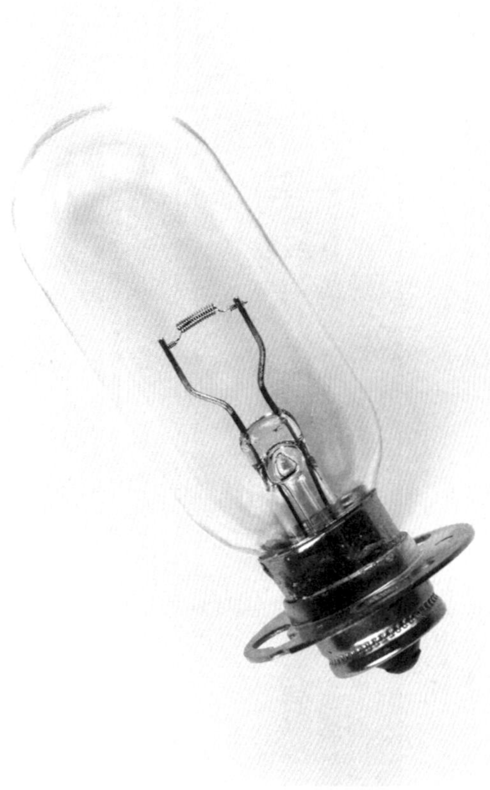

9.5 – **White-light exciter lamp.**

Watch for any gray or white spots which form on the quartz. This phenomenon is called **devitrification**; when it occurs, the quartz is beginning to weaken in this area. If left unchecked, this condition can cause a lamp to explode. Devitrification may be caused by lamp overheating, foreign material (possibly fingerprints) on the lamp, or by a lamp suffering a manufacturing defect. Replace the lamp if it exhibits any devitrification.

If the chrome-like ends of a xenon lamp, which conduct electricity to the anode and cathode, become discolored over time, the lamp is overheating. If you suspect overheating, have a service engineer check the lamphouse ventilation to ensure that the cubic feet per minute (CMF) exhaust is correct for your installation. Also, make sure the lamphouse fan is clean and running correctly.

Alignment: Whether the projector lamphouse employs carbon-arc or xenon lamp illumination, in order to achieve maximum light output and even screen illumination it is necessary that the light source is perfectly aligned with the projector optics. The center of the light source must be centered with the reflector(s), film aperture, and projection lens in both horizontal and vertical axis. Lamphouse alignment kits are offered by several manufacturers. One kit from the United States, the Align-O-Tron, employs a red laser and metal target piece.

White-light exciter lamps, one of many light sources for soundtrack readers, require **periodic calibration**. *[Figure 9.5]* As their filaments sag with age, the audio output is adversely affected. Periodic testing with the appropriate SMPTE optical sound test film (such as the *SMPTE Photographic (Optical) Sound Test Film P35-BT-50*) allows the projectionist to calibrate the equipment to compensate for **filament sag**.

SOUND SYSTEMS

Regular maintenance of the sound system is fundamental, and is usually contracted to a qualified **cinema sound engineer** with specialized knowledge, tools, and calibration films. Audio components addressed by the technician include:

- **A-chain audio for optical** (audio signal from sound reader,
   through pre-amplification and sound processing), which

includes position, width, uniformity, and focus of the slit optics and light, position of the solar cell, lateral position of the film, and pre-amplifier level.

- **A-chain audio for magnetic**, which includes lateral alignment, pre-amplifier level, and frequency response.
- **A-chain audio for digital**, which includes calibration of digital readers, adjustment or replacement of LEDs, and video-level assessment.
- **B-chain audio** (audio signal from output level, through amplifiers and speakers), which includes individual channel assessment for playback level, frequency response, and dead or under-performing speakers or power amplifiers.

The sound engineer should also be able to assist with **audio issues resulting from ground loops or insufficient grounding**. Proper installation of audio equipment provides a zero ohm difference between the chassis and ground of all equipment.

Electrical components for audio need a clean, cool environment for reliable operation, so it is important to keep their air filters clean.

CLEANING THE SCREEN

Projection screens should be replaced on a periodic basis, as it is difficult to clean them with good results. A ten-year life span, unless damage occurs sooner, is considered normal. Having a curtain in front of the screen, kept closed when not projecting, helps to keep the screen clean. The accumulation of dust in screen perforations may be removed by vacuuming from behind the screen with a soft brush. Removing dust from the front may be accomplished by carefully dusting the entire screen surface with a very soft cloth or screen brush. Exercise care not to scratch the screen surface through dust particles adhering to the screen or in the cloth itself. (When brushing the front screen surface, it is likely that you may end up with a streaked screen. This is especially true if the theater is heated with an oil-burning furnace and uses forced hot air to heat the room.)

Stains are best removed by sponging the area with a soft cloth moistened with warm water and mild soap, followed by blotting with a dry, soft absorbent cloth or tissue.

The screen area should be reinforced from behind during the cleaning process, so that the material is not stretched. Care should be taken not to let the water run down the front or back of the screen. Be aware that spot cleaning can compromise the uniformity of the projection area.

The cleaning procedures described here apply only to **matte surface** screens. Do *not* attempt to clean the front surface of a white-gain or silver-gain screen. (The term "gain" refers to the measure of reflectivity of a screen surface; white and silver indicate, respectively, the presence of magnesium oxide or silver-based compounds on the projection surface.)

Prevention and occasional screen replacement go a long way toward maintaining a desirable screen appearance.

DO'S AND DON'TS

ALWAYS

- Maintain a regular supply and an accurate inventory of the most important replacement parts for projection equipment.

- Research and cultivate possible sources for precision parts engineering related to film projection.

- Participate in, and actively promote, professional development and training in film projection.

- Establish and maintain a schedule for cleaning the projection booth and all its components.

- When cleaning the booth and its equipment, start from the top and work towards the bottom.

- Keep a clear and accurate maintenance log for each projector.

- Cultivate professional training for all projection staff on an ongoing basis.

NEVER

- Clean the sprocket drives when the projector is running.

- Spray compressed air directly towards the projector's optics, including lenses and sound readers.

- Clean the projector's lamphouse and optics when they are still hot.

- Use magnetized tools near film projectors.

- Clean the film path with film mounted on the projector.

- Handle the projector's xenon lamp with bare hands.

- Apply excessive amounts of lubricant to the parts of a projector and other equipment.

- Keep the projector's douser open with no film in the machine for more than 20 to 30 seconds at a time.

- Try to clean the front surface of a white-gain or silver-gain cinema screen.

292

293

294

295

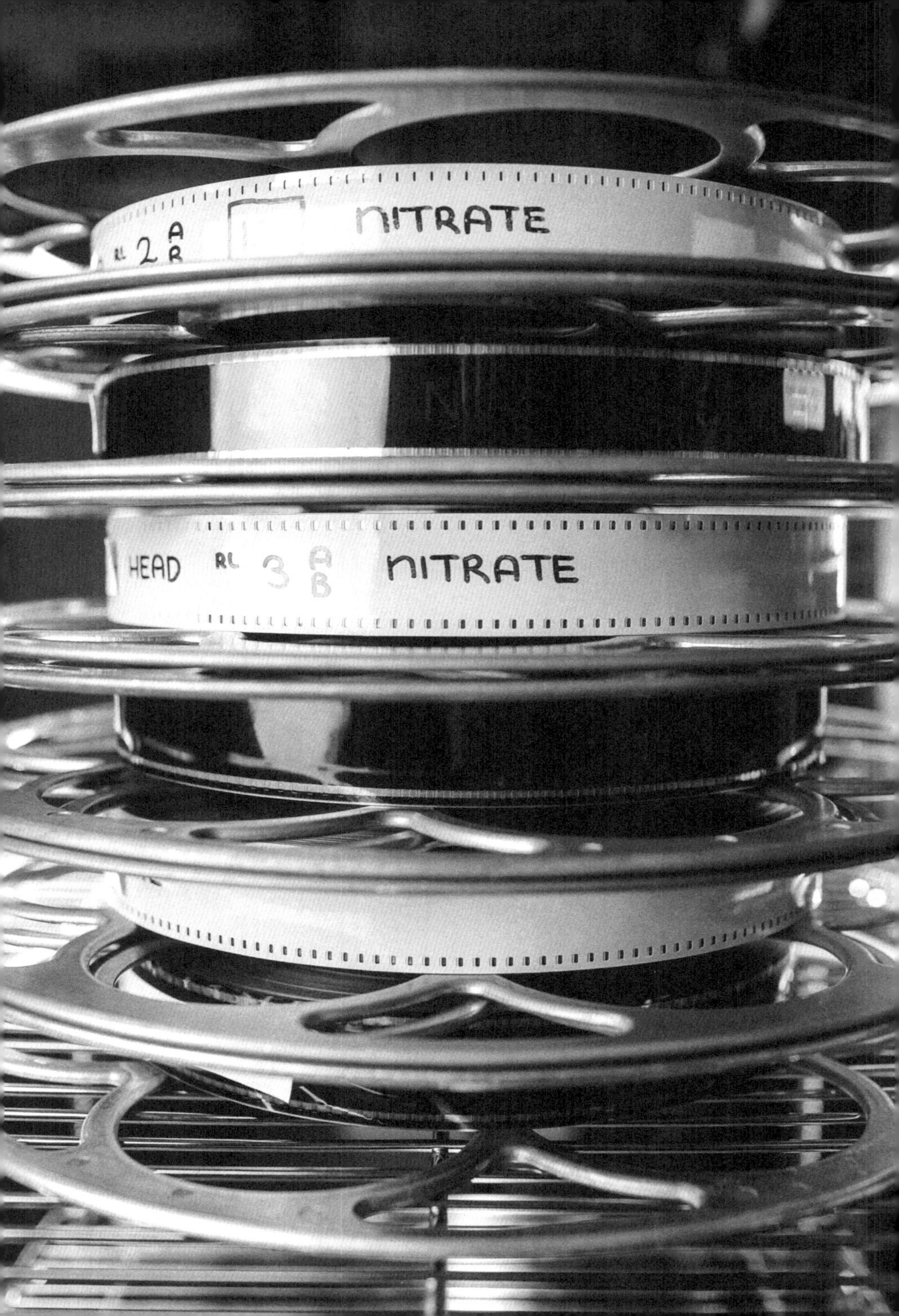

RL 2 A
B
NITRATE
HEAD RL 3 A
B
NITRATE

10

NITRATE FILM PROJECTION

FROM THE 1880s through 1951, cellulose nitrate film stock was manufactured for the production of 35mm motion picture film. Commonly known as "nitrate film," this film stock is highly flammable and impossible to extinguish once burning, as it creates its own oxygen. Nitrate fires burn fast and intensely, and produce toxic gases. Film history is populated with various disastrous fires at theaters, archives, and studio vaults; it is a material not to be taken lightly. In the United States, non-flammable, acetate-based safety film stocks were developed for non-commercial and home use in the 1910s (28mm) and 1920s (16mm) in response to the many concerns related to the potential danger involved in exhibiting nitrate film. Nitrate film is classified in the United States and in many other countries among the "flammable solid dangerous goods," subject to strict regulations for storing, transport, and projection facilities. Nitrate film prints must be stored properly and handled carefully.

Fig. 10.1 – **A 35mm nitrate print, wound onto aluminum house reels, carefully inspected and prepared for projection.**

HOW TO IDENTIFY NITRATE FILM

It is important to understand how to identify nitrate film, as it looks and feels similar to most standard safety-film stocks. Identification is often provided by printed information along the edges of the film stock.

Look at the margins of the print:

1. If you see the words "Nitrate Film" in crisp, **black letters**, the film stock is likely made of cellulose nitrate. *[Figure 10.2]* If these words appear in white letters or dull black letters, you are looking at a "print-through" edge code, which is information derived from a previous copy. *[Figure 10.3]* When identifying film stock, it is important to understand this distinction. In some instances, the "print-through" edge code for nitrate film may appear on a projection print struck on cellulose triacetate stock.
2. If you see **tick marks** that run into your print, you have nitrate film. *[Figure 10.4]*

16mm film was almost never manufactured on nitrate stock, so if you are planning to project this format, you almost certainly

10.2 – 10.4 –

(Top) 35mm nitrate print with a crisp black inscription "NITRATE FILM" edge code and clear inscription edge code printed through from a film element of a previous generation (*Mystery of the Wax Museum*, Michael Curtiz, US 1933).

(Middle) 35mm triacetate print with a crisp black inscription "SAFETY FILM" edge code and clear inscription "NITRATE FILM," printed through from a film element of a previous generation (*[Burton Holmes: Ireland]*, Burton Holmes, US, ca. 1928).

(Bottom) 35mm nitrate print with tick marks (*Scarface*, Howard Hawks, US 1932).

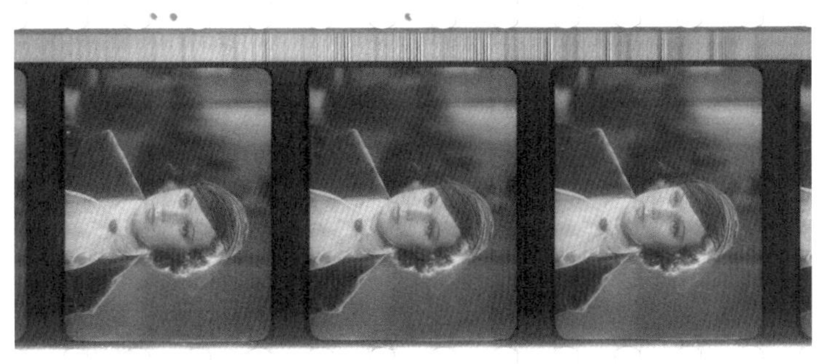

10.2

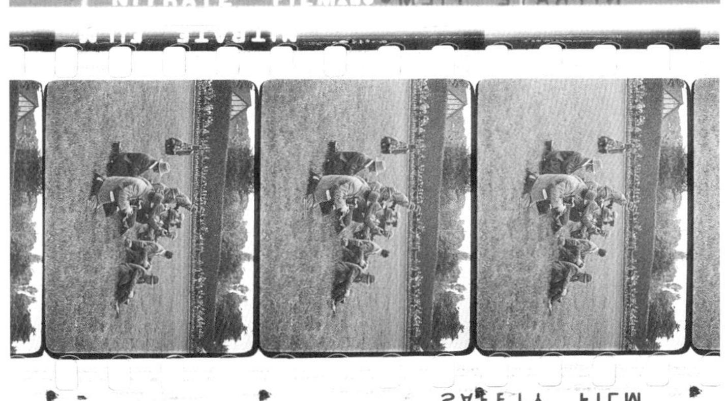

10.3

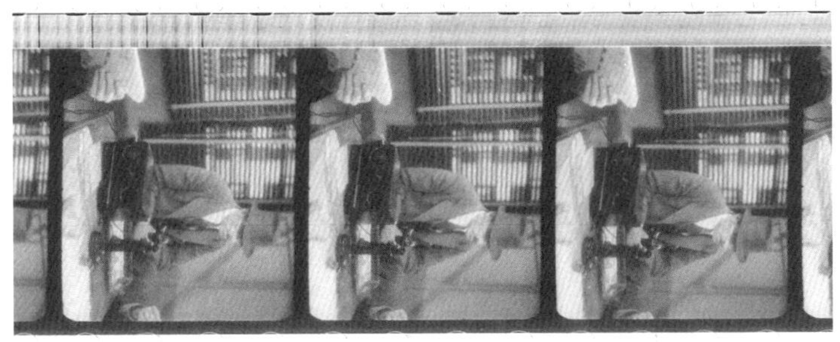

10.4

have safety film. 70mm projection prints were manufactured on safety film stock (acetate or polyester), with the exception of the 1930 Fox production *The Big Trail*, directed by Raoul Walsh.

WHY PROJECT NITRATE?

Archives and cinematheques strive to present the breadth and depth of cinema history to their audiences. As part of the evolution of motion picture film presentation, the chemical and optical properties of nitrate film stock, along with various types of photographic emulsions and a variety of color processes, provide a unique aesthetic experience, virtually unknown to audiences of the present time. Nitrate film screenings provide an opportunity to present a wider spectrum of film history through the exhibition of original prints.

PRECAUTIONS AND REGULATIONS

In order to project nitrate film, a projection booth and its equipment must be designed and manufactured specifically to exhibit this flammable film stock. Safety features must be incorporated within film projectors and the booth, and certification by a local authority having jurisdiction is also often required. Proper training of projectionists with approved procedures is a necessity.

Because of its chemical nature, nitrate film requires **special precautions** for projection. Nitrate prints should first be evaluated to determine their suitability for public exhibition. Assessment of shrinkage, damage, flexibility, and the general condition of a print is necessary to determine if the print can be projected safely, without risk of harm to projection staff or damage to the film.

There is no need to be afraid of nitrate film stock. A **healthy respect** for the proper storage, handling, projection, and shipping of nitrocellulose base film will benefit all those involved in the care and exhibition of this irreplaceable artifact.

First and foremost, it is important to check with your local and state government for the most current and concise **regulations for projection booth standards** (unfortunately, nitrate film projection is prohibited altogether in several countries). In North America, the **National Fire Protection Association (NFPA)** is a standards development organization which establishes and publishes voluntary consensus parameters and codes for fire, electrical, and building safety. A document titled *NFPA 40* provides a complete guide on the safe storage and handling of still and motion picture cellulose nitrate-based film located in film cabinets, vaults, archival vaults, projection booths, laboratories, and other venues. For those living outside the United States, NFPA's International Operations Department works to develop and increase global awareness of technical and educational information on this subject.

NFPA 40 covers all the issues insurance professionals, fire protection design engineers, film vault owners and operators, and enforcing officials need to know when cellulose nitrate film is archived in a facility, including construction requirements and arrangements of buildings, fire protection, storage and handling of nitrate film, and motion picture projection. Chapter 8 of the 2016 edition addresses projection booth specifications and requirements; Annex C.2 provides additional information. *NFPA 40* information can be accessed at nfpa.org/codes-and-standards/all-codes-and-standards/list-of-codes-and-standards/detail?code=40.

(A full bibliographic listing for this publication is also available in the "Suggested Readings" section of this book.)

THE NITRATE PROJECTION BOOTH

No combustible material is allowed in the booth. All furniture (including shelves, tables, and workstations) must be made of non-combustible materials. The only exceptions to the rule apply to the nitrate film itself, film cleaner, lubricants, and film cement. The booth should hold a fire resistance capacity of at least one hour. A minimum of two outwardly opening exit doors should be fire-approved and self-closing. These doors must be kept closed at all times.

Each opening (projection port) in the projection wall should be provided with a suspended steel-plate gravity shutter in order to isolate the booth from the auditorium in the event of a fire. These fire safety shutters must be arranged to close automatically in case of ignition, with the use of fusible links. The gravity shutters must also incorporate a manual release mechanism to close all shutters simultaneously. There should not be more than two projection ports per projector, one for the projectionist and one for the projector. The size of these openings must not exceed a very limited area within the wall behind the auditorium. *[Figure 10.5]*

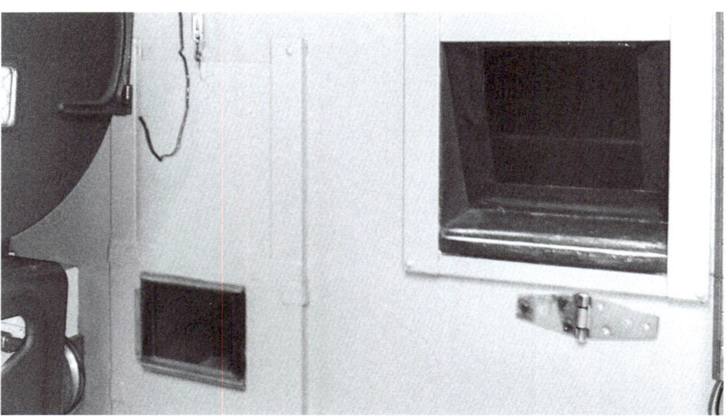

10.5 – **Suspended steel plate gravity shutters over projection and viewing ports in a projection booth. 35mm slide courtesy of Timothy J. Wagner.**

NITRATE-READY PROJECTORS

It is recommended that no more than two nitrate-compliant projectors be installed in any enclosed projection booth, although additional "safety film" projectors are permitted. As mentioned earlier, projectors designed to show nitrate film incorporate several safety features. These features include:

- **Enclosed feed and take-up magazines, along with enclosed picture and sound heads**. All of these must be closed during projection for the safety of the projectionist. The purpose is to contain a film fire, should one occur.
[Figure 10.6, see following pages]

- **Fire rollers** between the feed magazine and picture head, and between the sound head and take-up magazine. These sets of steel rollers, which the film passes through, are typically mounted in pitched castings, so that the rollers press together when no film is present. The purpose is to isolate the "feed" and "take-up" film reels in the event of a fire.
[Figure 10.7, see following pages]

- **Water-cooled gate** in the picture head. Circulating cold water through the water-cooled gate mechanism is intended to keep the gate as cool as possible, in order to minimize the amount of heat to which film, as well as fingers threading the projector, are exposed. *[Figure 10.8, see pages 306–307]*

- **Fire safety shutter mechanism**. Incorporated within the picture head, this mechanism includes a metal shutter to block the light, and therefore heat, from reaching the film aperture when the projector is stopped or running too slow. This safety feature is designed to minimize heat exposure to flammable nitrate film. *[Figure 10.9, see page 308]*

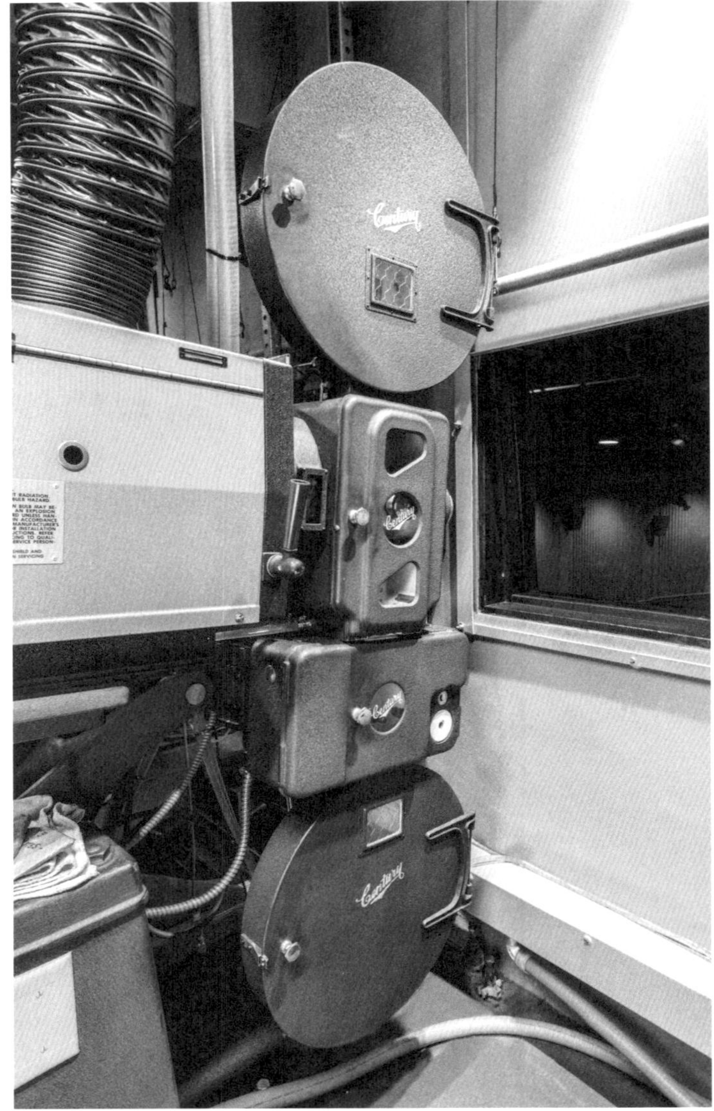

10.6 – Enclosed film path components of a Century Model C 35mm film projector (United States, ca. 1940).

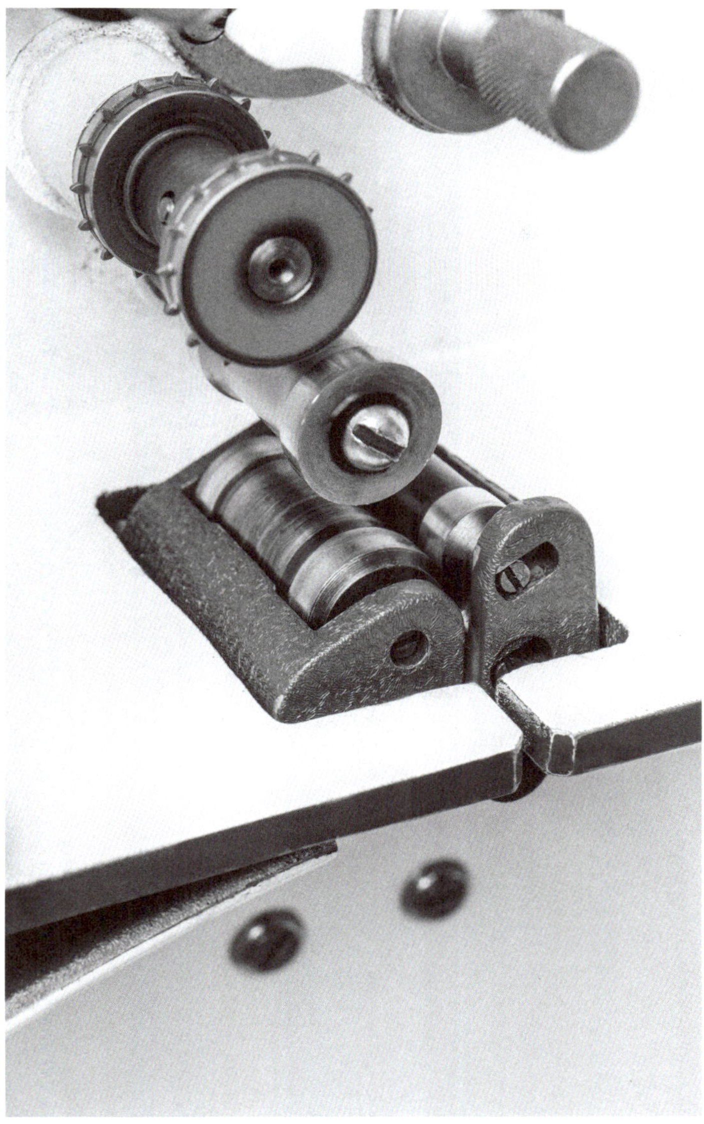

10.7 – Steel fire rollers between the sound head and take-up magazine of a Century 35mm film projector.

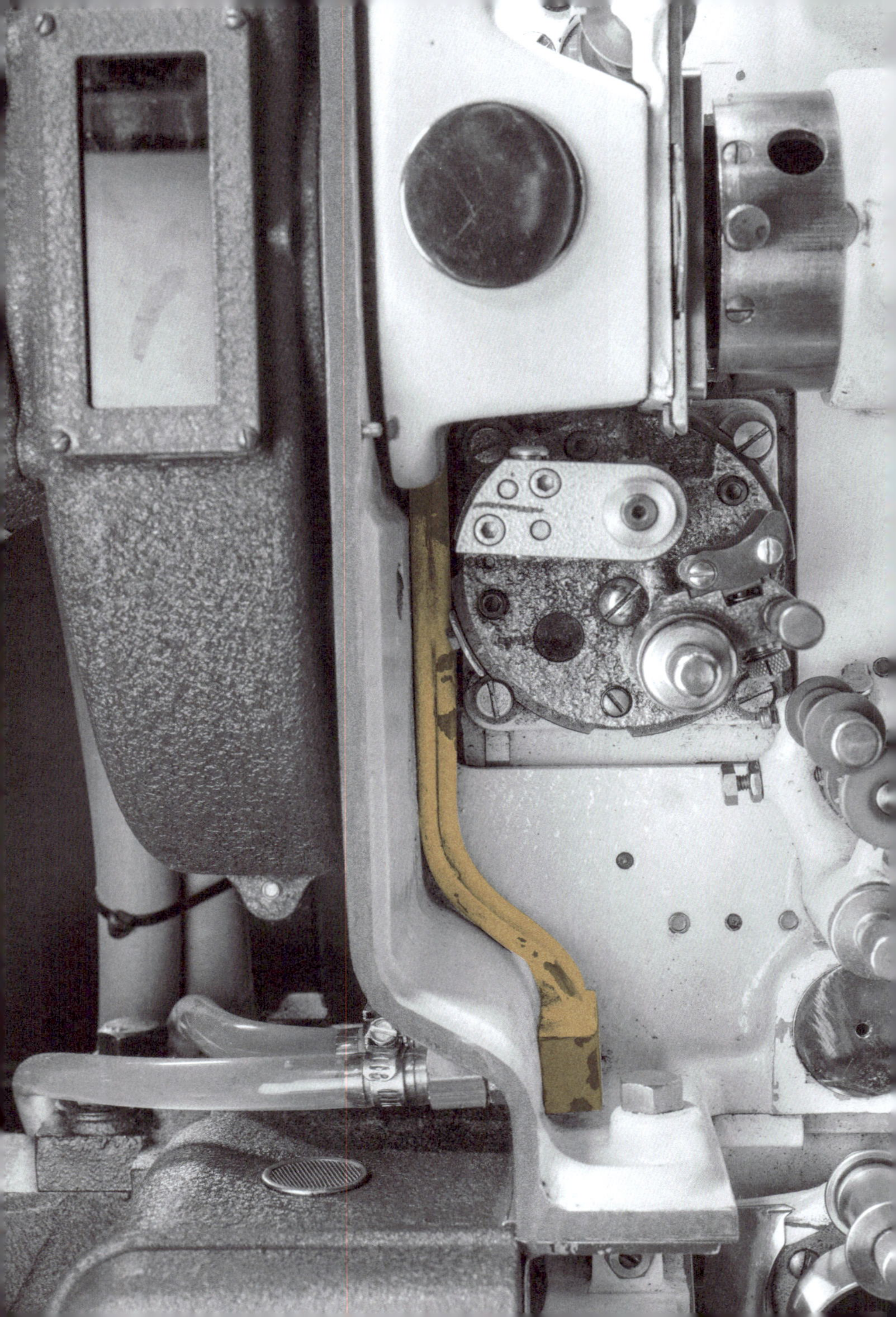

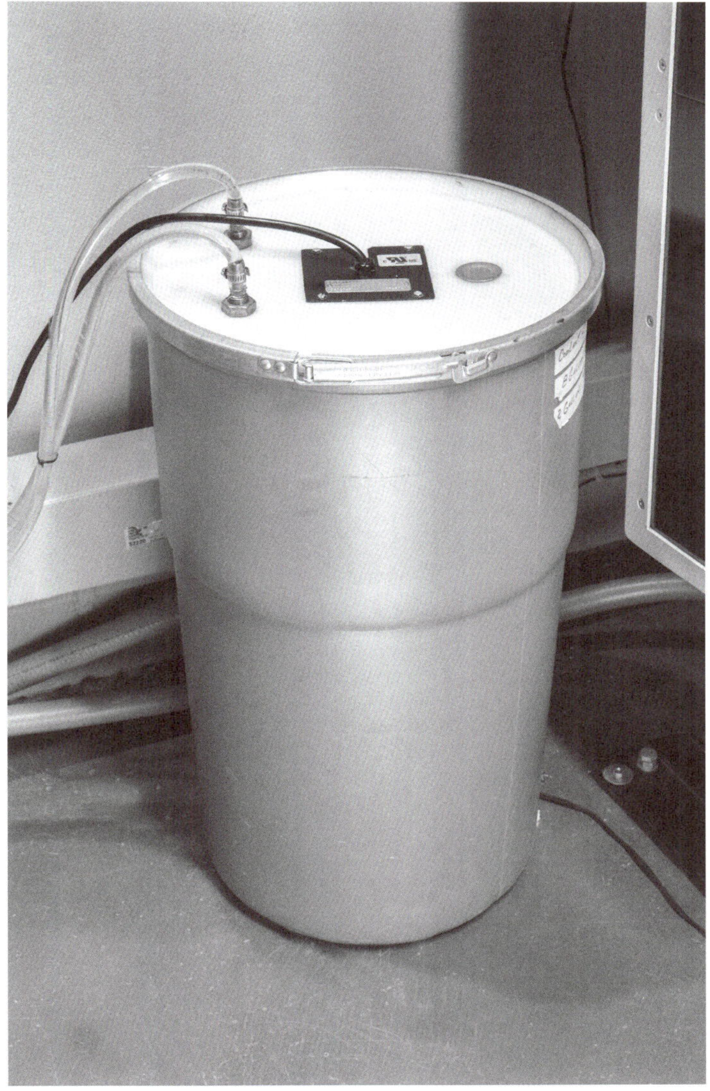

10.8 – The main components of a water-cooled gate: plumbing in a Century 35mm film projector picture head (left, highlighted in color); and a circulation pump/reservoir (right).

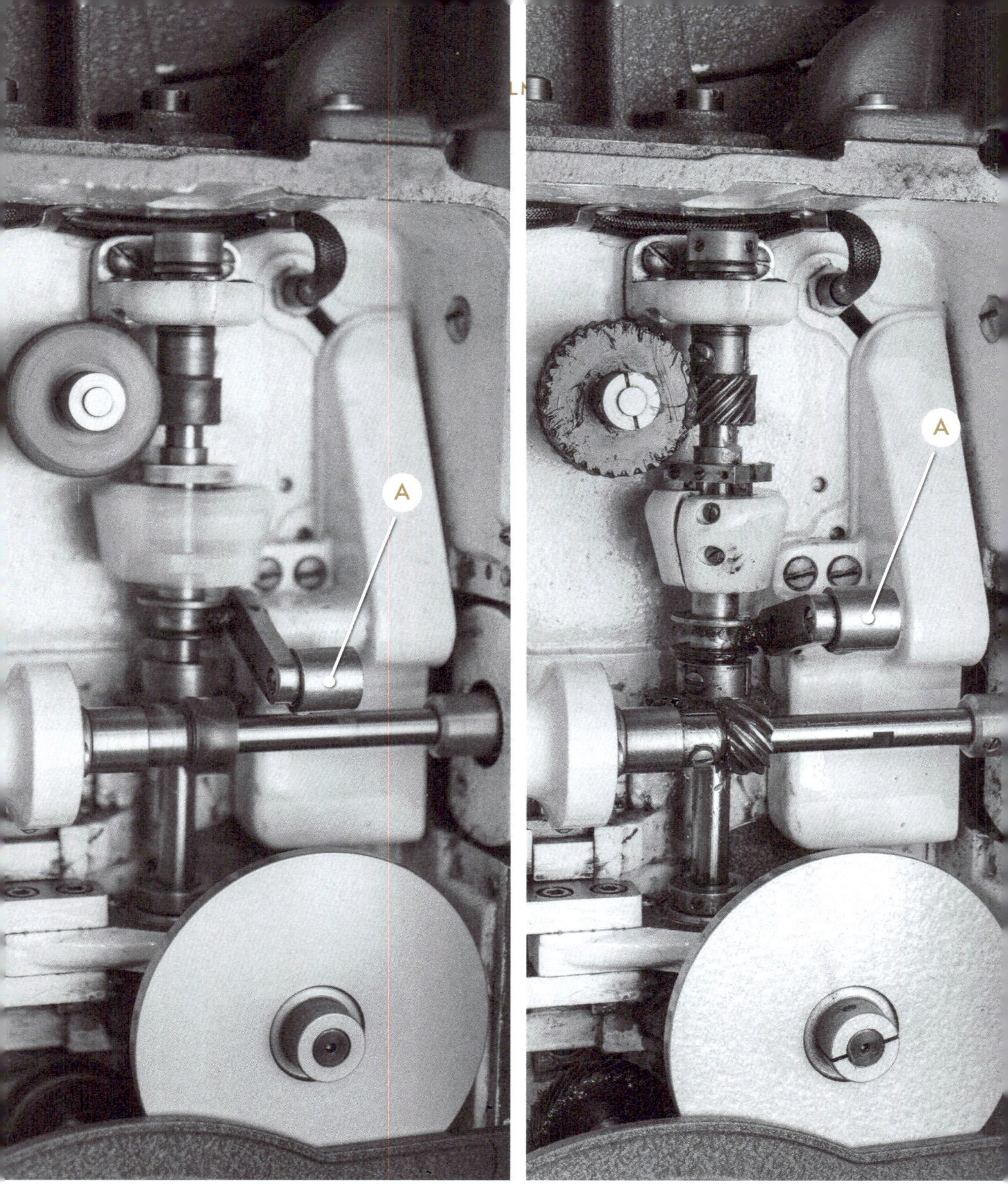

10.9 – **Fire shutter mechanism in a Century 35mm film projector, with motor running (left) and at rest (right).**

A. POSITION OF SHUTTER

Every **projector lamphouse must be vented to outside air** to exhaust the heat generated from the light source, which is most commonly — at the time of this writing — a xenon lamp. Lamphouses for carbon-arc lamps also vent smoke from the burning carbon rods. To minimize heat transfer to the film, whether nitrate or safety stock, it is important that the exhaust system is activated before the lamps are turned on. Additionally, some lamphouses incorporate **heat filters**, which deflect the infrared portion of the light spectrum (heat), while passing the visible light portion. For nitrate film projection, make sure the lamphouses include any heat filters they are designed to have.

Every lamphouse also contains a manual douser, which the projectionist must open to allow light to pass into the picture head of the projector. **The douser should never be opened until the projector is running, with film moving through the gate.** While this is important operational practice when projecting safety film, to prevent it from melting, this is of *critical* importance when projecting nitrate film, which will quickly ignite if exposed to the lamp while standing in the gate.

Traditionally, nitrate film projection requires **two projectionists**, one for each projector. The running **nitrate film should *never* be left unattended during a performance** (this rule applies to the projection of *all* motion picture film, regardless of its base, but is a matter of public safety in the case of nitrate film projection). Each projectionist should constantly monitor the film passage through the picture and sound heads. They should have close physical proximity to both the lamphouse douser and the projector motor switch. In the event of a film break (the most likely spontaneous damage to occur), the projectionist should *immediately* close the lamphouse douser and stop the projector motor, in order to (1) prevent the film from igniting in the gate, and (2) minimize damage from film building up within the projector.

NITRATE STORAGE
AND TRANSPORT

In the United States and in other countries where projection of flammable film is permitted, the amount of nitrate film allowed in a projection booth is strictly regulated. *NFPA 40* limits the amount of unenclosed nitrate film in a projection booth to 75 pounds. Greater amounts may be stored in a dangerous-goods approved cabinet. The cabinet must be non-combustible, large enough to hold a feature film, be self-closing, and certified to hold so-called "Type III" flammable solids. **Detailed specifications and regulations for proper storage and handling of cellulose nitrate film** can be found within *NFPA 40*. It is recommended that any amount of nitrate film in a projection booth is stored in an approved cabinet.

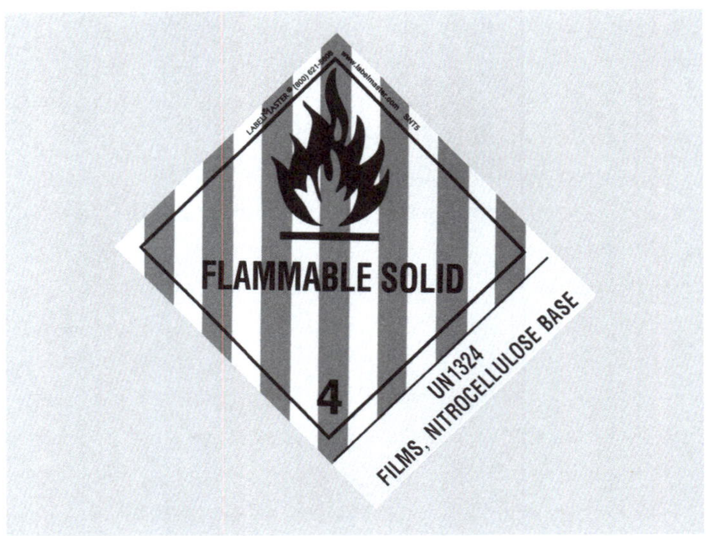

10.10 – Adhesive label for the shipment of 35mm nitrate film (Class 4 hazard label with UN ID number and proper shipping name for nitrate motion picture film stock).

Nitrate film is regarded as a hazardous material. It is classified as UN Hazard Class 4 – Flammable Solid. As such, cellulose nitrate film has strict regulations for domestic and international shipment. In some countries, to legally ship dangerous goods such as nitrate film, you must attend a training course and be certified. Within the United States, the federal government requires every shipper to have **job-specific dangerous-goods training** before tendering a dangerous-goods shipment to any carrier. This includes every person who performs any part of shipping dangerous goods, a process which also involves filling out with the utmost accuracy all the relevant shipping forms. Employees should be trained within 90 days of hiring, and training records must be maintained on file. In addition to initial training, recurrent training is required. *[Figure 10.10]*

Information on dangerous-goods shipping courses may be obtained from a dangerous-goods shipper, such as Federal Express, or through the International Air Transport Association (IATA). When planning the shipment of nitrate film, **always check the laws and regulations pertaining to the country where you work**. Do so periodically: rules are subject to frequent changes. Be aware that not all carriers will accept dangerous goods for transport.

DO'S AND DON'TS

ALWAYS

- Review and follow laws and regulations pertaining to the storage, handling, and projection of nitrate film in your region.

- Check and test safety equipment, such as port window shutters (and their rigging), water-cooling systems, and shutter mechanisms in the picture heads.

NEVER

- Project nitrate film without a minimum of two projectionists.

- Leave nitrate film unattended during projection.

- Store combustible material inside the projection booth.

313

314

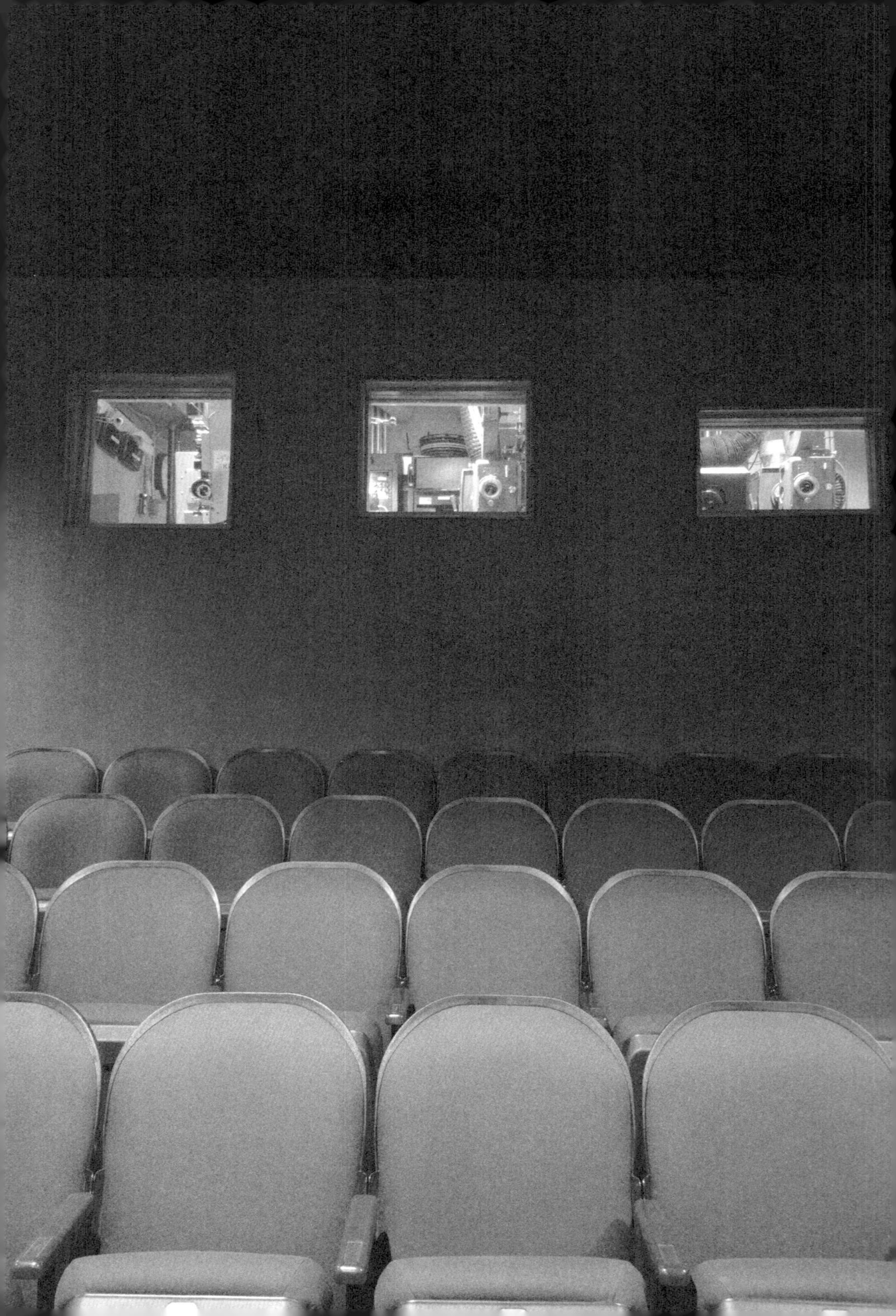

SO NOW YOU'RE A PROJECTIONIST. You are armed with the basic technical knowledge to safely and effectively project film.

You will be ignored by your audience. You will make mistakes. You will encounter show-stopping malfunctions and equipment breakdowns. You will fix them, and continue on. You will project shows for packed houses. You will project shows for audiences of one, the only patron to make it to the theater in a snowstorm. You will be the last person to leave the building at night, and you will still be rewinding film when your audience has climbed into their beds.

Your audience will rarely thank you. Count yourself blessed if you are mentioned during the introduction to a screening, or waved to through the port window; most of your audience will not know that you exist. Many of those who do will think you watch movies for a living. Your friends, family, and loved ones may never truly understand what it is you do in that cramped, shadowy booth every night.

Your reward must come from within. You will have flawed shows, yes — but you will also have brushes with perfection. You will know the indescribable feeling of closing the douser and raising the house lights at the end of a screening populated by seamless changeovers, sharp focus, and impeccable framing. And you will have screenings where you do everything perfectly, and then forget to mute the audio before the last reel's tail leader runs through the sound head.

But never let such hiccups dissuade you for long. You are an artist, and an artist should not fear failure, but rather embrace it as a tool for learning. Do no harm, but be relentless in your pursuit of The Perfect Show. Someday, you will have one. And it will feel amazing.

Share the knowledge you have acquired. Remember the moment you first touched film, and let that guide you when you take an apprentice under your wing.

Above all else, remember how fortunate you are to have the honor and privilege to project film. In those moments when your next reel is threaded and you are waiting for the changeover, watch the film as it winds its way through the projector. Listen to the click-click-click of the intermittent movement. Feel the warm enclosure of the lamphouse. Allow yourself to acknowledge this long-standing tradition, and cherish your place in this proud and unique lineage.

Be passionate. Be humble. Be the best you can be. You are an artist, a technician, a mechanic, and — in a way — a film curator. Maybe also a magician of some sort. You are all of these things, and more. You are a Projectionist. Now go make a show.

APPENDICES

APPENDIX A
SAMPLE INSPECTION REPORT

Film Title: ____

Play Date: ________________ Projectionist: ______________________

No. of Reels: ______________ FPS: ____________ ☐ 35 mm ☐ 16 mm

Source: ____

Aspect Ratio: ☐ 1.18 ☐ 1.33 ☐ 1.37 ☐ 1.66 ☐ 1.85 ☐ 2.39 ☐ 2.66

Sound: ☐ silent ☐ optical ☐ magnetic ☐ digital   Volume: __________

☐ mono 35   ☐ mono 16   ☐ Dolby A   ☐ Dolby SR

☐ Dolby SRD   ☐ DTS   ☐ SDDS   ☐ cyan dye

Base: ☐ nitrate ☐ acetate ☐ polyester   Stock: ________ Year: ________

Opens With:

Closes With:

Cues:

REEL 1 ____

REEL 2 ____

REEL 3 ____

REEL 4 ____

REEL 5 ____

REEL 6 ____

REEL 7 ____

REEL 8 ____

REEL 9 ____

REEL 10 ____

Take Up Instructions:

Notes:

Inspected by: ____________________ Date: __________________

SAMPLE PROJECTION BOOTH MAINTENANCE LOG

WEEKLY (NOTE DATE COMPLETED)										
Check 35mm drive chains										
Check 35mm sprocket drives										
Oil 35mm supply and take-up shafts										
Check 35mm/16mm intermittent oil levels										
Vacuum booth floor and equipment vents										
Clean projector and viewing ports										
Check removable rewind shafts for oiling										
MONTHLY (NOTE DATE COMPLETED)										
Check 35mm gears										
Oil sound head flywheel drum rollers										
Oil slip clutch on 35mm take-up shafts										
Check 16mm mechanism oil level										

EVERY TWO MONTHS (NOTE DATE COMPLETED)										
Check liquid level and pump intake in circulator reservoir; remove any buildup										
Exchange cleaning rags										

EVERY THREE MONTHS (NOTE DATE COMPLETED)										
Oil 35mm stack exhaust fan motor										
Vacuum the dimmer panel air filter										
Clean film threading bins										

EVERY SIX MONTHS (NOTE DATE COMPLETED)										
Oil 16mm stack exhaust fan motor										
Oil 16mm intermittent motor										
Oil 35mm lamphouse fans										
Check rewind bench motor brushes										
Check oil level in 35mm damping pots										
Replace 35mm exciter lamps										

EVERY YEAR (NOTE DATE COMPLETED)										
Oil 16mm supply and take-up reel arms										
Oil 16mm lamphouse fans										
Clean lamphouse reflectors										
Clean 16mm heat shields and negative lenses										
Vacuum/brush 35mm shutter blades										
Vacuum/brush the lamphouse fans										
Vacuum the rectifier interiors										
Have the curtain and masking pulleys lubricated										

EVERY TWO YEARS (NOTE DATE COMPLETED)										
Replace 16mm exciter lamps										

PREPARING THE SHOW: A CHECKLIST

1. SETTING THE PROJECTOR

- Aperture Plate and Lens
  - ☐ Use an aperture plate and lens that correspond to the film's designated aspect ratio
  - ☐ Use a lens that is properly calibrated for the given projector
- Checking the Equipment
  - ☐ Inspect all lenses and the port glass for cleanliness
  - ☐ Inspect the film path for deposits of dirt, dust, emulsion, and lubricants
  - ☐ Check lubricant levels on projectors with gear-based drive mechanisms
- Turning on the Equipment
  - ☐ Turn on the exhaust ventilation*
  - ☐ Turn on the rectifiers and power supplies*
  - ☐ Strike the projector lamps
  - ☐ Turn on the exciter lamps (if applicable)
  - ☐ Turn on the audio rack power and the sound equipment
  - ☐ Turn on the booth monitors

    *ALWAYS TURN ON THE EXHAUST AND RECTIFIERS FIRST.

2. THREADING THE PROJECTOR

- Reel Orientation
  - ☐ 35mm: counter-clockwise orientation, soundtrack outboard
  - ☐ 16mm: clockwise orientation, soundtrack inboard, perforations outboard (for single-perforation stock)

- Setting the Intermittent
    - ☐ Advance the projector motor manually until the intermittent sprocket is at rest
    - ☐ Advance the projector motor manually until the pull-down claw is retracted (16mm)
    - ☐ If the intermittent mechanism is used as the framing mechanism, adjust the position of the intermittent mechanism so that it is midway between its two extremes.
- Framing; Intermittent Sprocket
    - ☐ Line up the film frame with the projector aperture (35mm)
    - ☐ The perforations must be engaged with the intermittent sprocket (35mm)
    - ☐ The gate must be closed, with the film properly aligned within the trap (35mm)
    - ☐ The gate must be closed, and the projector motor manually advanced until the pull-down claw engages the perforations (16mm)
- Threading the Countdown
    - ☐ Determine the type of countdown being used (Academy or SMPTE)
    - ☐ Thread the countdown at 8 to 9 feet before the first image*

        *THE THREADING POSITION DEPENDS ON THE REFLEXES OF THE PROJECTIONIST, THE PROJECTOR RAMP-UP SPEED, AND THE PLACEMENT OF CUES ON THE PRINT.

- Upper Loop
    - ☐ The upper loop is formed between the drive sprocket and the gate
    - ☐ The perforations are engaged with the drive sprocket
    - ☐ The loop should not be too small or too large
    - ☐ The pad roller or shoe on the drive sprocket should be closed
- Lower Loop
    - ☐ The lower loop is formed after the intermittent sprocket
    - ☐ The perforations are engaged with the intermittent sprocket and the following sprocket

- ☐ The loop should not be too small or too large
- ☐ The pad roller or shoe on the sprockets should be closed
- Sound Head
  - ☐ The film is threaded around the sound drum and the tension rollers
  - ☐ There should be appropriate tension around the sound drum
  - ☐ There should be no fluctuations of pitch during playback
- Take-Up
  - ☐ The film is wrapped around reel hub in a clockwise fashion
  - ☐ All slack should be taken up
  - ☐ Take-up tension is engaged (where applicable)
  - ☐ Manually advance the film through the projector, looking and listening for signs of misthreading or equipment malfunction

3. SETTING THE AUDIO FORMAT, GATE TENSION, FOCUS, VERTICAL ALIGNMENT, SOUND LEVEL, AND MASKING

- Setting the Audio Format
  - ☐ Make sure that the proper audio format is selected on the cinema sound processor
- Setting the Gate Tension
  - ☐ Make sure that gate tension is adjusted to provide a stable image
- Setting the Focus and Framing
  - ☐ Adjust the focus until the image appears sharp at center and sides
  - ☐ The print's grain should be sharp
  - ☐ No frame lines should appear on the screen
  - ☐ Framing should be adjusted to present the intended composition
- Setting the Vertical Alignment
  - ☐ The anamorphic lens should be rotated to provide proper image orientation
- Setting the Sound Levels
  - ☐ Begin by playing the sound at the default level set for the theater
  - ☐ Walk around the theater and listen for both music and dialogue levels

    ☐ Check to ensure that all speakers are functioning properly

    ☐ There should be no fluctuations of pitch during playback

    ☐ Listen for feedback, dropout, or any other issues

- **Setting the Masking**

    ☐ Set the masking according to the print's aspect ratio

    ☐ Mask any unused (blank) screen space

    ☐ Avoid image spillover

4. MAKING ANY NECESSARY ADJUSTMENTS

    ☐ Check for any issues that become apparent while the film is running

    ☐ If possible, tend to any issues before the screening begins

5. UNTHREADING THE PROJECTOR

    ☐ Once the focus and sound level have been set, close the lamphouse douser and stop the projector motor

    ☐ Open the gate, and the pad rollers or shoes

    ☐ Carefully unthread the sprockets and rollers while avoiding any contact with the image area of the film

    ☐ Rewind the print and rethread the proper reels before showtime

SUGGESTED READINGS

Brown, Harold, *Physical Characteristics of Early Films as Aids to Identification*, 2nd Edition, edited by Camille Blot-Wellens (Brussels: FIAF, 2019)

Cleveland, David, and Brian Pritchard, *How Films Were Made and Shown. Some Aspects of the Technical Side of Motion Picture Film, 1895–2015* (Manningtree, UK: David Cleveland, 2015)

Kattelle, Alan, *Home Movies: A History of the American Industry, 1897–1979* (Nashua, NH: Transition Publishing, 2000)

Kodak Motion Picture Film, 5th Edition, Kodak Publication No. H-1, Cat. 155 2280; Minor Revision, June 2000 (Rochester, NY: Eastman Kodak Company, 2000)

Lee, William E., and Charleton C. Bard, "The Stability of Kodak Professional Motion-Picture Film Bases," in *SMPTE Journal*, vol. 97, no. 11, November 1988, pp. 911-914

Motion-Picture Projection and Theatre Presentation Manual (New York: Society of Motion Picture and Television Engineers, 1969)

NFPA 40: Standard for the Storage and Handling of Cellulose Nitrate Film (Quincy, MA: National Fire Protection Association, 2015)

Sætervadet, Torkell, *The Advanced Projection Manual* (Oslo: Norwegian Film Institute / Brussels: International Federation of Film Archives, 2006)

Shanebrook, Robert L., *Making Kodak Film*, 2nd Edition (Rochester, NY: Robert L. Shanebrook, 2016)

SMPTE Standard 196M-1995, Indoor Theater and Review Room Projection – Screen Luminance and Viewing Conditions (White Plains, NY: Society of Motion Picture and Television Engineers, 1995)

SMPTE Standard 301-1999, Theater Projection Leader, Trailer, and Cue Marks (White Plains, NY: Society of Motion Picture and Television Engineers, 1999)

White, Deane R., Charles J. Gass, Emery Meschter, and Wilton R. Holm, "Polyester Photographic Film Base," in *SMPTE Journal*, vol. 64, no. 12, December 1955, pp. 674-678

Paolo Cherchi Usai is Senior Curator of the Moving Image Department at the George Eastman Museum and Adjunct Professor of Film at the University of Rochester. He is founder or co-founder of the Pordenone Silent Film Festival; of the L. Jeffrey Selznick School of Film Preservation; and of the Nitrate Picture Show, established in 2014. Among his published works are *Silent Cinema: A Guide to Study, Research and Curatorship* (2019); *The Griffith Project* (1999–2008, 12 volumes); and *Film Curatorship: Archives, Museums, and the Digital Marketplace* (2008). He is the author of the feature-length films *Passio* (2007), adapted from his book *The Death of Cinema: History, Cultural Memory, and the Digital Dark Age* (2001), and *Picture* (2015), with live music performance by the Alloy Orchestra.

Spencer Christiano is Chief Projectionist of the Moving Image Department at the George Eastman Museum, where he oversees technical operations in two archival exhibition spaces. He teaches film inspection and projection to students of the L. Jeffrey Selznick School of Film Preservation. He has lectured on film projection for the University of Rochester, and at the 2016 Film Preservation and Restoration Workshop at the National Film Archive of India in Pune. He also served as Technical Manager of the MuCCC Theater in Rochester, where he is an Artist in Residence. His work as a playwright includes *Endangered Features* (2016), about the world of film archiving, film projection as a technical art, and the evolution of cinema exhibition from its analog roots to cutting-edge digital.

Catherine A. Surowiec is an independent film historian, researcher, and editor. She began her career at the film archive at

The Museum of Modern Art, New York; subsequent freelance work has been wide-ranging. Publications on which she has worked in an editorial capacity or as author/contributor include *Rediscovering French Film* (1983), *Accent on Design: Four European Art Directors* (1992), *The LUMIERE Project: The European Film Archives at the Crossroads* (1996), *This Film Is Dangerous: A Celebration of Nitrate Film* (2002), *Film Curatorship* (2008), *Ealing Revisited* (2012), *The Dawn of Technicolor* (2015), *King of Jazz: Paul Whiteman's Technicolor Revue* (2016), and FIAF's *Journal of Film Preservation*. She has edited the catalogue of the Giornate del Cinema Muto (Pordenone silent film festival) since 2000.

Timothy J. Wagner is a film archivist and projectionist. He served from 2001 to 2017 as Film Technician and Projection Manager at the George Eastman Museum, where he was in charge of preparing and shipping film prints to be exhibited at archival venues, supervising film equipment maintenance and repair, and teaching the technique of film inspection to students of the L. Jeffrey Selznick School of Film Preservation. He has extensively lectured on motion picture film and archival film projection. During his tenure at the museum, Wagner also contributed to the ongoing maintenance and operation of the institution's screening venues. A graduate of SUNY Buffalo and of the Selznick School, Wagner currently serves as film archivist at the Indiana University Libraries Moving Image Archive.

THE GEORGE EASTMAN MUSEUM

The George Eastman Museum holds unparalleled collections of photographs, motion pictures, photographic and cinematic technology, and photographically illustrated books, totaling more than four million objects. A world leader in film preservation and photograph conservation, the Eastman Museum educates archivists and conservators from around the world through its academic and archival training programs. The museum's film preservation strategies focus on the forgotten works of early cinema and on orphan films that would otherwise be lost through chemical decomposition. Established as an independent nonprofit institution in 1947, it is one of the largest film archives in the United States and the world's oldest photography museum. The museum is located in Rochester, New York, on the site of the National Historic Landmark house and gardens of George Eastman, the philanthropist and father of popular photography and motion picture film.

THE L. JEFFREY SELZNICK SCHOOL OF FILM PRESERVATION

Established in 1996 by the son of film producer David O. Selznick, The L. Jeffrey Selznick School of Film Preservation at the George Eastman Museum is the longest-standing program of its kind worldwide, and the first in the United States. Its courses are organized into two parallel strands: a one-year Certificate Program, and a two-year Master of Arts Program in Film and Media Preservation, currently held in partnership with the University of Rochester. The hands-on, full-immersion training programs, led by an international team of specialists, provide students with comprehensive knowledge on the theories, methods, and practices of film and media preservation, along the full spectrum of analog and digital laboratory techniques. The Selznick School's practicum projects include 35mm film projection and the actual preservation of films in photochemical and digital formats.

INDEX

Page numbers in bold indicate illustrations.

335